Anglican Religious Life

2012–2013

A Year Book of
Religious orders and communities in
the Anglican Communion,
and tertiaries, oblates, associates and companions

Published by
Canterbury Press Norwich
a publishing imprint of Hymns Ancient & Modern Ltd *(a registered charity)*
13–17 Long Lane, London EC1A 9PN
www.canterburypress.co.uk

ISBN: 978-1-84825-089-5

Agents for Canterbury Press outside the UK:

Australia	Rainbow Book Agency	www.rainbowbooks.com.au
Canada	Novalis Books	www.novalis.ca
Europe (continental)	Durnell Marketing	www.durnell.co.uk
Ireland	Columba Bookstores	www.columba.ie
New Zealand	Church Stores	christianbooksnz.com/churchstores
South Africa	Pearson South Africa	www.pearson.com
USA	Westminster John Knox	www.wjkbooks.com
West Indies	Hugh Dunphy	www.bloodaxe.com

The Editorial committee of ARLYB and the publishers wish to thank
The Society of the Faith
for supporting the publication of this *Year Book.*

Drawings by Sister Mary Julian Gough CHC
The cover design is by Leigh Hurlock

Key to the photographs on the cover, clockwise from top left:
Religious at the 2010 conference in the Solomon Islands on peace-making;
LBF Brother in Australia;
Stream-cleaning at Malling Abbey, UK;
SSF life profession in Seoul, Korea;
SSJD Sisters in Canada.

Printed and bound by CPI Group (UK) Ltd, Croydon, CR0 4YY

Contents

Foreword
by
Rt Revd John Pritchard, Bishop of Oxford

Alnmouth Friary; room 15; bliss. That was where I used to go on retreat when I was in the north of England. It was a superb place with its panoramic view of sea, sky and cliff top. Then there was the space, the worship, the acts of grace (a tot of whiskey arriving late one evening, left by a generous guest but surplus to Community requirements). To a weary bishop it was a glimpse of the hospitable heart of God.

Obviously there are many different styles of Religious life, but there is only one God calling us irresistibly to transformation. This *Year Book* celebrates that richness and that potential for renewal.

Moreover, our Religious Communities act as reminders of the depth and complexity of faith. In an age of 'coin-operated' religion where 'outcomes' are valued more highly than wisdom, our Communities are signs of contradiction in a self-absorbed (not to say self-opinionated) culture. Their counter-cultural life demands of their brothers and sisters self-knowledge, discipline and clarity of purpose if they are to sustain their trajectory towards God. The rest of us need not only their constant intercession but also their desire to return the loving gaze of God. In this they model the purpose of creation, which is precisely to live and flourish in that gaze of Divine Love. No wonder we need our Religious Communities: they go before us as spiritual adventurers.

From the vantage point of a place on the Advisory Group on the Relations of Bishops and Religious Communities, and being a Visitor to a number of those Communities, I particularly welcome the explorations going on between traditional Religious Communities with all their accumulated experience and wisdom, and the new Religious communities which are springing up energetically and looking for guidance. Most of these new communities are not sufficiently mature yet to find a place in the *Year Book*, but they are bubbling up just below the surface. God is always at work renewing his Church: we are simply called to 'catch the wave' of the Spirit and hang on to our surf-board!

What is never negotiable, however, is the primary vocation of Religious Communities to live in the gaze of God and to experience for and with the rest of us the blistering caress of God's love.

How lost we would be without you. Thank you for staying close to the fire.

+ *John Oxon*

A Prayer for Vocations to the Religious Life

Setting a particular Sunday each year as a Day of Prayer for Vocations to the Religious Life was begun in 1992. This is currently the **Fourth Sunday after Easter**. All are also invited to pray each Friday for the life and work of the Religious communities in the Church, using the following prayer, written by a Little Brother of Francis, originally for communities in Australia and New Zealand.

**Lord Jesus Christ
in your great love you draw all people to yourself:
and in your wisdom you call us to your service.
We pray at this time you will kindle in the hearts of men and women
the desire to follow you in the Religious life.
Give to those whom you call, grace to accept their vocation readily
and thankfully, to make the whole-hearted surrender
which you ask of them, and for love of you, to persevere to the end.
This we ask in your name. Amen.**

A NOVENA OF PRAYER FOR RELIGIOUS LIFE

Day 1: 2 Thessalonians 1: 3
We give thanks for Religious communities throughout the world.

Day 2: Romans 14: 7–9
We give thanks for members in our communities who have died.

Day 3: Acts 15: 36–40
We pray for those who have left our communities.

Day 4: Ephesians 4: 1–6
We give thanks for our own vocations.

Day 5: 1 Thessalonians 5: 12–14
We pray for our leaders and for all who make decisions.

Day 6: Titus 2: 7–9
We pray for novice guardians and all who teach in our way of life.

Day 7: 1 Corinthians 12: 27–31
We pray that we will be faithful to our vows.

Day 8: Acts 2: 44–47
We pray for all who seek to know and to do your will and that men and women will be led to join our communities.

Day 9: 2 Corinthians 4: 16–18
We recognize that the future is in God's hands. We pray that the Holy Spirit will help and support us as we live in the Light of Christ.

We give thanks for the Religious Life in all its forms

1 Community of All Hallows *in the UK*
   All Saints Sisters of the Poor *in the UK & the USA*
   Society of the Precious Blood *in Lesotho, South Africa & the UK*
2 Community of the Holy Spirit *in the USA*
   Community of St Mary *in Malawi, the Philippines & the USA*
3 Community of the Resurrection *in the UK*
   Community of the Resurrection of Our Lord *in South Africa*
4 Community of Saint Francis & Society of Saint Francis *in Australia, Brazil,*
   Korea, New Zealand, Papua New Guinea, the Solomon Islands, the UK & the USA
   Little Brothers of Francis *in Australia*
   Society of the Franciscan Servants of Jesus & Mary *in the UK*
   The Third Order SSF *throughout the world*
5 Community of the Servants of the Will of God *in the UK*
   Community of Sisters of the Church *in Australia, Canada, Solomon Islands & UK*
6 Brotherhood of St Gregory *in the USA*
   Christa Sevika Sangha *in Bangladesh*
   Church Mission Society *throughout the world*
7 Community of Jesus' Compassion *in South Africa*
   Community of the Holy Name *in Lesotho, South Africa, Swaziland & the UK*
8 Society of the Servants of Jesus Christ *in Madagascar*
   Order of Julian of Norwich *in the USA*
   Society of Our Lady of the Isles *in the UK*
9 Community of St Denys *in the UK*
   Society of the Sacred Advent *in Australia*
10 Community of St Laurence *in the UK*
   Chita che Zita Renoyera (Holy Name Community) *in Zimbabwe; and* Chita che
   Zvipo Zve Moto (Community of the Gifts of the Holy Fire) *in Zimbabwe*
11 Order of St Benedict *in independent Abbeys and Priories throughout the world*
   Benedictine Community of Christ the King *in Australia*
   Benedictine Community of the Holy Cross *in the UK*
   Benedictine Community of Our Lady and St John *in the UK*
12 Community of the Holy Transfiguration *in Zimbabwe*
   Community of the Transfiguration *in the Dominican Republic & the USA*
   Oratory of the Good Shepherd *in Australia, north America, South Africa & the UK*
13 Community of the Glorious Ascension *in France & the UK*
   Brotherhood of the Ascended Christ *in India*
   Sisters of Jesus' Way *in the UK*
14 Community of the Servants of the Cross *in the UK*
   Order of the Holy Cross *in Canada, South Africa & the USA*
   Society of the Holy Cross *in Korea*
   Society of the Sacred Cross *in the UK*
15 Community of St Mary the Virgin *in the UK*
   Society of Our Lady St Mary *in Canada*

in the Church, and today we pray especially for:

16 Order of the Teachers of the Children of God *in the USA*
Community of the Companions of Jesus the Good Shepherd *in the UK*
Community of the Good Shepherd *in Malaysia*
17 Melanesian Brotherhood *throughout the Pacific region*
Community of the Sisters of Melanesia *in the Solomon Islands*
18 Companions of St Luke – OSB *in the USA*
Company of Mission Priests *in the UK*
Order of the Community of the Paraclete *in the USA*
19 Order of the Holy Paraclete *in Ghana, Swaziland & the UK*
Community of the Holy Name *in Australia*
20 Society of St Margaret *in Haiti, Sri Lanka, the UK & the USA*
Community of Nazareth *in Japan*
21 Community of St Clare *in the UK*
Little Sisters of St Clare *in the USA*
Order of St Helena *in the USA*
22 Community of the Sacred Passion *in the UK*
Community of St Mary of Nazareth and Calvary *in Tanzania & Zambia*
23 Community of Celebration *in the UK & the USA*
Community of St John the Evangelist *in the Republic of Ireland*
24 Community of St John Baptist *in the UK & the USA*
Worker Brothers & Sisters of the Holy Spirit *in Australia, Canada, Haiti & USA*
25 Community of St Paul *in Mozambique*
Society of St Paul *in the USA*
Sisterhood of the Holy Nativity *in the USA*
26 Order of St Anne *in the USA*
Community of the Sisters of the Love of God *in the UK*
27 Community of St John the Divine *in the UK*
Sisterhood of St John the Divine *in Canada*
Society of St John the Divine *in South Africa*
Brothers of St John the Evangelist *in the USA*
Society of St John the Evangelist *in north America & the UK*
Sisters of Charity *in the UK*
28 Society of the Sacred Mission *in Australia, Lesotho, South Africa & the UK*
Sisters of the Incarnation *in Australia*
29 Community of St Michael & All Angels *in South Africa*
Community of St Peter (Woking) *in the UK*
Community of St Peter, Horbury *in the UK*
Society of the Sisters of Bethany *in the UK*
30 Community of St Andrew *in the UK*
Community of the Sacred Name *in Fiji, New Zealand & Tonga*
31 Congregation of the Sisters of the Visitation of Our Lady *in Papua New Guinea*
Community of the Blessed Lady Mary *in Zimbabwe*
Community of St Aidan & St Hilda *in the UK*
Sisterhood of St Mary *in Bangladesh*

News
of
Anglican
Religious Life

CSF house, Metheringham, Lincolnshire, UK, in the snow.

Earthquakes

The years 2010–11 have seen some devastating earthquakes around the world and Anglican Religious have been both directly affected and also involved in a ministry to others caught up in these natural disasters.

On 12 January 2010, lives and homes in Haiti were shattered by an earthquake. Casualty figures were enormous, as were the numbers of injured. Those who survived had to cope – and still do – with the destruction of buildings and roads that will take years to rebuild. The Sisters of St Margaret in the capital Port-au-Prince, along with the residents of their old people's home, were directly hit by the tremors. Miraculously none of the Sisters or those who live with them was killed or seriously injured. However, the convent was rendered uninhabitable – the kitchen had collapsed, the upstairs library had fallen into the chapel below. Holy Trinity Cathedral nearby was a ruin too. The Sisters, and the elderly for whom they care, found refuge in a soccer field at a nearby college, sleeping in tents. Gradually, over the months since, the Sisters have been recreating their ministries and places to live. First priority was shelter for the elderly of the Foyer Notre Dame. Then the schools, which became operative again by April 2010. The Sisters aid the youngsters with their tuition fees and books. Food is still scarce, as is fresh water, but the Sisters help whoever they can in the Cathedral complex. Electricity supply is unpredictable. Nevertheless, hope is not lost, despite the continuing trials. As Sister Marie Margaret puts it, "I do know and believe that God is guiding us to get completely out of this dark tunnel."

The Community of the Sacred Name in Christchurch, on the south island of New Zealand, were hit by a major earthquake there during the night of 4 September 2010. The red brick convent was so badly damaged that it will have to be demolished. The Sisters were mercifully unhurt but had to move into the much smaller Retreat House, which was not damaged then. Before any decisions could emerge as to the community's future in Christchurch, another earthquake struck on 22 February

A CSN group outside the red brick convent which was damaged in the first earthquake.

2011. As this one occurred at lunchtime, casualties in the city were far higher. Again, the Sisters escaped unhurt, but this time the Retreat House suffered cracks in its concrete base. The sisters evacuated to Ashburton, one hour to the south, and at the time of writing no firm plans have been made as to the future shape of CSN's presence in Christchurch.

On 11 March 2011, it was Japan's turn to suffer an earthquake, the biggest on the Richter scale that nation has ever suffered since records have been kept. The Community of Nazareth resident at Mitaka, a town within the Tokyo conurbation, were unharmed. Most of the appalling devastation was not caused by the tremors and aftershocks, but by the tsunami, and that affected predominantly the north-eastern seaboard of Japan. The dangers of radiation from the damaged nuclear installations on the coast were a major concern.

The tremendous work of reconstruction in these areas of the world will take years to complete. The memory of the events for those who experienced them will be ever present in the mind. All who pray will ask for courage and energy to be granted to all those who have suffered and still suffer. They will ask too that the Religious communities are able to be a blessing and a strength to those around them, and continue to be beacons of hope amidst the adversity.

Living anew

Several communities have been involved in building new monasteries and convents or have opened new houses since the last edition of the Year Book. Some of these are shown in illustrations on the section title pages to follow.

One issue that has figured strongly in some of the new buildings is that of sustainability. The Benedictines, formerly at Burford in the UK, moved into their new home at Mucknell late in 2010. At the new abbey, the community are seeking "to live more simply, sustainably and more lightly on the earth." Wherever practical, the existing farm buildings have been retained for re-use, whilst the materials of what was demolished have been recycled. Arrangements for heating, lighting and insulation minimise energy use. Renewable fuel sources and technologies are used. There is a rainwater harvesting system. Foul water is disposed of using an on-site biological treatment system and reed beds in swales. Waste is minimised through recycling and composting. The garden is organic, including a large walled kitchen garden, and an orchard has been planted, so that the community can produce food for itself and others. The brothers and sisters hope in their life-style to echo the delight God has in creation (picture page 175).

The Community of the Holy Cross moved into their new home at Costock, UK, – not far from their previous home at Rempstone – in March 2011. This too has been designed with environmental factors given significance. The new building has solar panels for energy supply, and the surrounding land is being utilised with ecological balance in mind. Not only will the Community continue (as at Rempstone) to grow much of its own food, it has also planted areas to encourage bees and butterflies and other wildlife, whilst a further area has already been planted with saplings to create more woodland.

The buildings themselves incorporate the existing farm structures. The early

18th century farmhouse is restored as the guest house, the barns as the community enclosure, refectory, reception rooms and cloister, all surrounding the garth. In the centre of the garth, a new chapel has been built, stunning in its simplicity, elegant in its proportions. The venerable tradition of CHC has been poured into a new form, and the centrality of prayer and contemplation is geographically at the centre of all the Community will do in their new home *(picture page 9)*.

Other new buildings illustrated are the CSF house at Metheringham in Lincolnshire, UK, which is a former old rectory *(see pages 1 & 187)*, the new wing at Malling Abbey *(see page 19)* and the new home of the monks formerly at Elmore Abbey, now resident in the cathedral close at Salisbury, UK *(see page 181)*.

Walsingham update

Sister Mary Teresa SSM writes: For the Sisters at the SSM Priory at Walsingham, UK, 2010 proved to be a challenging year. As it dawned, things looked promising, as four serious young aspirants were exploring a possible vocation with us. This gave us fresh hope and a sense of expectancy.

At the end of May, Sister Phyllis fell and needed surgery on her femur. Although this healed well, she became bewildered, and her confusion advanced with such rapidity that she lost all her reasoning powers and needed to be admitted to a specialist care home. Sadly, she can never return home. Then, two years after major surgery, Sister Joan Michael's cancer returned and she lost her long and courageous battle, dying on 7 December. Before her death, the first of our aspirants, Rose, was received as a postulant. Three weeks later, Mother Carolyne Joseph told the Chapter that she and Sisters Wendy Renate and Jane Louise, had decided to enter the Roman Catholic Ordinariate. They left the Community on 2 December.

At the Priory, this meant there were just four older Sisters and Rose. The future for us looked very bleak, but we knew it was not the time for hasty decisions. We needed time and space to review the whole situation to discern the way ahead.

However, not one of us felt we could just give up, close down this autonomous house of the Society, send Rose away and tell the aspirants there would be no future Noviciate. In addition, Sister Caroline Jane CSP, from St Peter's Woking, had for some time been considering transfer to Walsingham and now made her decision to ask to do so. To give up now was certainly not the spirit of our Founder, John Mason Neale, nor that of SSM! Echoing in our ears was his maxim: "The impossible *must* be done!" With this in mind, we have now elected Sister Mary Teresa as Mother, re-opened the Noviciate, accepted Sister Caroline Jane to explore transfer – and wait to see what transpires.

Humanly speaking, we know this must seem quite mad. Under God, what might have seemed an apparent death must issue in resurrection, whatever the outcome. We are well aware of our fragility: we know postulants do not necessarily stay the course, but we are more than prepared to take the risk, and so, it seems, are they. Who knows? God is the God of the impossible. Whatever happens in the end, we shall be able to rest in the peace and the certainty that we have tried to do what we feel to be God's Will – and that is all that really matters.

All shall be well and all manner of things shall be well!

News from SHC

The Society of the Holy Cross from Korea closed their mission house in the UK in November 2010 after three years of experiment because it was too difficult to obtain visas. Instead they are assisting in the training and nurture of novices in Myanmar (Burma), Singapore and Hong Kong, with the aim of opening Religious communities in each Province in the future. Two girls from Myanmar are coming to Korea for their formation. They will live with SHC until they make their Profession. It will take a year at least for them to learn the Korean language, with then 2–3 years in the novitiate and 3–4 years for junior and senior profession. Sister Margaret CGS will stay with SHC in Seoul for a month in mid-2011 to share in the formation process. A team of five women and two priests from Hong Kong Province has already visited Seoul for a few days in February 2011 to explore Religious community life.

Love Fulfilled

Sisterhood of the Epiphany

Mother Winifred SE died on 26 May 2010, the last surviving member of a sisterhood founded in 1902. The Oxford Mission to Calcutta had brought into being the Brotherhood of the Epiphany, and when the Brothers appealed to their supporters in Britain for women to assist, four volunteered. Under the leadership of Edith Langridge, an Oxford graduate, they arrived in Calcutta at the end of 1902, and in February 1903 went to Barisal (now in Bangladesh), where their mother house was established. They engaged in educational, evangelistic and medical work, particularly among women, and helped to transform many lives with their various ministries. From the beginning, they had determined to create a Religious community, and a Rule, based on that of St Benedict, evolved. Others joined them over the succeeding decades; and, in time, they also opened an orphange and primary school in Behala, near Calcutta. The climate and political conditions made this a tough vocation to maintain, with some Sisters having to withdraw because of health problems. However, over their hundred-year history, thirty-eight Sisters persevered and died in vows, with two others transferring to other communities: Leonore, who died as a CSF Sister, and Mother Sushila, who founded the Christa Sevika Sangha. In the 1990s, the three SE Sisters remaining in Bangladesh returned to Britain to spend their final years with the Community of All Hallows in the UK. Sister Florence remained in India until her death in 2004 at the age of 100. Winifred took over as Mother from Joan in 1997; the latter died in 1999, followed by Sister Rosamund in 2003. With Winifred's death, the Sisterhood's mission is fulfilled.

Community of the Holy Family

Sister Jean CHF died on 27 November 2010, the last of the Community of the Holy Family, founded in the 1890s by Agnes Mason. The foundress was a graduate of Newnham, Cambridge, UK, as were two of the three others noviced in August 1896. From the beginning therefore, although some Sisters would pursue nursing and other activities, most of the Sisters focussed on an educational ministry, the community opening schools in London and Kent, before finally establishing their main work at Baldstow near St Leonard's-on-Sea in 1913. They also ran a training college at Naini Tal, in Lucknow diocese, in India for many years. The Mother Foundress and other Sisters wrote books and articles, and were keen to remain in touch with academic life, so a house of study was maintained for some years in Cambridge. The more contemplative aspect of Religious life was represented by the Sisters opening St Pega's Hermitage, near Peterborough, eventually taken over by the Society of the Precious Blood. Through so many avenues, the Sisters CHF influenced many lives over the hundred years of their witness. Mother Agnes, professed in 1898, became the first Mother Superior. She resigned in 1933 and died in 1941 aged 92. The work continued under her successors, Mildred (1933–58) and Gwendolen (1958–92), but the number of vocations declined and by the time Kathleen Mary became Mother in 1992, there were only a few Sisters remaining. In January 1997, the last three Sisters moved to live in the gatehouse at Malling Abbey to live under the care of the Benedictine community there. Kathleen Mary died in 2002, Phyllis Ella in 2006; Jean's death after 64 years in profession completed the story. For all that these sisters achieved and were, thanks be to God!

Alton Abbey's founder

The library of books on the history of Anglican Religious life has been supplemented by a new study of one of the lesser-known community founders. Charles Plomer Hopkins began the Order of St Paul in 1884, a community that is now the Benedictine Community of Our Lady & St John at Alton Abbey in Hampshire, UK. R W H Miller has now published a study of his life, in particular his political work with the seamen's union, at a time when men at sea were frequently treated unfairly by shipping employers. The study is entitled *Priest in Deep Water: Charles Plomer Hopkins and the 1911 Seamen's Strike* (Lutterworth Press, Cambridge, UK, 2010).

The book is full of interesting details both of the life of contemporary seafarers and also the evolution, through the ministry to them, of OSP. Born originally in the USA (though with a British mother), Hopkins spent much of his early life in Burma, where his American father worked as a river pilot. Charles grew up to be a talented musician who became organist at the local cathedral. Hopkins soon also developed a successful chaplaincy to the seaman who would arrive in the local port far from home and with few places to go. Encouraged by the local bishop, this led to Hopkins being ordained. The development of a Religious community was his answer to the problem of how to increase the number of port chaplaincies of the type he pioneered. The most prominent houses in Britain were at Barry (in Wales) and Greenwich in London. A 'mother house' was created in Hampshire, UK, which is now Alton Abbey. One of Hopkins's innovations was to allow women to join the Order, although only a few took up the opportunity. However, Sister Frances persevered and when Hopkins died in 1922, she succeeded him as superior.

Hopkins's work for seaman and his crucial role in their union's political struggles, especially the 1911 strike, is thoroughly explored in the heart of this book and forms an interesting illustration of how Anglican Religious have been influential outside the Church as well as within it.

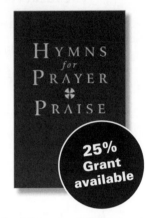

Articles

The chapel at the new CHC convent at Costock, UK.

Reflections on New Monasticism
by Abbot Stuart OSB

The rich proliferation of experience in the field of new monasticism reflects fresh life. It heralds, I believe, the beginning of a new age, a new way of 'being Church'. The era of Christendom – the religious culture that has dominated Western society since the fourth century – is over, however much many church-going Christians may not recognize or wish to admit it. When Christianity was established as the official religion of the Roman Empire and its successor states, what developed was church and state becoming the twin pillars of a sacral culture, each supporting the other. This is no longer true and the great institutions of that era are now crumbling, even where they haven't already disappeared. We are therefore entering a new era and a new paradigm is beginning to emerge.

There are hints that behind the materialism that has marked the recent 'consumer society', there is growing a search for spirituality – rather than formal institutional religion – which will affirm the global interdependence of all peoples and honour the many different forms the quest for spiritual integrity will take. The expressions of Christian new monasticism are attempts to live the Christian gospel with a fresh integrity. The temptation is to seek the recognition and approval of the institutional Church – but in a new era, I think we should sit light to seeking formal regulation and structure for these communities too soon, while at the same time seeking to protect people from abuse. It's a tricky tightrope to tread if these communities are to be truly prophetic, because by their very nature they will challenge much of the 'double think' of the established churches and, not least, denominationalism itself.

A second temptation is to focus on the natural desire to increase the numbers of

the core community rather than deepen the life of the members in the Christ-life and leave the increase to the Holy Spirit. Seeking to create community is like seeking to create happiness. Christian community results from engaging together in rediscovering the Church's original mandate to be a missionary people, a community on the move, as were the first Christians – focusing outward rather than inward. No community is static but always in flux as existing members 'journey' and new people come. One of the vital missional elements in community is to create an atmosphere in which the visitor can encounter Christ: *'Where two or more are united in my name, there am I among them.'* (Matthew 18.20). This can only be achieved by engaging in the paschal mystery. Jesus' new commandment to *'Love one another as I have loved you'* (John

Abbot Stuart OSB

15.12), requires us to lay down our lives for each other – our way of doing things, our opinions, etc. When we know how to peel a potato, can we allow someone else to do it a different way?! It takes courage to risk, and courage is the fruit of trust, and trust can take years to grow.

Many, if not most, of us who are attracted to community life are damaged and fearful people, and when we live at close quarters with each other, it doesn't take long before some of the deep buttons begin to be pushed. St Benedict tells us to *'support with the greatest patience one another's weaknesses of body and character'* (Rule, chapter 72). It's not an easy thing when we find ourselves irrationally irritated by someone from whom we have no escape! Fear of conflict will impede the growth of trust in a community; it is vital to address it and not to be afraid to seek help from outside the community. It is important, too, not to underestimate the difficulty of holding together those who temperamentally need clearly-defined boundaries and expectations with those who temperamentally need to travel light. The great thing is to be able to see difference as gift, as invitation to grow in mutual charity, rather than as hindrance to a peaceful life in community. There is a common and mistaken assumption that members of a community will be naturally compatible: it was not so among the men Jesus chose as his disciples – Matthew was a tax collector for the Romans and Simon the Zealot was a violent Jewish nationalist – and it is not so now.

I am reminded of something Brother Ramon SSF used to say. He believed that when the Religious life was recovered in the Church of England in the nineteenth century, a great mistake was made in adopting the Roman Catholic pattern of many different orders, some 'active' and others 'contemplative', rather than following the Orthodox model of having only one monastic order with different expressions so that, as people journeyed, there could be times and levels of withdrawal and others of missional engagement, as appropriate. One of the gifts of 'traditional' monastic life is its 'long haul' perspective of life commitment: a life commitment to live with the same bunch of people come what may, so that rather than walk away, one has to work through the difficulties. Important, too, is that this is a two-way commitment: the community's life commitment to the individual gives that member security to face the dark, frightening issues that normally lie buried, too deep to be faced and healed, and supports them as they do so. And the fruit of that is – or should be – a depth of acceptance and freedom among the members of the community that means that other people can be welcomed and accepted as they are – as people were by Jesus.

One important element in many of the new monastic communities is the presence of children. Benedict had children (though not usually the children of his monks!) in his monasteries, 'given' by parents to be members of the monastic community, to be brought up and educated and become adult monks. Children are an aid in 'sitting light' to the less important structures and opening us to the immediacy of the demands of charity. They also have the capacity to prick our bubbles of self-importance and self-righteousness and keep our feet on the ground: *'How can you say you love God whom you cannot see, when you do not love your neighbour whom you can see?'* (1 John 4.20).

When God invites groups of individuals to journey together into community, it is usual to find that, once the initial flush of enthusiasm is over, the members discover that they are not naturally compatible soul mates. This is why it is always useful to have a wise person around who can 'hold the boundaries' and help the community to deepen. The prime vocation of the monastic is the choice of God and the gospel-life and not to the community; that is secondary. Whereas the demands of charity and the community can be all too obvious and insistent, very often God seems to disappear and we are left floundering. Again, there is need for wise accompaniment for each individual as well as for the community as a whole. When the almost overwhelming temptation is to assume that it is all a big mistake, and we feel ready to throw in the towel and give up, this is precisely the moment to stay put and explore the invitation to growth.

The trouble is that at the moment there seems to be a dearth of humble, mature wisdom in this field. We are at the beginning of a new era and there are very few obviously holy 'starez' or 'gurus' to turn to for counsel. They do exist – very often in the most unlikely places, and like the *starez* of the Russian forests and the gurus of India they have to be searched out and, often, persuaded that they might have wisdom to share; wisdom gained from their own journey into God and their humanity (there is a great truth that the wiser one is, the less wise one feels – just as the holier one is, the less holy one feels). Their circumstances and religious traditions may be very different from those of the new monastics, but if their wisdom is of God it will cross these differences. Jesus' 'new commandment' remains the same for all time and for all who seek to follow him: *'Love one another as I have loved you – Follow me.'*

It is a great joy when we see very different expressions of monastic communities, 'new' and 'old', working together. We need each other, and we need to be able to draw on each other's experience and wisdom. It is vital that the 'new monastic communities' both share with each other (not least by using the website: *new-monasticism-network.ning.com*) and also develop strong relationships with some of the more traditional monastic communities so that such treasures as they have – both spiritual and material – can be shared and a strong, vibrant network of community life be part of the Church as it emerges into the new era.

The article above is an edited version of the Abbot's contribution to Graham Cray et al, New Monasticism as Fresh Expression of Church, *Canterbury Press, Norwich, 2010.*

Be the change you want to see:
Becoming communities of formation
by Brother Clark Berge SSF

One of the surprising developments during my first year in office as Minister General of SSF was the decision to look at formation. This was made by our First Order Chapter – a gathering when sisters and brothers from all the provinces meet together, which only happens once every three years. The decision grew out of a series of complaints, which matured into observations: we were having a hard time getting members to serve as novice guardian because we were not very clear about what formation meant. Few brothers or sisters felt they had the skills to be novice guardian.

To implement the decision, a series of international conferences was planned, the first being a three-week program with the task of developing an international curriculum for initial formation. We gathered in New York at Little Portion Friary during July 2009. From the beginning challenging issues arose.

ISSUE 1: WILLINGNESS TO CHANGE

First was the hurdle that many communities want new members, but refuse to change when the new members come. The result is that communities lure new members in saying they want to grow, but then "torture" them by refusing to change to incorporate new members in a life-giving way. At times, the example of the professed can be a process of deformation and eccentricity. Therefore, Don Bisson, a Marist brother, helped us see that flexibility and willingness to change are qualities that communities require if they are to be an effective place of formation. Therefore formation cannot be solely the job of one designated person; rather it is the work of the entire community. So we must become communities of formation.

The underlying lesson for us was the willingness to do things differently in order to further the Kingdom's goals. This was reinforced by a field trip to the Poverty Initiative at Union Seminary where we spoke to people about identifying and training leaders among America's poor. They not only give potential leaders solid teaching and orientation, they listen to them and incorporate their ideas in the work of the organization. We also visited the Ecclesia Ministries and learned about forming non-traditional ways of working; for example, homeless people were not comfortable in beautiful Episcopal churches, so they took church outside to them instead.

ISSUE 2: VALUING EVERYONE'S EXPERIENCE

There is nothing so formative as "walking a mile in another's shoes." This was one of the challenges that came from Dr. Kwok Pui-Lan, a professor at the Episcopal Divinity School. She asked us questions about our homes, our ministries, and our hopes for our curriculum. Then she observed that our Order is made up of nations that were formerly part of the British Empire, and asked how we grappled with this colonial heritage. We talked about the valuing of experience of all members, the need for financial self-sufficiency (not to rely on financial support from the "home" country). There are many insidious ways that colonial attitudes make an impact on our work and devalue non-Western cultures. It was important, she said, actually to go to the different countries.

A prominent labor organizer gave us a helpful formula: conscientization + commitment = change (C + C = C). Becoming aware of a problem, or what a person has to offer, is the first challenge. Add to this a commitment to learn about and do something about a situation. Then you have the way to change. When he learned that literacy is one of the major challenges among some of our brothers, he showed us drawings he uses as "texts" to assist in the process of reflection and awareness.

ISSUE 3: EVERYONE HAS LEADERSHIP POTENTIAL

There are no excuses not to engage people in formation. All of us are capable of growing and changing, and we can teach people to become leaders. Likewise, we can teach literacy, the lack of it does not disqualify one from being part of a community's formation process. It became clear that our community is training

Brother Clark Berge SSF (centre) at the Formators' Conference, SI, 2010

men and women to be leaders, and it will require a diversified approach and a commitment to living differently. God calls each of us to a ministry; each of us has responsibilities. We are all leaders.

A WAY FORWARD

We decided that our curriculum would have to provide a road map, but leave the details of implementation up to the several provinces. We will address the challenges (like literacy) best at the local level. Now, if you join SSF in Papua New Guinea, or Brazil, in Korea or UK, every member will struggle with the same topics, reach for similar milestones. The result, we hope, will be a flexible community that welcomes new members and listens to their voices, honoring their experiences. New members will feel empowered to develop ministry initiatives and take responsibility for themselves and the community.

Immediately after we developed the curriculum, we identified parts of it that sound good on paper, but few of us had any notion how to implement. For instance, how do we teach a core Franciscan value on "being peacemakers"? This gave us part of our agenda for the next year's conference.

HEALING, TEACHING SKILLS AND PEACEMAKING

Setting three goals for the second formators' conference, we wanted to heal some of the colonial past, to develop teaching skills that could transform novices and the community as a whole, and to learn about being peacemakers. We met in the Solomon Islands. Brothers and sisters from developed nations learned much about life in a developing nation, and some of us felt chastened by the experience! We followed a curriculum called the Anti-violence Project with two amazing facilitators. We soon learned some very specific ways to teach about peace as well as discovering a wealth of different ideas about how to teach.

DISCERNMENT

The third conference is already in the works, in a process of discernment. Working collaboratively and cross-culturally is an exciting experience. As we reflect on our community life, we have had to pray hard about some things. We've made changes. New members are joining. Now is not the time to rest on our laurels. New members bring new perspectives, new opportunities.

Formation: some thoughts

by Sisters Margaret Theresa & Clare Louise SLG

assisted by Sister Isabel SLG

What should be our approach to Formation in the 21st Century? How can we best pass on our Community's ethos?

Many experiencing a call to the Religious Life are older than was usual thirty years ago and have considerable experience of life. They may have held responsible positions in secular employment. They may have been in a long-term relationship or married. Some will have been Christians for many years; others will have come to faith more recently. This can result in a diverse novitiate. This presents many challenges. Also, there are fewer aspirants and that may mean a novitiate of only one or two. The lack of a peer group is especially challenging for a lone novitiate member, as well as for the community as a whole. It is probably more keenly felt in larger than smaller communities. The image of grafting newcomers onto the trunk of the community is one worth keeping in mind. An assistant Novice Guardian can also be a support – to both Guardian and novice.

A community may even be without anyone at all in the novitiate for a number of years. Nevertheless, to retain the office of Novice Guardian enables the community as a whole to be ready still to welcome newcomers. The Guardian should keep in touch with others in that role, continue their own formation in guardianship and keep up-to-date with current issues. Hosting inter-novitiate study days is another way in which Novice Guardians can keep active in their office and whole communities can once again have first-hand experience of those in formation.

It seems advisable to involve all the life professed in discerning whether or not a candidate should be received into the novitiate. It is the whole community that newcomers are seeking to join. This helps to ensure that the wisdom of all members is available in the discernment process. While the Novice Guardian should oversee the study schedule and retain overall responsibility for training, the involvement of more of the professed, by providing 'classes' for example, is one way of enabling the grafting process to take effect. For experienced Religious to meet with those who have newly-joined helps the latter to interact at a deeper level than is often possible through recreational encounters, by engaging together with a specific theme. Where there is a larger novitiate, it may be appropriate for each member to have a life professed companion or mentor in addition to the Guardian. Our experience has shown that the same two people meeting most weeks for both a 'direction' session and a 'class' can become very hard work. The right distinction between the two types of encounter is easily blurred; it can be hard for the relationship to grow and dependency can become a problem; the dynamic needs some variation. Here also discernment is required for too many different approaches can be confusing for the newcomer.

Returning to study, it is sometimes useful for this to be provided from outside the community. Novitiate members can enrol in courses, either locally for those in urban situations, or by correspondence; they can hear talks from outside people and via the inter-novitiate study programme. For many years now, there have been meetings of novices from the various communities for shared study, and an annual conference. Though widely appreciated, the sessions have lacked a comprehensive plan, being organised mostly on an *ad hoc* basis. Over the past year, with the encouragement of the Leaders, the Novice Guardians have been seeking to establish a three-year course of inter-novitiate study with a planned syllabus of subjects, comprising residential sessions held at various host communities, study days and the annual conference. Fairacres hosted the first such residential study session in January 2011. Twelve participants from eight different communities met from Monday evening until Thursday morning to study early monasticism with Brother Thomas OSB and Sister Benedicta Ward SLG. The novices appreciated the teaching offered and the chance to meet with others, and we, as the host community, enjoyed having such a large group of novices with us. These inter-novitiate study events provide an appropriate setting for novices to meet as a peer group, and to form friendships that may last throughout their community lives. Communities have an opportunity to enlist the teaching skills of outside speakers for their novices – while all share the cost involved.

There are other ways in which communities can share resources. Most have a person who is an expert in a particular area or has a deep love for some aspect of the Religious life that they can share. The inter-novitiate study course gives the opportunity for these gifts to be shared and be used to enrich the formation of novices in all our communities, not just one. Even communities currently without novices can host an event – and also those who no longer expect to receive newcomers, as they too have wisdom and experience to pass on. Each community has its own gifts, resources and unique charism to share. However, it is essential that a balance be maintained, so that novices remain confident their own community will provide training and support, both before and after life profession. The experience of those who have trodden the path before them, with its difficulties, doubts and struggles, is an important gift for newer members.

While aloneness before God in prayer is essential, there is also the need for friendship and companionship. Therefore, particularly for lone novices, inter-novitiate contact between scheduled study events is something to be encouraged. In the past there have been fears that a community might 'lose' someone by allowing visits to another community. Yet being drawn to another community can equally well be the call of God and if that proves to be so, there is no loss incurred by anyone.

However bewildering the rapid changes in our world, the challenge for Religious communities is to hold fast to what they have whilst adapting the training they provide. What aspirants receive from the community in the early stages must be authentic enough to carry them forward in faith and commitment to Life Profession and beyond.

Spiritual Direction
by Father Bill Scott

I have no sense of direction! The age of the Sat Nav is a great joy to me and enabled me to have a solitary holiday in France visiting everywhere I wanted to see by simply sitting back and doing as I was told. When we turn to Spiritual Direction it is helpful not to see it as a kind of Sat Nav issuing instructions and reminding constantly of the speed limit, but much more a discerning of the direction which God appears to wish a person to follow. A Spiritual Director is not there to dictate but simply to be, perhaps asking some questions and reflecting peoples' feelings and decisions back to them in order that they may be open to God in the ordinary events of their lives and in their prayer and sacramental acts.

The term, "Spiritual Director" is not a universally acceptable one, some preferring, "Soul Friend", "Godly Chum", "Fellow Traveller" and so on. Words are important, but I cannot help feeling that some things can become all too ridiculous. So for the purposes of this short article I will stick with "Spiritual Director".

There are volumes written on the subject but I would like to pick out a few aspects which are meaningful to me both as Director and Directee.

Firstly, the providing of a safe place where someone can feel secure and open. That is why confidentiality is as important as in the Confessional. When we feel safe we can relax, unwind, be open and honest and not worry about being thought strange or naughty! If someone feels awkward with the Director then the process is not fulfilling its potential. We all have moments of fear, but if fear dominates then it is time to change Director.

Secondly, the Director needs to be a listener. She or he is not there to do all the talking. I once was directed by an Irish Sister who did talk non-stop but knew exactly what was going on in my life. She had some mystical perception or second sight. We are not all thus endowed and so while the Director may well at times express ideas, opinions and gentle encouragement, these ought not to dominate.

Thirdly, as humans we do need help about the direction of our lives. We sometimes need a helping hand regarding how we pray, or what books to read. The Director might well try at times to lead the Directee towards a place where he or she may be better able to face barriers and grow closer to God.

Fourthly and not far from the last point, the Director has to be sensitive to the Directee's image of God. People can tend to flagellate themselves and be over harsh and judgmental about themselves. The Director is responsible for kindly and gently attempting to plant a more positive image of the God who loves, and to help people to realize that the aim of the whole spiritual journey is to accept God's love because it is only in that acceptance that we grow and are transformed.

The View from the Kennel
by an Old Dog
(otherwise Brother Anselm SSF)

Formation is not just a matter for novices and their guardians; the advent of new ideas and new methods are as significant to the senior members of a community as to the new recruits. Here, Brother Anselm SSF – after over fifty years as a Religious – reflects on the challenge for the older generation as Religious life faces change.

Old dogs are proverbially either reluctant to, or simply unable to, learn new tricks. If they are also burdened with an old-fashioned conscience and in the habit of self examination (remember?), they are confused old dogs – tormented with the questions: 'Is this old dog incapable of learning a new trick – and therefore innocent of culpable, selfish obstinacy?' or, 'Is this old dog reluctant to learn a new trick if that involves leaving a comfort zone for the sake of the gospel?' 'Am I an old dog in a new manger?' .

I was professed in 1960. Our Franciscan *Principles* were written (in India) before 1930 and are still read daily in portions over a period of one month, so we are perhaps over-familiar with them and have stopped noticing that they are peppered with allusions and assumptions which sound, to say the least, quaint. We are encouraged, monthly, to value simple living, silence, study, sacramental absolution, unquestioning obedience to superiors – all the old virtues and practices which, taken together made up the experience called 'The Religious Life' and which attracted vocations and which were expected of us by the Church. So, we take *The Principles* on our lips, they enter our ears – and then what? To the newcomer they must sound archaic and strange and attempts have been made to update them, and to make them intelligible to those from other English-speaking cultures – yet, somehow they seem to me to lose in those processes a certain something which, in the quaint original, spoke with eloquence and integrity of the kingdom, and of the gospel.

The bedrock of the quaint original *Principles* was the "Master's Law of Renunciation and Sacrifice", and the outworking of that Law, its incarnation, is in the practices outlined above. We are now told that slavish conformity to the rules is a denial of the gospel and a travesty of the kingdom of God – that a questioning of what used to be unquestioned is literally vital to the continuing life of the Religious life. I believe, in gloomier moments, that it's all too easy to forget about the simple living, the silence, the study, penitence, obedience – anything that constitutes an infringement of what can be thought of as my human rights – and to dress up all that forgetting as the grand quest for the renewed Religious life. There is, undeniably, the danger of hiding behind the old routines and thus escaping the life giving challenges of reform – but often, as I see it, those challenges are made the occasion of embracing the ways of the world in that we find ourselves enjoying the cosy lifestyles of middle-class affluence, and yielding to the enticements of digital entertainments and surfing the web. What has happened to the Master's Law? Is it possible somehow to safeguard silence, poverty, and ordinary hard work?

The above rather muddled observations are a part of being old. I have long had the reputation of being an Eeyore (from A A Milne's *Winnie the Pooh* stories), and to Eeyore I could add Gus the Theatre Cat, from the stage musical *Cats* (do you remember his view of the training of stage kittens?) – and if I didn't believe that many Religious, being also old, share some of this confusion, pain even – I'd keep it all to myself as perfect joy. Perhaps the old dogs should leave all this agonising behind – after all, we are old – accept with gratitude the changes which God sends us, and devote our dwindling energies to safeguarding, fostering, promoting in ourselves what the *Principles* describe as the three notes of the Order –

HUMILITY – LOVE – JOY, the oldest tricks of all?

Directory of traditional celibate Religious Orders and Communities

The new south wing at Malling Abbey, UK.
(photo courtesy of Paul Riddle)

20

Section 1

Religious communities in this section are those whose members take the traditional vows, including celibacy. For many, these are the 'evangelical counsels' of chastity, poverty and obedience. In the Benedictine tradition, the three vows are stability, obedience and conversion of life, celibacy being an integral part of the third vow.

These celibate communities may be involved in apostolic works or be primarily enclosed and contemplative. They may wear traditional habits or contemporary dress. However, their members all take the traditional Religious vows. In the Episcopal Church of the USA, these communities are referred to in the canons as 'Religious Orders'.

There are an estimated 2,082 celibate Religious in the Anglican Communion, (949 men and 1,133 women).

The approximate regional totals are:

Africa:	338	(Men 43, Women 295)
Asia:	71	(Men 14, Women 57)
Australasia & Pacific:	898	(Men 682, Women 216)
Europe:	507	(Men 123, Women 384)
North & South America & Caribbean:	268	(Men 87, Women 181)

International telephoning

Telephone numbers in this directory are mainly listed as used within the country concerned. To use them internationally, first dial the international code (usually 00) followed by the country code (see list below).

Australia	+ 61	India	+ 91	Solomon Islands	+ 677
Bangladesh	+ 880	Republic of Ireland	+ 353	South Africa	+ 27
Brazil	+ 55	Japan	+ 81	Sri Lanka	+ 94
Canada	+ 1	Korea (South)	+ 82	Spain	+ 34
Fiji	+ 679	Lesotho	+ 266	Swaziland	+ 268
France	+ 33	Malaysia	+ 60	Tanzania	+ 255
Ghana	+ 233	New Zealand	+ 64	UK	+ 44
Haiti	+ 509	PNG	+ 675	USA	+ 1

Society of
All Saints
Sisters of
the Poor

ASSP

Founded 1851

All Saints Convent
St Mary's Road
Oxford OX4 1RU
UK
Tel: 01865 249127
Email: leaderassp
@socallss.co.uk

Website: www.
asspoxford.org

Mattins   6.30 am

Terce or Eucharist
9.00 am

Eucharist 12.00 noon
or   Midday Office
12.15pm

Vespers   5.30 pm

Compline
8.00 pm

Variations on Sundays,
Saturdays
& major festivals

Office book
ASSP Office, based on
Anglican Office Book
1980

God calls us to be channels of God's love to those who are in need because of age, health or social circumstances, wherever we believe the Holy Spirit is leading us.

The heart of our Community life is the worship of God in the daily Office and the Eucharist. We set aside time for prayer and spiritual reading. We have meals together in refectory, make time for each other and share in day-to-day decision-making. We consider vocation to be ongoing and look for God in new situations.

The Convent adjoins St John's Home, which cares for frail, elderly people and has plans for developing dementia care. On the same site, Helen and Douglas House offer respite and end-of-life care for children and young people with life-shortening conditions. Across the road, the Porch Steppin' Stones is a day centre for homeless or vulnerably-housed people. These all have separate management but Sisters are involved in a variety of ways.

Our guest house gives a warm welcome to individuals or groups needing retreat or spiritual refreshment. Sisters also offer Spiritual Direction and the ordained Sister has ministered in Oxford parishes and chaplaincies.

SISTER JEAN RAPHAEL ASSP
(Community Leader, assumed office 18 October 2010)
SISTER FRANCES DOMINICA ASSP
(Assistant Community Leader)

Sister Margaret	Sister Ann Frances
Sister Jean Margaret	Sister Margaret Anne
Sister Helen Mary	*(priest)*
Sister Mary Julian	Sister Jane

Obituaries
4 Sep 2010   Sister Helen, aged 83, professed 55 years, Revd Mother 1989–2006

Associates and priest Friends
Those who want to commit support for the community and, where possible, practical help may be invited to become Associates or Priest Friends.

Community Publication
New Venture, published annually in November. Order from the Society of All Saints.

Community Wares
All Saints Embroiderers make, repair and remount vestments, frontals etc.

Guest and Retreat Facilities
Brownlow House, our guest house with six en-suite rooms, including one double and one twin, and the Upton Room accommodating meeting of up to fifteen people. Self-catering facilities are available. *Email: guestsister@socallss.co.uk*

Bishop Visitor: Rt Revd Bill Ind

Other Addresses
St John's Home *(for the elderly)*, St Mary's Road, Oxford OX4 1QE, UK
Tel: 01865 247725   Fax: 01865 247920   Email: admin@st_johns_home.org
All Saints Embroidery, All Saints Convent, St Mary's Road, Oxford OX4 1RU, UK,   *Tel: 01865 248627*

Associated Houses
Helen and Douglas House, 14a Magdalen Road, Oxford OX4 1RW, UK
Tel: 01865 794749   Fax: 01865 202702   Email: admin@helenanddouglas.org.uk
Website: www.helenanddouglas.org.uk   Registered Charity No: 1085951
The Porch Steppin' Stone Centre, All Saints Convent, St Mary's Road, Oxford OX4 1RU, UK
Tel: 01865 728545   Email: info@theporch.fsbusiness.co.uk
Website: www.theporch.org.uk   Registered Charity No: 1089612

Community History & Books
Peter Mayhew, *All Saints: Birth & Growth of a Community*, ASSP, Oxford, 1987.
Kay Syrad, *A Breath of Heaven: All Saints Convalescent Hospital*, Rosewell, St Leonard's on Sea, 2002.
Sister Frances Dominica ASSP, *Just My Reflection: Helping families to do things their own way when their child dies*, Darton, Longman & Todd, London, 2nd ed 2007, £6.50.
Behind the big red door: the story of Helen House, Golden Cup, Oxford, 2006, £12.00

Registered Charity: No. 228383

All Saints Convent
PO Box 3127
Catonsville
MD 21228-0127
USA

Tel: 410 747 4104
Fax: 410 747 3321

Three All Saints Sisters went to Baltimore, Maryland, and the community house they began became an independent house in 1890.

In September 2009, the majority of the members of this American community of All Saints Sisters were received into the Roman Catholic Church.

Whilst still living at the Convent in Catonsville with the rest of the community, two sisters remain in the Anglican Communion.

Website
www.
asspconvent.org

Sister Virginia of All Saints *(sometime Mother)*
Sister Barbara Ann of All Saints

Brotherhood of the Ascended Christ

BAC

Founded 1877

Brotherhood House
7 Court Lane
(Rustmji Sehgal
Marg)
Delhi 110054
INDIA
Tel: 11 2396 8515
or 11 2393 1432
Fax: 11 2398 1025
Email:
dbs@bol.net.in

**Morning Worship &
Eucharist**
7.00 am

**Forenoon Prayer
(Terce)**
9.00 am

Midday Prayer (Sext)
12.45 pm

**Afternoon Prayer
(None)**
3.50 pm

Evening Worship
7.30 pm

**Night Prayer
(Compline)**
9.10 pm

Today, the Brotherhood has one bishop, three presbyters, one lay-brother and three lay-probationers who belong to the Church of North India. Since the earliest days, the Brotherhood has had a concern for serving the poor and underprivileged. In 1975, the Delhi Brotherhood Society was set up to organise social development projects in the poorer parts of Delhi. The work and social outreach of the Brotherhood is with and not for the poor of Delhi. The Brotherhood has initiated programmes of community health, education, vocational training and programmes for street and working children.

IAN WEATHRALL BAC
(Head, assumed office 27 March 2004)
COLLIN THEODORE BAC *(Assistant Head)*

Monodeep Daniel   Raju George
Solomon George
     Probationers: 3

Associates and Companions
There are twenty-three Presbyter Associates and eight Lay Companions who follow a simple Rule of Life adapted to their individual conditions.

Community Publication
Annual Newsletter and Report (free of charge).

Community History
Constance M Millington, *"Whether we be many or few": A History of the Cambridge/Delhi Brotherhood*, Asian Trading Corporation, Bangalore, 1999. Available from the Brotherhood House.

Guest and Retreat Facilities
The Brotherhood House at Court Lane has a large garden and well-stocked library. It is used as a centre for retreats, quiet days and conferences. The small Guest Wing receives visitors from all over the world. There are four rooms. Both men and women are welcome.

Most convenient time to telephone:
7.30 am – 8.30 am, 4 pm – 5 pm (Indian Standard Time)

Office Book
The Church of North India Book of Worship & Lesser Hours & Night Prayer (BAC)

Bishop Visitor: Rt Revd Dr P P Marandih

Chama cha Mariamu Mtakatifu
(Community of St Mary of Nazareth and Calvary)

CMM

Founded 1946

The Convent
Kilimani
PO Box 502
Masasi, Mtwara
TANZANIA

Morning Prayer
5.30 am

Mass
6.30 am

Midday Prayer
12.30 pm

Evening Prayer
3.00 pm

Compline
8.30 pm

The Community was founded in 1946 when the first girls took vows, and was under the Community of the Sacred Passion (CSP) until 1968, when they left them and Sister May Elizabeth was elected first Mother Superior CMM.

Bishop Frank Weston is the Grandfather Founder of CMM, while Bishop William Vincent Lucas is the Father Founder CMM. Both were Universities' Missionaries to Central Africa. CMM Sisters are trying their best to keep the aims of the founders: to serve God, His Church and His people.

Since then, there are eleven Houses in Tanzania and one in Zambia. Sisters do different services in the stations where they live, according to the demands and resources. At the time being, the Community is busy to raise up the standard of education of the members, so that it copes with the duties they face.

SISTER GLORIA PRISCA CMM
Revd Mother Superior, assumed office 22 May 2004)
SISTER HELEN CMM *(Sister Superior, Mother House)*
SISTER MARTHA BRIJITA CMM
(Sister Superior, Northern Zone)
SISTER MAGDALENE CMM
(Sister-in-charge, Mother House)

Sister Rehema	Sister Mercy
Sister Cesilia	Sister Lidia
Sister Ethel Mary	Sister Stella
Sister Neema	Sister Agness Margreth
Sister Ester	Sister Merina Felistas
Sister Christine	Sister Jane
Sister Tabitha	Sister Rabeca
Sister Eunice Mary	Sister Dorothy
Sister Joy	Sister Perpetua
Sister Franciska	Sister Jennifer
Sister Anjela	Sister Anjelina
Sister Anna	Sister Julia Rehema
Sister Prisca	Sister Joceline Florence
Sister Nesta	Sister Jane Rose
Sister Bertha	Sister Susana Skolastika
Sister Aneth	Sister Anna Beatrice
Sister Mary	Sister Mariamu Upendo
Sister Agatha	Sister Josephine Joyce
Sister Lucy	Sister Skolastika Mercy
Sister Berita	Sister Mary Prisca

Sister Paulina Anna
Sister Janet Margaret
Sister Thecla Elizabeth
Sister Janet Elizabeth
Sister Edna Joan
Sister Josephine Brijita
Sister Dainess Charity
Sister Agnes Edna
Sister Jane Felistas
Sister Asnath Isabela
Sister Ethy Nyambeku
Sister Vumilia Imelda
Sister Anna Mariamu
Sister Debora Skolastika
Sister Foibe Edina
Sister Veronika Modesta
Sister Harriet Helena
Sister Hongera Mariamu
Sister Lulu Lois

Sister Martha Anjelina
Sister Lucy Lois
Sister Penina Skolastika
Sister Anet Olver
Sister Roda Rahel
Sister Edith Natalia
Sister Harriet
Sister Victoria
Sister Violet Jaqueline
Sister Debora Dorothy
Sister Nesta Sophia
Sister Lea Felicia
Sister Hongera Elizabeth
Sister Edith Grace
Sister Elizabeth Getrude
Sister Benadeta Jane
Sister Philippa Sapelo
Sister Joan Patricia
Sister Jessie Mary

Sister Imani
Sister Antonia Tereza
Sister Veronica Rita
Sister Violet Minka
Sister Beata
Sister Hope
Sister Erica Mary
Sister Rose Monica
Sister Thecla Leticia
Sister Mariamu
Sister Emma Agatha
Sister Joyce Agnes

Novices: 19
Postulants: 5

Community Wares
Vestments, altar breads, agriculture products, cattle products, crafts, candles.

Office Book: Swahili Zanzibar Prayer Book & The Daily Office SSF

Bishop Visitor: Rt Revd Patrick P Mwachiko, Bishop of Masasi

Other addresses

PO Box 116, Newala
Mtwara Region
TANZANIA
Tel: 023 2410222

PO Box 162, Mtwara
TANZANIA
Tel: 023 2333587

PO Box 45, Tanga
Region, TANZANIA
Tel: 027 2643245

PO Box 195, Korogwe
Tanga Regio
TANZANIA
Tel: 027 2640643

The Convent, PO Kwa
Mkono Handeni
Tanga Region
TANZANIA

Ilala, PO Box 25068,
Dar es Salaam
TANZANIA
Tel: 022 2863797

PO Box 150, Njombe
TANZANIA
Tel: 026 2782753

PO Box 6, Liuli, Mbing
Ruvuma Region
TANZANIA

Sayuni Msima
PO Box 150
Njombe
TANZANIA
Tel: 026 2782753

Fiwila Mission
PO Box 840112
Mkushi
ZAMBIA

Mtandi, Private Bag,
Masasi
Mtwara Region
TANZANIA
Tel: 023 2510016

Chita Che Zita Rinoyera

(Holy Name Community)

CZR

Founded 1935

St Augustine's
Mission
PO Penhalonga
Mutare
Zimbabwe
Tel:
Penhalonga 22217

Bishop Visitor:
Rt Revd
Julius Makoni

Our Community was started by Father Baker of the CR Fathers at Penhalonga, with Mother Isabella as the founder. The CZR Sisters were helped by CR Sisters (Liz and Lois), and later by OHP Sisters (especially Lila, Mary Francis, Joyce and Hannah). When they left, Sister Isabella was elected Mother.

Today the CZR Sisters work at the clinic and at the primary and secondary schools. Some do visiting and help teach the catechism. We make wafers for several dioceses, including Harare. Some of the Sisters look after the church, seeing to cleaning and mending of the church linen. We have an orphanage that cares for thirty children, with an age range of eighteen months to eighteen years.

In 1982, half the Sisters and the novices left CZR and created another community at Bonda. Six months later, some of those Sisters in turn went to found Religious Life at Harare. In 1989, some of the Bonda community left to go to Gokwe and begin Religious Life there. So CZR has been the forerunner of three other communities in Zimbabwe. Please pray that God may bless us.

MOTHER BETTY CZR
(Reverend Mother, assumed office 2007)

Sister Stella Mary   Sister Elizabeth
Sister Anna Maria   Sister Emilia
Sister Hilda Raphael Sister Annamore
Sister Felicity   Sister Sibongile

Community Wares
We sell chickens, eggs, milk, cattle (two or three a year) and wafers.

Community of the Blessed Lady Mary

CBLM

Founded 1982

The Sisters care for orphans on St John's Mission, Chikwaka, and do parish work there and on the two missions of Christ the King, Daramombe, and St Francis Mission, Sherugi, in the diocese of Masvingo.

MOTHER SYLVIA CBLM
(Reverend Mother)

Address
Sister Dorothy   Sister Jasmine
Sister Anna   Sister Praxedes
Sister Faustina

Shearly Cripps Children's Home, PO Box 121 Juru, ZIMBABWE
Bishop Visitor: Rt Revd Chad Gandiya

Chita che Zvipo Zve Moto

(Community of the Gifts of the Holy Fire)

CZM

Founded 1977

Convent of Chita
che Zvipo Zve Moto
PO Box 138
Gokwe South
ZIMBABWE
Telefax: 263 059 2566

House Prayer 5.00 am

Mattins followed by
meditation 5.45 am

Holy Communion
6.00 am

Midday prayers
12 noon

Evensong
followed by
meditation 5.00 pm

Compline 8.30 pm

Office Book
Book of Common
Prayer & CZM Office
Book 2002

Bishop Visitor
Rt Revd Ishmael
Mukuwanda, Bp of
Central Zimbabwe

The Community is a mixed community of nuns and friars, founded by the Revd Canon Lazarus Tashaya Muyambi in 1977. On a visit to St Augustine's Mission, Penhalonga, he was attracted by the life of the CR fathers and the CZR sisters. With the inspiration of the Spirit of the Lord, he believed it was of great value to start a Religious community. The first three sisters were attached to St Augustine's for three months. The first convent was officially opened in 1979 and the initial work was caring for orphans at St Agnes Children's Home.

In January 2000, Canon Muyambi stepped down from leadership, believing the Community was mature enough to elect its own leaders, which it did in March 2000. The Community have a Rule, Constitution and are governed by a Chapter. They take vows of Love, Compassion and Spiritual Poverty. The Community is progressing well with young people joining every year. Each member is qualified or skilled in one trade or another.

SISTER PHOEBE CZM *(Archsister in charge)*
FRIAR JOSHUA CZM *(Archfriar)*
(both assumed office December 2006)

Sister Gladys A
Sister Eugenia
Sister Elizabeth
Sister Eustina
Sister Lydia
Sister Anna Kudzai
Sister Vongai Patricia
Sister Gladys B
Sister Teresah
Sister Alice
Sister Tendai A
Sister Itai
Sister Juliet
Sister Constance
Sister Tirivatsva

Sister Lilian
Sister Cynthia
Sister Precious
Sister Joyline
Sister Vongai
Friar Tapiwa Costa
Friar Brighton

Novices: 3
Sister Benita
Sister Tendai B
Sister Blessing

Postulants: 2

Other addresses in Zimbabwe
St Patrick's Mission Branch House, P. Bag 9030, Gweru
St James Nyamaohlovu Bulawayo P. Bag, Matebeleland
30 Berwick Road, South Downs, Gweru

Community Wares
Sewing church vestments, school uniforms, wedding gowns; knitting jerseys; garden produce; poultry keeping.

Christa Sevika Sangha
(Handmaids of Christ)

CSS

Founded 1970

Jobarpar
Barisal Division
Uz Agailjhara 8240
BANGLADESH

Oxford Mission,
Bogra Road
PO Box 21
Barisal 8200
BANGLADESH
TEL: 0431 54481

Morning Prayer

Holy Communion

Midday Prayer

Quiet Prayer together

Evening Prayer

Compline

Office Book
Church of Bangladesh
BCP &
Community Office
Book
(all Offices are in
Bengali)

The Community was founded in 1970 and was under the care of the Sisterhood of the Epiphany until 1986, when its own Constitution was passed and Sister Susila SE was elected as Superior.

The Sevikas supervise girls' hostels and a play-centre for small children. They also help in St Gabriel's School and supervise St Mary's Asroi (Home) at Barisal. The Community also produces for sale a wide variety of goods and produce.

MOTHER SUSILA CSS
(Mother Foundress, 25 January 1970; elected Reverend Mother CSS in July 1986)

Sister Ruth	Sister Dorothy
(House Sister, Jobarpar)	Sister Margaret
Sister Jharna	Sister Kalyani
(House Sister, Barisal)	Sister Shefali
Sister Sobha	Sister Shalomi
Sister Agnes	Sister Shikha

Fellowship of the Epiphany
The Oxford Mission Fellowship of the Epiphany was founded in 1921 for friends of the Mission in India, Bangladesh, the British Isles and elsewhere. There is also a Prayer Fellowship group.

Community Wares
Vestments, children's clothes, embroidery work, wine, wafers, candles. Farm produce: milk, poultry, fish. Land produce: rice, fruit, coconuts & vegetables. Twenty-four books translated into Bengali are for sale.

Community Publication
The Oxford Mission News, twice a year. Write to Oxford Mission, PO Box 86, Romsey, Hampshire SO51 8YD.
Tel: 01794 515004 Annual subscription: £4.00, post free.

Community History
Brethren of the Epiphany, *A Hundred Years in Bengal,*
ISPCK, Delhi, 1979
Mother Susila CSS, *A Well Watered Garden,*
(editor: M Pickering), Oxford Mission, Romsey, 2000
available from O. M. address above, £5 including p & p.

Guest and Retreat Facilities
Two rooms for men outside the Community campus. One house (three beds) for women. Donations received.

Bishop Visitor
Rt Revd Paul S Sarker, Bishop of Dhaka

Community of All Hallows

CAH

Founded 1855

All Hallows Convent
Belsey Bridge Road
Ditchingham
Bungay, Suffolk
NR35 2DT
UK
Tel: 01986 892749
(office) Mon-Fri

01986 895749
(Sisters)

Fax: 01986 895838

Email:
allhallowsconvent
@btinternet.com

Lauds 7.30 am

Eucharist
8.00 am (9.30 am Sat,
10.00 am Sun)

Sext 12.15 pm

Evening Prayer
5.30 pm

Compline 8.00 pm

Office Book
Daily Prayer

Registered charity
No 230143

We are a group of women with diverse personalities and gifts called together in a common commitment to prayer and active work under the patronage of the Saints. Central to our life are the daily Eucharist and the Divine Office, combined with time for personal prayer, meditation and spiritual reading. Together they draw us deeper into the desire to "serve Christ in one another and love as He loves us". This overflows into our active works – particularly in our ministry of hospitality, expressed mainly through our Guest Houses, Spiritual Direction, and leading Retreats for individuals and small groups. It also includes some pastoral ministry at our All Hallows Hospital and Nursing Home, which were founded and developed by us, but now form a separate Charity. In addition there is a large Conference Centre and a Day Nursery within our grounds. Our former convent building opposite is now home to an Emmaus community for the homeless.

The ministry of hospitality and prayer continues to flourish at our house in Rouen Road, Norwich, which is closely linked with the adjacent Julian Shrine and Centre.

All enquiries about the life and work of CAH should be directed in the first place to the leaders at the Convent.

SISTER ELIZABETH CAH & SISTER SHEILA CAH
(Joint Leaders, assumed office 7 July 2010)
SISTER PAMELA CAH *(Assistant Leader)*

Sister Violet   Sister Edith Margaret
Sister Winifred   Sister Rachel
Sister Jean   Sister Anne
Sister Margaret

Obituaries
11 Nov 2009   Sister Winifred Mary, aged 90,
               professed 37 years
26 May 2010   Mother Winifred SE, aged 87,
               professed 48 years, Revd Mother SE 1999–2010

Companions, Oblates, Associates and Contact Members
COMPANIONS, OBLATES, ASSOCIATES and CONTACT MEMBERS offer themselves to God within the community context in a varying degree of 'hands-on' commitment. Apply to the Convent for details.

Community Publication
A newsletter is circulated yearly at All Saints tide. To be included on the mailing list, please write to All Hallows Convent at the address above.

A group at All Hallows.

Other addresses and telephone numbers
All Hallows Guest House
Tel: 01986 892840

All Hallows House, St Julian's Alley, Rouen Road, Norwich NR1 1QT, UK
Tel: 01603 624738

Community Wares: A wide selection of photography cards.

Community History and books
Sister Violet CAH, *All Hallows, Ditchingham*, Becket Publications, Oxford, 1983.
Mother Mary CAH, *Memories*, privately published 1998.
Sister Winifred Mary CAH, *The Men in my Life*, privately published 2009.
Sister Violet CAH, *A Book of Poems*, privately published 2011.

Guest and Retreat Facilities: Enquiries about staying at our guest house should be addressed to Barbara Pascali, All Hallows House, address above.

Most convenient time to telephone:
9.00 am – 12 noon; 2.15 pm – 4.30 pm; 7.00 pm – 7.45 pm

Bishop Visitor
Rt Revd Graham James, Bishop of Norwich

Benedictine Community of Christ the King

CCK

Founded 1993

344 Taminick Gap Road
South Wangaratta
Victoria 3678
AUSTRALIA
Tel/Fax: 3 57257343
Email: cck94
@bigpond.com

Monastic Mattins & Prayer Time
4.30 am

Lauds 6.00 am

Eucharist & Terce
8.00 am

Sext 12 noon

None 1.15 pm

Vespers & Prayer Time 5.00 pm

Compline 7.15 pm

Office Book
The Divine Office is based on the Sarum Rite, using AAPB for the Psalms. Whenever the Office is sung, it is in Plainsong using BCP Psalms.

The Community of Christ the King is a Traditional Anglican Benedictine order, enclosed and contemplative. Its members endeavour to glorify God in a life of prayer under the threefold vow of Stability, Conversion of Life and Obedience. They follow a rhythm of life centred on the worship of God in the Daily Eucharist and sevenfold Office. The convent nestles at the foot of the Warby Ranges in Victoria, Australia. It is surrounded by attractive flower gardens, a citrus orchard and a kitchen garden. The fruit and vegetables ensure a certain amount of self-sufficiency, and afford the opportunity and privilege of manual labour, essential to the contemplative life. Hospitality aimed at helping visitors deepen their spiritual lives through prayer is a feature of the life. The property, with its extensive views, bush walks and seclusion, is ideally suited to relaxation, quiet reflection and retreat. It is ringed by fourteen large crosses providing opportunity for meditation on the way of the cross, and for prayer in solitude. We hold silent retreats and hope to develop this outreach.

MOTHER RITA MARY CCK
(*Revd Mother, assumed office 31 July 1997*)
SISTER PATIENCE CCK (*Assistant*)

Oblates: An Order of Benedictine Oblates has been established, open to women and men, clerical and lay.

Community Publication
The Community publishes a letter twice a year, sent free of charge to all interested in CCK (approximately 300 copies).

Community History
Dr Lesley Preston, *Called to Pray: Short History of the Community of Christ the King*, Benedictine Press, Camperdown, VIC., Australia, 2009. Available from Dr E M Crowther, 31 Hazlewood Close, Kidderminster, Worcs., DY11 6LW (for the price of the postage).

Guest and Retreat Facilities
We cater for those who want to deepen their life in Christ. There is a guest house which can accommodate three people (women or men): a self-contained cottage. There is no charge. A flat is attached to the chapel. A large fellowship room provides for parish quiet days and study groups. The original farmhouse is also available.

Most convenient time to telephone:
10 am – 12 noon, 2 pm – 4 pm, 6.45 pm – 7.40 pm.

Visitor: Father Bernard McGrath OSB

Community of the Companions of Jesus the Good Shepherd

CJGS

Founded 1920

The Priory
25 Woodstock
Road West,
Begbroke
Oxfordshire
OX5 1RJ
UK
Tel: 01865 855326
or
01865 855320

Email:
cjgs@csjb.org.uk

Lauds   7.30 am

Tierce   9.00 am

Eucharist   9.15 am

Midday Office
12.00 noon

Vespers   5.00 pm

Compline   8.30 pm

Registered Charity:
No. 270317

When the Community was founded, the first Sisters were all teachers living alone or in small groups but coming together during the school holidays. In 1943, West Ogwell House in South Devon became the Mother House and the more usual form of conventual life was established as well. The work of Christian education has always been of primary concern to the Community, whether in England or overseas, although not all the Sisters have been teachers.

In 1996, the Community moved to Windsor to live and work alongside the Community of St John Baptist, while retaining its own ethos. The Community aims 'to express in service for others, Christ's loving care for his flock.' At present, this service includes involvement in lay and ordained local ministry training; offering companionship to those seeking to grow in the spiritual life through spiritual direction and quiet days; and especially the befriending of the elderly, lonely, deaf and those in need.

In 2012, the Community expect to move with CSJB to Ripon College, Cuddesdon, OX44 9EX.

MOTHER ANN VERENA CJGS
(Mother Superior, assumed office 20 March 1996)
SISTER FLORENCE CJGS *(Assistant Superior)*
Sister Kathleen Frideswide

Obituaries
7 Jan 2010   Sister Evelyn Theresa, aged 89,
                    professed 54 years, Mother Superior 1984–1996

Associates
Associates of the Community are members of the Fellowship of St Augustine. They follow a rule of life drawn up with the help of one of the Sisters. They give support to the Community through their prayer, interest and alms, and are remembered in prayer by the Community. They and the Community say the 'Common Devotion' daily. They are truly our extended family.

Community Publication
CJGS News. Contact the Mother Superior.

Office Book: Common Worship with additions from the old CSJB Office.

Bishop Visitor: Rt Revd Dominic Walker OGS,
                  Bishop of Monmouth

Community of the Glorious Ascension

CGA

Founded 1960

Brothers:
The Priory
Lamacraft Farm
Start Point
Kingsbridge
Devon TQ7 2NG
UK

Tel & Fax:
01548 511474
Email: ascensioncga
@fsmail.net

Sisters:
Prasada
Quartier Subrane
Montauroux
83440 Fayenne
Va
FRANCE

Tel/Fax: 04 94477426

Registered Charity:
No. 254524

The Community seeks to live a common-life centred upon daily work, prayer and worship. The corporate pattern of the monastic life is at the heart of our life together; which aims to be informal and inclusive both in worship and hospitality. From its beginning, CGA has had a vibrant sense of mission which we try to maintain through our friendship with those who stay or visit, and also through involvement with people in the local area.

BROTHERS

BROTHER SIMON CGA
(Prior, assumed office 20 May 1993)
Brother David
Brother John

SISTERS

SISTER JEAN CGA *(Prioress)*
Revd Sister Cécile

Community Publication
CGA *Newsletter*, published annually. Write to the Prior.

Guest and Retreat Facilities
The priory in Devon offers accommodation for retreats or holiday in self-catering cottages. A purpose-built barn enables us to offer hospitality to local groups and churches on a daily basis.

Bishop Visitor: Rt Revd Edward Holland

Community of the Good Shepherd

CGS

Founded 1978

Christ Church Likas
PO Box 519
88856 Likas
Sabah
MALAYSIA
Tel: 088 383211

Residential address:
MQ8, Jalan Teluk
Likas
Kota Kinabalu
88400 Likas
Sabah
MALAYSIA

Morning Prayer
&
Evening Prayer
daily

Compline
7.45 pm

Holy Communion
8.00 am
(1st Thu of month)

The CGS Sisters in Malaysia were formerly a part of the Community of the Companions of Jesus the Good Shepherd in the UK *(see separate entry)*. They became an autonomous community in 1978. Their Rule is based on that of St Augustine and their ministry is mainly parish work.

In October 2000, the Sisters moved to Kota Kinabalu, the capital of Sabah, and have settled in at Likas, just opposite to Christ Church. Since 24 April 2010, Revd Yong Thiam Choy of All Saints' Cathedral has been the chaplain for the Community. The Diocesan project of building a new Community House has been completed, and occupied in November 2007. It has a spacious ground in front with cool breezes from Likas Bay beyond. There are rooms for visitors and enquirers to Religious Life.

In Kota Kinabalu, the Community, with the help of the associates, see the need to supply wafers to the Diocese and to gather the associates to pray for the Diocese.

SISTER MARGARET LIN-DIN CGS
(Sister-in-charge, assumed office 1978)

Postulants: 2

Associates
In Kota Kinabalu, some committed Christian women from the three Anglican Churches join in fellowship with the Community and have become associate members. They follow a simple rule of life to support the Community through prayer and to share in the life and work of the Community. Whenever they can, they come to join the annual retreat.

Community Wares
Stoles and wafers
                    (to supply the Sabah diocese at present).

Office Book
ASB and the Service Book of the Province of the Anglican Church in S E Asia.

Bishop Visitor
Rt Revd Albert Vun Cheong Fui, Bishop of Sabah

Benedictine Community of the Holy Cross, Costock

CHC

Founded 1857

Holy Cross Convent
Highfields
Nottingham Road
Costock   LE12 6XE
UK

Tel: 01509 852761
Fax: 01509 853051
Email: sisters@
holycrosschc.org.uk

Website: www.
holycrosschc.org.uk

(SOUTHWELL DIOCESE)

Matins   6.15 am

Lauds   7.30 am

Terce   9.15 am

Mass   9.30 am
(subject to change)

Sext   12.15 am
(subject to change)

None   1.30 pm

Vespers   4.30 pm
(4.00 pm Thu & Fri)

Compline   8.00 pm

The Community of the Holy Cross was founded in 1857 by Elizabeth Neale (sister of John Mason Neale, the hymnographer), at the invitation of Father Charles Fuge Lowder. The foundation was intended for Mission work in Father Lowder's parish of London Docks, but succeeding generations felt that the Community was being called to a life of greater withdrawal, and in the twentieth century the Benedictine Office, and later the *Rule of St Benedict*, were adopted.

The Community aims to achieve the Benedictine balance of prayer, study and work. All the work, whether manual, artistic or intellectual, is done within the Enclosure. The daily celebrations of the Eucharist and the Divine Office are the centre and inspiration of all activity.

Apart from worship, prayer and intercession, and the work of maintaining the house, garden and grounds, the Community's works are: the publications and greetings cards described below; providing retreats and quiet days; and dealing with a large postal apostolate.

SISTER MARY LUKE WISE CHC
(Mother Superior, elected 8 November 1991)
SISTER MARY JULIAN GOUGH CHC *(Assistant Superior)*
Sister Mary Michael Titherington
Sister Mary Bernadette Priddin
Sister Mary Joseph Thorpe
Sister Mary Cuthbert Aldridge
Sister Mary Hannah Kwark
Sister Mary Catherine Smith

Oblates and Associates

The Community has women Oblates who are attached to it in a union of mutual prayers. Each has a rule of life adapted to her particular circumstances. Oblates are not Religious but they seek to live their life in the world according to the spirit of the *Rule of St Benedict*. There are also Associates who have a much simpler rule.

Community Wares

A great variety of prayer and greeting cards are available for sale. Some are produced by the sisters and others are from a number of different sources.

Community Publications: A *Newsletter* published in the Spring. Available free from the Publications Secretary.

Office Book: CHC Office

Bishop Visitor: Most Revd Dr David Hope

Registered Charity: No 223807

Community History
Alan Russell, *The Community of the Holy Cross Haywards Heath 1857 – 1957: A Short History of its Life and Work*, 1957.
A leaflet: *A short history of the Community of the Holy Cross.* Available from the Publications Secretary.

Guest and Retreat Facilities
There is limited accommodation for residential, private retreats. The Community also provides for Quiet Days for individuals or groups up to twenty. The Guest House is closed at Christmas.

Community of the Holy Name

CHN

Founded 1888

Community House
40 Cavanagh Street
Cheltenham
Victoria 3192
AUSTRALIA

Tel: 03 9583 2087
Fax: 03 9585 2932
Email: chnmelb
@bigpond.com

Eucharist 7.30 am

Mattins 9.00 am

Midday Office
12.45 pm

Vespers 5.30 pm

Compline 7.30 pm

The Community of the Holy Name was founded in 1888 within the Diocese of Melbourne by Emma Caroline Silcock (Sister Esther). The work of the Community was initially amongst the poor and disadvantaged in the slum areas of inner-city Melbourne. Over the years, the Sisters have sought to maintain a balance between a ministry to those in need and a commitment to the Divine Office, personal prayer and a daily Eucharist.

For many years, CHN was involved in institutions, like children's homes and a Mission house. There were many and varied types of outreach. The Holy Name Girls' High School was established in Papua New Guinea, and the indigenous Community of the Visitation of Our Lady fostered there.

Today, Sisters are engaged in parish work in ordained and lay capacities, and in a great variety of other ministries, including hospital chaplaincies, both general and psychiatric, spiritual companionship and leading of Quiet Days and retreats. The offering of hospitality to people seeking spiritual refreshment or a place away from their normal strains and stresses has become an important part of our life and ministry.

Other Australian Addresses
St Julians, 33 Lorna Street, Cheltenham, VIC 3192
25 Lorna Street, Cheltenham, VIC 3192
68 Pickett Street, Footscray, VIC 3011
2/7 James Street, Brighton, VIC 3186
8/7 James Street, Brighton, VIC 3186

Community Wares
Cards are sold at the Community House.

CAROL CHN
(Mother Superior, assumed office 12 April 2011)

Andrea	Hilary	Margaret Anne	Sheila
Avrill	Jean	Margot	Sheila Anne
Betty	Jenny	Pamela	Shirley
Elizabeth Gwen	Josephine Margaret	Philippa	Valmai
Felicity	Lyn	Penelope	Winifred Muriel
Francine	Maree	Ruth	

Obituaries
11 Dec 2010   Hilda, aged 80, professed 43 years

Oblates and Associates
The Order of Oblates is for women and men who desire to lead lives of prayer and dedication in close association with the Community. The Oblates have a personal Rule of Life based on the Evangelical Counsels of Poverty, Chastity and Obedience and renew their dedication annually.

The Associates and Priests Associate support and pray for the Community. In some areas they have regular meetings for fellowship. Priests Associate offer the Eucharist with special intention for the Community and seek to promote the Religious Life.

Community Publication
An *Associates Letter* is published four times a year. Write to Sister Avrill, the Associates Sister, for a subscription, which is by donation.

Community History
Sister Elizabeth CHN, *Esther, Mother Foundress*, Melbourne, 1948.
Lynn Strahan, *Out of the Silence*, OUP, Melbourne, 1988.

Guest and Retreat Facilities
Day groups of up to twenty-five people are welcome in the Prayer Group and Gathering Space. There is accommodation for six residential guests at the Community House and a Sister is available for help and guidance if requested. St Julian's Retreat and Spirituality Centre accommodates ten guests in affordable and comfortable surroundings.

Most convenient time for guests to telephone: 10am – 12.30 pm, 2pm – 5pm

Office Book: CHN adaptation of the Anglican Office Book

Bishop Visitor: Most Revd Dr Philip Freier, Archbishop of Melbourne

EDITORS' NOTE: *The Community of the Holy Name in the UK and Africa, which forms several of the subsequent entries in this directory, is a community entirely distinct from CHN in Australia. Although sharing the same name, the two communities were founded independently of each other.*

Community of the Holy Name

(UK Province)

CHN

Founded 1865

Convent of
the Holy Name
Morley Road
Oakwood
Derby
DE21 4QZ
UK

Tel: 01332 671716
Fax: 01332 669712

Email: bursarsoffice
@tiscali.co.uk

Website:
www.chnderby.org

Bishop Visitor
Rt Revd
John Inge
Bishop of Worcester

The Sisters combine the life of prayer with service to others in their evangelistic and pastoral outreach and by maintaining their houses as centres of prayer where they can be available to others. They run a small guest house in Derby. In our houses, and from the Convent in Derby, the Sisters are involved in parish work, hospital visiting, retreat-giving and work among the wider community, and with those who come for spiritual guidance.

The members of the Fellowship of the Holy Name are an extension of its life and witness in the world. We encourage those who wish to live alongside for a period of time.

SISTER MONICA JANE CHN
(Provincial Superior, assumed office 10 January 2004)
SISTER JEAN MARY CHN *(Assistant Superior)*

Sister Judith	Sister Elizabeth Clare
Sister Ruth	Sister Diana
Sister Marjorie Jean	Sister Edith Margaret
Sister Barbara	Sister Pauline Margaret
Sister Joy	Sister Carol
Sister Brenda	Sister Pippa
Sister Verena	Sister Rosemary
Sister Constance	Sister Irene
Sister Lilias	Sister Lynfa
Sister Theresa Margaret	Sister Elaine Mary
Sister Mary Patricia	Sister Julie Elizabeth
Sister Lisbeth	Sister Linda Frances
Sister Vivienne Joy	Sister Catherine
Sister Charity	Sister Lucie Elizabeth

Obituaries

14 Jan 2010	Sister Dorothy, aged 89, professed 40 years
25 Jul 2010	Sister Christine, aged 63, professed 8 years
6 Sep 2010	Sister Penelope, aged 86, professed 61 years
2 Nov 2010	Sister Francesca Mary, aged 94, professed 57 years

Fellowship of the Holy Name

The Fellowship is comprised of ecumenically-minded Christians who feel called to share with the Community in their life of prayer and service.

Members have a personal Rule of Life, which they have drawn up in consultation with a particular Sister. This will keep in contact and help with a regular review. This rule

Prime
7.45 am

Eucharist
8.00 am
(12.20 pm Tue & Thu)

Mattins
9.15 am
(8.45 am Tue & Thu)

Midday Office
12.45 pm
(12.05 pm Tue & Thu)

Vespers
5.00 pm

Compline
9.15 pm
(8.45 pm Sat)

Office Book
Daily Office CHN

**Most convenient time
to telephone:**
10.00 am – 12.30 pm
2.00 pm – 5.00 pm
5.30 pm – 9.00 pm

Registered Charity:
No. 250256

includes daily private prayer, regular prayer and worship with the local Christian community, as well as time and space for their own well-being and creativity. Each rule varies with the individual. A six-month probation living the rule is required before formal admission to the Fellowship. This usually takes place at the Convent in the context of the Eucharist. There are regional meetings for members living in the same area, and the Community distributes newsletters throughout the year and encourages members to contribute articles for the Community magazine.

Other Addresses
Cottage 5, Lambeth Palace, London SE1 7JU
Tel: 020 7928 5407

64 Allexton Gardens, Welland Estate, Peterborough PE1 4UW
Tel: 01733 352077

Community History
History of the Community of the Holy Name, 1865 to 1950, published by CHN, 1950.
Una C. Hannam, *Portrait of a Community,* printed by the Church Army Press, 1972.

Community Publication
Community magazine – contact the editor

Community Wares
Various cards.

Booklet of Stations of the Cross, from original paintings by Sister Theresa Margaret CHN, with biblical texts. Can be ordered from the Convent: £5.00 each, or for orders of ten or more £4.50 each. Icons are also available.

Sister Pauline Margaret CHN, *Jesus Prayer,* £3.50. Can be ordered from the Convent or SLG Press.

Sister Verena CHN, *A Simplified Life,* Canterbury Press, Norwich. Available at convent £10.

Guest and Retreat Facilities
There are opportunities for individuals to make a private retreat at the guest house, and Sisters would be prepared to give help and guidance if requested. Six single rooms, one double – see our website.

Community of the Holy Name
(Lesotho Province)

CHN

Founded 1865 (in UK)
1962 (in Lesotho)

Convent of the Holy
Name
PO Box 22
Ficksburg 9730
SOUTH AFRICA
Tel: 22400249
Email: cohona
@datacom.co.ls
Website:
www.chnderby.org

Morning Prayer
6.30 am
(6.45 am Sun)

Terce
7.45 am (Sun only)

Eucharist
7.00 am (8.00 am Sun;
12 noon Wed)

Midday Office   12.15
pm (12.30 pm Sun,
11.45 am Wed)

Evening Prayer
5.00 pm

Compline   8.15 pm

Office Book
South African Prayer
Book, supplemented
by CHN Office Book

The Basotho Community of St Mary at the Cross was founded in Leribe, Lesotho, in 1923, under the Community of St Michael & All Angels, Bloemfontein. In 1959, CHN Sisters were invited to take over this work and started at Leribe in 1962. They had invited the Sisters of S. Mary at the Cross to become members of CHN and the full amalgamation of the two communities was completed in 1964. As a multi-racial community, the witness against racism at a time when apartheid was in the ascendant in South Africa was an important strand of the Community's vocation. New members have joined the Community in succeeding years, and they have continued the evangelistic and pastoral work which is also an important part of the CHN vocation. Sisters are involved in children's work, prison visiting, as well as other outreach in both Lesotho and South Africa. There is a church sewing room and wafer room. The Sisters in Leribe run a hostel for secondary school students who live too far away to travel daily. Some Sisters are 'Volunteers of Love' for families where there is HIV/AIDS. This work is enabled and strengthened by the daily round of prayer, both corporate and private, which is at the heart of the Community's Rule. A daily Eucharist at the centre of this life of prayer is the aim, but in some houses this is not always possible owing to a shortage of priests. There is a small guest house.

SISTER JULIA CHN
(*Provincial Superior, assumed office April 2007*)
SISTER MPOLOKENG CHN *(Assistant Superior)*

Sister Calista
Sister Alphonsina
Sister Hilda Tsepiso
Sister Maria
Sister Lucia
Sister Angelina
Sister Mary Selina
Sister Josetta
Sister Gertrude

Sister Ryneth
Sister Lineo
Sister Exinia Tsoakae
Sister Leboheng
Sister Malineo
Sister Malefu
Sister Molehobeng
Sister Mookho
Sister Maseeng

Other houses
For other houses, please contact the main house.

Community Wares
Church sewing (including cassocks, albs & stoles); communion wafers; Mothers Union uniforms; mohair and woven goods from the Leribe Craft Centre and the disabled workshop, started by the Community.

Bishop Visitor: Rt Revd Adam Taaso

Community of the Holy Name

(Zulu Province)

CHN

Founded 1865 (in UK)
1969 (in Zululand)

Convent of the Holy
Name
Pt. Bag 806
Melmoth 3835
Zululand
SOUTH AFRICA
Tel: 3545 02892
Fax: 3545 07564

Email:
chnsisters
@telkomsa.net

Website:
www.chnderby.org

Terce   6.30 am

Eucharist
6.30 am (Wed & Fri)
6.45 am (Tue & Thu)
4.30 pm (Mon)

Mattins   8.30 am

Midday Office
12.30 pm

Evening Prayer
4.00 pm (Mon & Wed)
5.00 pm (Tue & Thu)
4.30 pm (Fri)

Compline   7.45 pm

The Community of the Holy Name in Zululand was founded by three Zulu Sisters who began their Religious life with the Community in Leribe. All three Provinces of CHN have the same Rule of life, but there are differences of customary and constitutions to fit in with cultural differences. The daily life of the Community centres around the daily Office, and the Eucharist whenever the presence of a priest makes this possible.

The Sisters are involved extensively in mission, pastoral and evangelistic work. The Zulu Sisters have evangelistic gifts which are used in parishes throughout the diocese at the invitation of parish priests. Several Sisters have trained as teachers or nurses. They work in schools or hospitals, where possible within reach of one of the Community houses. Their salaries, and the handicrafts on sale at the Convent at Kwa Magwaza, help to keep the Community solvent.

MOTHER NOKUBONGWA CHN
(Provincial Superior, assumed office February 2008)
SISTER BENZILE CHN (Assistant Superior)

Sister Gertrude Jabulisiwe	Sister Patricia
Sister Claudia	Sister Phindile
Sister Olpha	Sister Nqobile
Sister Nesta Gugu	Sister Fikile Cynthia
Sister Nokuthula Victoria	Sister Sibekezelo
Sister Sibongile	Sister Xolisile
Sister Zodwa	Sister Philisiwe
Sister Mantombi	Sister Ntsoaki
Sister Bonakele	Sister Nomathemba
Sister Nonhlahla	Sister Thandukwazi
Sister Jabu	Sister Zamandla
Sister Thulisiwe	Sister Bongile
Sister Thembelihle	Sister Maureen
Sister Sebenzile	Sister Thembsile
Sister Samkelisiwe	Sister Neliswa
Sister Thandazile	Sister Hlengiwe
Sister Thandiwe	Sister Nkosikhoma
Sister Nondumiso	
Sister Thokozile	Novices: 3
Sister Duduzile	

Office Book
Offices are mainly in Zulu, based on the South African Prayer Book & the CHN Office Book.

Community Wares
Vestments, cassocks, albs and other forms of dressmaking to order.

Other Houses
Usuthu Mission, PO Box 8, Luyengo, SWAZILAND
PO Box 175, Nongoma 3950, SOUTH AFRICA
St Benedict House, PO Box 27, Rosettenville 2130, SOUTH AFRICA

Bishop Visitor: Rt Revd Dino Gabriel, Bishop of Zululand

Community of the Holy Spirit

CHS

Founded-1952

454 Convent Ave
New York
NY 10031-3618
USA

Tel: 212 666 8249
Fax: 801 655 8249

Email: chssisters
@chssisters.org

Website
www.chssisters.org

The daily schedule varies with the seasons. Please call ahead for current schedule. Monday is a Sabbath in each house of the Community, during which there is no corporate worship.

Each person is given an invitation to follow Christ. The Sisters of our monastic community respond to that invitation by an intentional living out of the vows of poverty, chastity, and obedience within the structure of a modified Augustinian Rule. Through the vow of poverty, we profess our trusting dependence upon God by embracing voluntary simplicity and responsible stewardship of creation. Through chastity, we profess the sanctity of all creation as the primary revelation of God. Through obedience, we profess our desire to be dependent on God's direction and to live and minister in ways that respect all creation, both now and for generations to come. Compassionate, respectful love is God's gift to life. Prayer and the worship of God are the lifeblood and heart of our Community and the source of inspiration for all that we undertake. Through our prayer, worship, and creative talents we encourage others to seek God. Through our ministries of hospitality, retreat work, spiritual direction, and education through simple, sustainable, spiritual living, we seek to grow in love and communion with all whose lives touch us and are touched by us. We also provide spiritual support for women and men who wish to be linked with our Community as Associates. By adopting a personal rule of life, they extend the Community's ministry through prayer, worship and service.

SISTER HELÉNA MARIE CHS *(June 2001)*
SISTER FAITH MARGARET CHS *(June 2001)*
SISTER CATHERINE GRACE CHS *(June 2001)*
(Community Council)

Sister Élise
Sister Mary Christabel
Sister Mary Elizabeth
Sister Jerolynn Mary
Sister Dominica
Sister Emmanuel
Sister Maria Felicitas

Sister Leslie
Sister Claire Joy
Sister Carol Bernice

Resident Companions:
Revd Suzanne Guthrie
William Consiglio

Associates
From the Community's early days, Christian women and men have sought an active association with the Sisters, wishing to live out their baptismal commitments by means of a rule of life.

The Community provides four rules: Fellowship, St Augustine, Confraternity and Priest Associate. Each consists of prayer, reading, self-denial and stewardship. Each provides an opportunity for growth toward God and daily renewal of life in Christ. Each calls for a commitment to pray daily for the Sisters and all others in their life, worship and ministry, using the collect for Pentecost and the Lord's Prayer.

In consultation with the Sister for Associates, they may formulate their own rule if the ones provided cannot be fulfilled as they stand, or if they need to be expanded. As far as is possible Associates support the Community through gifts of time, talents and financial resources. There is an annual fee of $50, if possible.

Other Address
The Melrose Convent – Bluestone Farm and Living Arts Center
118 Federal Hill Road, Brewster, NY 10509-5307, USA
Tel: 845 278 9777   Fax: 425 944 1085   Email: Melrose@chssisters.org

Community Wares: [From Bluestone Farm]:
Maple syrup, honey, eggs, and other food items as available.

Community Publication: Monthly electronic newsletter.
Please send email address to *inquiries@chssisters.org.*

Community History: The Revd Mother Ruth CHS, *"In Wisdom Thou Hast Made Them"*, Adams, Bannister, Cox, New York, 1986

Guest and Retreat Facilities
The Longhouse at Melrose; seven rooms, total capacity eight. Closed irregularly; call in advance to make reservations.
Visit *www.chssisters.org* for further information.
Tel: 845 278 9777 ex 30   Email: BFLCreservations@chssisters.org

Most convenient time to telephone:
Generally, phones are staffed irregularly between 9.00 am and 5.00 pm EST Tuesday through Saturday, though you may leave a message at any time.

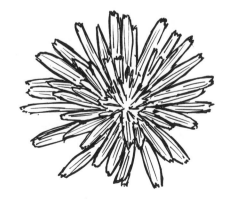

Office Book: CHS Office book

Bishops Visitor:
Rt Revd Mark H. Andrus,
Bishop of California
Rt Revd Catherine S. Roskam,
Suffragan Bishop of New York

Community of the Holy Transfiguration

CHT

Founded-1982

St David's Bonda
Mission
P Bag T 7904
Mutare
ZIMBABWE

Bishop Visitor
Rt Revd Peter Hatendi,
Bishop of Manicaland

The Community started in 1982 with eight members who broke away from the Community of the Holy Name (Chita Che Zita Renoyera). The Community is stationed at St David's Bonda Mission and it is an open community. We assist the Church in evangelistic work and other ministerial duties. Some members are employed by the diocese as priests and some as Evangelists. We run an orphanage with a maximum number of thirty young children. As of now, the age-group is going beyond this age range because of the HIV/AIDS pandemic. We are also a self-reliant community through land tilling and poultry. We look forward to opening branch houses in the near future.

SISTER MILDAH CHT
(Mother, assumed office 2006)

Sister Gloria
Sister Winnie
Sister Francesca
Sister Lucy
Sister Merina
Sister Gloria Mary
Sister Violet

Sister Dorothy
Sister Felicity
Sister Letwin
Rev Friar
Fungayi Leonard
Evangelist Friar Henry

Community of Jesus' Compassion

CJC

Founded 1993

PO Box 153
New Hanover
3230
SOUTH AFRICA
Tel: 033 502 0010

Tel: 033 502 0200
(for 2nd CJC house)

Founded in the Diocese of Natal by a sister from the Community of the Holy Name in Zululand, CJC have been based in Newcastle and Ixopo. However, the sisters have now settled at New Hanover, which is half an hour's drive from the cathedral city of Pietermaritzburg.

The main work of the sisters is evangelising in the local parish and children's ministry. The Sisters care for around thirty-five children, which is demanding, but good progress is being made.

On the 19th December 1998, the first professions within the community were received. The Community's formal recognition by the Church of the Province of South Africa followed in 2000 with the first life professions.

In 2006, Sister Thandi became the first nun in the diocese to be ordained to the stipendiary ministry, and she now serves in a parish in Durban. Her priesting followed in June 2007.

Community Wares
Girdles, Prayer Book and Bible covers, vegetables.

Bishop Visitor: Rt Revd Rubin Phillip, Bishop of Natal

Morning Prayer,
followed by Terce
5.30 am

Midday Prayer
12.30 pm

Evening Prayer
4.30 pm

Compline
8.15 pm

MOTHER LONDIWE CJC
(Mother Superior, assumed office 8 January 2000)
SISTER THANDI CJC *(Assistant Superior)*

Sister Yeki	Sister Nonhlanhla
Sister Nontombi	Sister Celiwe
Sister Zandile	Sister Ncebakazi
Sister Jabulile	Sister Mbali
Sister Nontokozo	Sister Thelma
Sister Thokozile	Sister Ayanda
Sister Nqobile	*Novices: 2*

Office Book: Anglican Prayer Book 1989 of the Church of the Province of Southern Africa
Midday Office book & Celebrating Night Prayer

Community of Nazareth CN

Founded 1936

4-22-30 Mure
Mitaka
Tokyo 181-0002
JAPAN
Tel: 0422 48 4560
Fax: 0422 48 4601

Morning Prayer
6.25 am

Eucharist 7.00 am

Terce 8.15 am

Sext 12 noon

None after lunch

Evening Prayer
5.00 pm

Night Prayer 8.15 pm

Under the guidance of the Sisters of the Community of the Epiphany (England), the Community of Nazareth was born and has grown. The Community is dedicated to the Incarnate Lord Jesus Christ, especially in devotion to the hidden life which he lived in Nazareth.

In addition to the Holy Eucharist, which is the centre and focus of our community life, the Sisters recite a sixfold Divine Office. We run a Retreat house and make wafers. We welcome enquirers and aspirants.

SISTER NOBU CN
(Reverend Mother)

SISTER MIYOSHI CN *(Assistant Mother)*

Sister Yachiyo	Sister Asako	Sister Junko
Sister Kayoko	Sister Setsuko	
Sister Chizuko	Sister Yukie	

Obituaries

12 Jul 2007	Sister Chiyo, professed 55 years
8 Feb 2008	Sister Haroko, professed 53 years
14 Jul 2010	Sister Sachiko, professed 44 years

Associates: Clergy and laity may be associates.

Other Address: 81 Shima Bukuro, Naka Gusuku Son, Naka Gami Gun, Okinawa Ken 901-2301, JAPAN

Community Wares: Wafers.

Guest and Retreat Facilities: There are twenty rooms available, for men or women, but not children. The suggested donation is ¥6,000 per night, including three meals.

Office Book: BCP of Nippon Seiko Kai Office Book

Bishop Visitor: Rt Revd Jintarō Ueda, Bishop of Tokyo

Benedictine Community of Our Lady & Saint John

Alton Abbey

OSB

Founded 1884

Alton Abbey
Abbey Road
Beech
Alton
Hampshire
GU34 4AP
UK
Tel: 01420 562145
& 01460 563575

Email: abbey@
domghill.mail1.co.uk

Morning Prayer
6.30 am

Conventual Mass
9.00 am   (10 am Sun)

Midday Office
12.00 noon

Evening Prayer
5.00 pm

Night Prayer
8.30 pm   (7.30 pm Sun)

The monks follow the Rule with its balance of prayer, work and study, supported by the vows of stability, conversion of life and obedience. A wide ministry of hospitality is offered, and visitors are welcome at the daily Mass and Divine Office. The purpose built monastery is built around two cloister garths; the Abbey Church dates from the beginning of the twentieth century. Set in extensive grounds, with contrast between areas that are cultivated and others that are a haven for wildlife, the Abbey is situated about four miles from Alton.

RT REVD DOM WILLIAM HUGHES OSB
(Abbot, assumed office 6 September 2010)
VERY REVD DOM ANDREW JOHNSON OSB *(Prior)*

Rt Revd Dom Giles Hill
Revd Dom Nicholas Seymour *(Guest Master)*
Dom Anselm Shobrook
Rt Revd Dom Timothy Bavin

Postulants: 2

Oblates
For details of the Oblates of St Benedict, please contact the Oblate Master.

Community Wares
Altar bread and incense: contact Alton Abbey Supplies Ltd.   Tel: 01420 565977

Guest and Retreat Facilities
Guest house facilities for up to eighteen persons, for both group and individual retreats. There is a programme of retreats each year, available from the Guestmaster. No smoking in the house.

Most convenient time to telephone: 4.00 pm – 4.30 pm.

Office Book: Alton Abbey Office Book

Website: www.altonabbey.org.uk

Bishop Visitor: Rt Revd Michael Scott-Joynt, Bishop of Winchester

Registered Charity: No. 229216

Community of the Resurrection

CR

Founded 1892

House of the
Resurrection
Mirfield
West Yorkshire
WF14 0BN
UK
Tel: 01924 494318
Fax: 01924 490489
Email:
community
@mirfield.org.uk

Website: www.
mirfieldcommunity.
org.uk

Mattins
6.45 am (7.30 am Sun)

Midday Office
12.00 noon

Mass   12.15 pm
On festivals on week
days, the time of Mass
may change.

Evensong   6.00 pm

Compline   9.15 pm

Office Book
CR Office

Registered Charity
No. 232670

The Community consists of priests and laymen living a life of worship, work and study within the monastic life. They undertake a wide range of pastoral ministry including retreats, teaching and counselling.

GEORGE GUIVER CR
(assumed office 29 December 2002)
OSWIN GARTSIDE CR *(Prior)*

Dominic Whitnall	Nicolas Stebbing
Roy France	John Gribben
Timothy Stanton	Peter Allan
Vincent Girling	Andrew Norton
Eric Simmons	Philip Nichols
Aidan Mayoss	Thomas Seville
Robert Mercer *(bishop)*	Steven Haws
Simon Holden	Barnabas Siddle
Crispin Harrison	*Novices: 2*
Antony Grant	

Obituaries

13 Sep 10   Zachary Brammer, aged 78, professed 50 years

Oblates

OBLATES, clergy and lay, are those who desire to make a special and permanent offering of themselves to God in association with the Community of the Resurrection.

Companions

COMPANIONS seek to live the baptismal vocation of all Christians through a commitment to each community to which they belong and also to the Community of the Resurrection; a commitment to Eucharistic worship, corporate and private prayer and the use of the sacrament of reconciliation; a commitment of time, talents and money. Those who wish to be Companions keep their commitments for at least a year before being admitted, and thereafter, with all Companions, renew their commitment each year. All Companions have a spiritual director or soul friend with whom their commitments are discussed and who undertakes to support them on their journey.

Associates

ASSOCIATES have a less demanding relationship with the Community for whatever reason, but do have an obligation of prayer and worship. For more information contact the Chaplain to the Companions at Mirfield.

Community Publication: CR Quarterly. Write to the Editor. Many subscribe to this who are not Oblates, Companions or Associates. The minimum annual subscription is £15.00.

Community History: Alan Wilkinson, *The Community of the Resurrection: A centenary history*, SCM Press, London, 1992.

Community Wares: Postcards of the buildings, theological and spiritual books, leaflets on prayer, CDs of Community's music, clothes with logo: apply to Mirfield Publications at the House of the Resurrection.

Guest and Retreat Facilities
Retreats are listed on the website.
HOUSE OF THE RESURRECTION
Twenty-four single rooms, two double rooms, nine en-suite rooms, one small flat.

Most convenient time to telephone: 9.00 am – 12 noon, 2.00 pm – 6.00 pm

MIRFIELD CENTRE
The Centre offers a meeting place at the College for about fifty people. Small residential conferences are possible in the summer vacation. Day and evening events are arranged throughout the year to stimulate Christian life and witness.

The Mirfield Centre (College of the Resurrection), Mirfield, West Yorks WF14 0BW, UK
Tel: 01924 481920   Fax: 01924 418921   Email: centre@mirfield.org.uk
COLLEGE OF THE RESURRECTION
The College, founded in 1902 and run by its own independent Council, trains men and women and also provides opportunities for others to study for degrees.
Acting Principal: Fr Peter Allan CR
College of the Resurrection, Mirfield, West Yorkshire WF14 0BW, UK
Tel: 01924 481900   Email: registrar@mirfield.org.uk

Bishop Visitor: Rt Revd Graham James, Bishop of Norwich

Community of the Resurrection of Our Lord CR

Founded 1884

St Peter's, PO Box 72
Grahamstown 6140
SOUTH AFRICA
Tel & Fax:
046 622 4210

This Community was founded in 1884 by Bishop Allan Becher Webb and Cecile Isherwood to undertake pastoral and educational work in Grahamstown. These two types of work, and later Social Welfare work, have predominated in the Community's undertakings throughout its history. The regular life of monastic Offices and personal prayer and intercession has always been maintained, both in the Mother House (Grahamstown) and all branch houses, wherever situated. It is still maintained in Grahamstown, the only centre where the Community life continues, our numbers being now much reduced. The Sisters are involved in various ministries: at the Cathedral and other churches as needed; in the Raphael Centre for people suffering from HIV/Aids etc; in visiting at Old Age Homes and the hospital; soup kitchens; and needlework/banners.

Bishop Visitor: awaiting election

Email: comres
@imaginet.co.za

Morning Office
6.30 am

Eucharist 7.00 am
(Sun, Tue, Thu & Fri)
(at the Cathedral
Mon & Wed)

Midday Office
followed by silent
intercession
12.30 pm

Evening Office
followed by silent
intercession 5.30 pm

Compline 7.30 pm

Greater Silence: 9 pm

Office Book
Anglican Prayer Book
1989, CPSA; Traditional
Midday Office &
Compline

Community Wares
Cards, banners and
girdles.

MOTHER ZELMA CR *(priest)*
(Mother Superior, assumed office 24 November 2005)
SISTER KEKELETSO CR *(Assistant Superior)*
Sister Dorianne
Sister Carol *(priest)*

Postulants: 2

Oblates and Associates

OBLATES OF THE RISEN CHRIST live under a Rule drawn up for each individual according to circumstances, on their observance of which they must report monthly to the Oblate Sister.

ASSOCIATES undertake a simple Rule, including regular prayer for the Community. Priest Associates undertake to give an address or preach on Religious Vocation at least once a year.

FRIENDS are interested in the Community and pray for it, and keep in touch with it.

There is a Fellowship Meeting twice a year, after Easter and near the Foundress's birthday on 14 November.

Also there is a Festival gathering of UK Associates at St Peter's Bourne, Whetstone, north London, on the Saturday nearest to St Peter's Day, 29 June, each year, at which two Sisters from South Africa are always present to preserve our links with the UK.

Community Publication: A Newsletter is sent out three times a year to all bishops and Religious communities of CPSA, and also to all the Oblates and Associates of the Community.

Guest and Retreat Facilities: Ten or more guests can be accommodated; though prior consultation is needed. The charge is negotiable. There is also a guest flatlet for two.

Community History and Books

A pictorial record of the Community's history, with commentary, was published in its centenary year, 1984. It was a collaborative work.

Lives of Mother Cecile and her successor, Mother Florence, have been published, in each case written by 'a Sister':

A Sister of the Community (compiler), *Mother Cecile in South Africa 1883–1906: Foundress of the Community of the Resurrection of Our Lord,* SPCK, London, 1930.

A Sister of the Community, *The Story of a Vocation: A Brief Memoir of Mother Florence, Second Superior of the Community of the Resurrection of Our Lord,* The Church Book Shop, Grahamstown, no date.

Guy Butler, *The Prophetic Nun,* Random House, 2000. (Life and art works, with colour illustrations, of Sisters Margaret and Pauline CR, and Sister Dorothy Raphael CSMV.) This is a coffee-table type book available in South Africa and the UK.

Community of the Sacred Name

CSN

Founded 1893

300 Tuam Street
Christchurch 8011
NEW ZEALAND
Tel: 03 366 8245
Fax: 03 366 8755
Email: comsacnm
@extra.co.nz

Morning Prayer
6.40 am

Mass
7.30 am

Terce   9.00 am

Midday Office
12 noon

Vespers   5.15 pm

Compline
7.30 pm

Office Book
Communities
Consultative Council

Community Wares
Embroidery,
cards, vestments.

Bishop Visitor
Rt Revd
Victoria Matthews

The Community of the Sacred Name was founded in Christchurch in 1893 by Sister Edith (Deaconess). She was released from the Community of St Andrew in London to establish an indigenous community to respond to the needs of the colonial Church. A wide variety of teaching, childcare and parish work has been undertaken over the years. Today there are three houses. Since 1966, the Sisters have run a large children's home in Fiji. In 1997, the Sisters undertook work in Tonga, helping in the Church in various ways. The major work is ecclesiastical embroidery. Underpinning all the work is a life of worship.

MOTHER KELENI CSN
(Mother Superior, assumed office 9 November 2006)
SISTER MELE CSN *(Assistant)*

Sister Annette	Sister Judith	Sister Vutulongo
Sister Brigid	Sister Miria	Sister Kalolaine
Sister Lu'isa	Sister Manu	Sister Sandra
Sister Anne	Sister Alena	
Sister Litia	Sister Fehoko	

Obituaries
19 Aug 2009   Sr Rose Ana, aged 77, professed 41 years

Oblates and Associates
The Community has Oblates, men and women called by God to live the contemplative life in the world.
We also have Companions, Associates, Friends of Polynesia and the Guild of Help. These may be women or men, priests or lay people.

Community History: Ruth Fry, *The Community of the Sacred Name – a Centennial History,* PPP Printers, PO Box 22.785, Christchurch, New Zealand, 1993

Guest and Retreat Facilities
Since the earthquakes of 2010–11 there are no more guest/retreat facilities in our Community, until we find out the future of our buildings.

Most convenient time to telephone: 9.15 am – 5.15 pm

Community Publication
Community *Newsletter*, published at Easter, Holy Name and Christmas. Write to the Reverend Mother.

Other addresses
St Christopher's Home, PO Box 8232, Nakasi, Suva, FIJI   Tel: 679 341 0458

PO Box 1824, Nuku'alofa, TONGA   Tel: 27998

Community of the Sacred Passion

CSP

Founded 1911

Convent of
the Sacred Passion
22 Buckingham
Road
Shoreham-by-Sea
West Sussex
BN43 5UB
UK
Tel: 01273 453807
Email: communitysp
@yahoo.co.uk

Other Address:
725 Wandsworth
Road
London SW8 3JF
UK

Morning Prayer
7.10 am

Prayer before noon
8.05 am

Mass
9.30 am (Mon, Thu,
Fri)

Midday Office
12.10 pm

Evening Prayer
6 pm

Compline 7.30 pm

The Community was founded to serve Africa by a life of prayer and missionary work, bringing to Africans a knowledge of God's love. After the Church in Tanzania gained independence, and the Community of St Mary of Nazareth and Calvary (CMM), which they nurtured, became self-governing, CSP withdrew from Tanzania and now offers support from England. Much of the help is channelled through CMM to whom they offer encouragement, advice and financial support. The Sisters also collect money for some of the work that they founded, including the Polio Hostel at Kwa Mkono, caring for disabled children, and, in this year of the centenary, the Sisters are hoping to help raise funds for the Nursing School at Muheza. At Shoreham, the Sisters offer hospitality for small day events and meetings. They are involved in guidance of individuals and have various contacts in the local community. The Sister who lives in Clapham is involved with the World Community for Christian Meditation and has contacts with people of various faiths. Prayer remains the foundation of the life of the Community.

MOTHER PHILIPPA CSP
(Revd Mother, assumed office 30 August 1999)
SISTER JACQUELINE CSP *(Deputy Superior)*

Sister Etheldreda	Sister Rhoda
Sister Dorothy	Sister Angela
Sister Thelma Mary	Sister Lucia
Sister Joan Thérèse	Sister Mary Kathleen
Sister Gillian Mary	

Obituaries
12 Aug 2010   Sister Mary Joan,
                          aged 89, professed 54 years

Oblates: Men and women who feel called to associate themselves with the aims of the community, by prayer and service, and by a life under a Rule. Their own Rule of Life will vary according to their particular circumstances. Oblates are helped and advised by the Oblates' Sister.

Associates: Men and women who share in the work of the community by prayer, almsgiving and service of some kind. They pray regularly for the community.

Priest Associates: Pray regularly for the community and offer Mass for it three times a year, of which one is Passion Sunday (the Sunday before Palm Sunday).

Friends: Pray regularly for the community and help it in any way they can.

Community History
Sister Mary Stella CSP,
*She Won't Say 'No': The
History of the Community
of the Sacred Passion*
privately published,
1984.

Bishop Visitor
Rt Revd Ian Brackley
Bishop of Dorking

All those connected with the community are prayed for daily by the Sisters and remembered by name on their birthdays. They receive the four-monthly intercession paper, and newsletter.

Guest and Retreat Facilities
One room with self-catering facilities in our smaller house, five minutes walk from the main house. Donations. Women only for overnight stay.

Most convenient time to telephone: 4 pm – 7.30 pm.

Community of St Andrew CSA

Founded 1861

Correspondence address:
Revd Mother Lillian,
CSA
40 Homecross House
21 Fishers Lane
Chiswick
W4 1YA
Email:
lillianmorris959@
btinternet.com
Tel: 020 8747 0001

Office Book
Common Worship –
Daily Prayer

Registered Charity
No 244321

In the mid 19th century a young woman, Elizabeth Ferard, realising that women had minimal opportunities for service in the Church, felt called to restore the diaconate of women. After spending several months with a Lutheran deaconess community at Kaiserswerth and some time with a community of Anglican Sisters of Mercy at Ditchingham, she was authorized by the then Bishop of London, Archibald C Tait, to begin an Institute to train women to be Deaconesses. A few women began to train together as a community on St Andrew's Day, 30 November 1861. Elizabeth was commissioned by the Bishop as the first Deaconess of the Church of England on 18 July 1862, and her companions about a year later. The Bishop would lay his hands on the head of each person to be made Deaconess, give her his blessing and she would be admitted to the Community of the London Diocesan Deaconess Institution (c.1868), which from c.1887 was known as the Community of St Andrew. About that time the Community evolved into a Religious Community. Thus the dual vocation of life commitment in community and ordained ministry within the life of the Church. The fundamental ministry is the offering of prayer and worship, evangelism, pastoral work and hospitality, now mainly through retirement ministries. In 2011 we celebrate our 150th anniversary as a Community and in 2012 the 150th anniversary of the Deaconess Order.

Community Publications
St Andrew's Review & *St Andrew's Newsletter.* Write to Sister Teresa. *Distinctive Diaconate News* & *Distinctive News of Women in Ministry*, both edited by Sister Teresa CSA: for UK addresses, £2 each payable to 'Distinctive Diaconate'; for other postal zones, please enquire.

REVD MOTHER LILLIAN CSA *(deacon)*
(Mother Superior, 1982–94, 2000–)
Revd Sister Donella CSA *(deacon)*
resident at 40 Homecross House, 21 Fishers Lane, Chiswick, W4 1YA
Tel: 020 8747 0001

Revd Sister Patricia *(deacon)* *(020 8742 8434)*
resident at: St Mary's Convent & Nursing Home, Burlington Lane, Chiswick,
London W4 2QE

Sister Pamela *(deaconess)*
resident at: 17 War Memorial Place, Harpsden Way,
Henley on Thames, Oxon RG9 1EP
Tel: 01491 572224

Revd Dr Sister Teresa *(priest)*
resident at: St Andrew's House, 16 Tavistock Crescent, London W11 1AP
Tel: 020 7221 4604   Email: teresajoan@btinternet.com

Obituaries
24 Apr 2011   Revd Sister Denzil *(priest)*, aged 91, professed 49 years
25 May 2011   Sister Dorothy *(deaconess)*, aged 97, professed 56 years

Associates
Our Associates are part of our extended Community family. They may be men, women, clergy or lay, and follow a simple Rule of Life, which includes praying for the Sisters and their work. The Sisters pray for the Associates every day.

Community History
Sister Joanna [Baldwin], Dss. CSA, "The Deaconess Community of St Andrew", *Journal of Ecclesiastical History*, Vol. XII, No.2, October 1961, 16pp.

Henrietta Blackmore, editor, *The Beginnings of Women's Ministry: The Revival of the Deaconess in the 19th-Century Church of England*, Boydell & Brewer, Woodbridge, 2007, ISBN 978-843-308-6.

Sister Edna Mary [Skinner], Dss. CSA, *The Religious Life*, Penguin, Harmondsworth, 1968.

Bishop Visitor
Rt Revd & Rt Hon Richard Chartres, Bishop of London

Head Sister Elizabeth Ferard,
First Deaconess of the Church of England

Community of St Clare

OSC

Founded 1950

St Mary's Convent
178 Wroslyn Road
Freeland
Witney
OX29 8AJ
UK
Tel: 01993 881225
Fax: 01993 882434

Email: community
@oscfreeland.co.uk

Morning Prayer
7.30 am

Eucharist
8.30 am

Midday Prayer
12.30 pm

Evening Prayer
5.30 pm

Night Prayer
8.00 pm

Office Book
The Daily Office SSF

Bishop Protector:
Rt Revd
Michael Perham,
Bishop of Gloucester

The Community of St Clare is part of the Society of St Francis. We are a group of women who live together needing each other's help to give our whole lives to the worship of God. Our service to the world is by our prayer, in which we are united with all people everywhere. We have a guest house so that others may join in our worship, and share the quiet and beauty with which we are surrounded. We try to provide for our own needs by growing much of our own food, and by our work of printing, wafer baking, writing and various crafts. This also helps us to have something material to share with those in greater need.

SISTER PAULA FORDHAM OSC
(Abbess, elected 30 January 2007)
SISTER ALISON FRANCIS HAMILTON OSC *(Assistant)*

Sister Clare Lowe   Sister Mary Margaret
Sister Damian Davies   Broomfield
Sister Kathleen Marie Staggs Sister Susan Elisabeth Leslie
Sister Mary Kathleen Kearns
                                      Novices: 1

Obituaries
19 Dec 2010   Sister Michaela Davis ,
                         aged 85, professed 29 years

Community Wares
Printing, cards, crafts, altar breads.

Guest and Retreat Facilities
Men, women and children are welcome at the guest house. It is not a 'silent house' but people can make private retreats if they wish. Eleven rooms (some twin-bedded). Donations, no fixed charge. Closed for two weeks mid-May and two weeks mid-September, and 16 Dec-8 Jan. Please write to the Guest Sister at the Convent address.

Most convenient time to telephone:
6.00 pm – 7.00 pm – on Convent telephone: *01993 881225*

Address of the Guest House (for guests arriving)
The Old Parsonage, 168 Wroslyn Road, Freeland,
Witney OX29 8AQ, UK   *Tel: 01993 881227*

Community History
Petà Dunstan, *This Poor Sort*, DLT, London 1997,
                                      pp157–167

Community of St Francis

CSF

Founded 1905

Minister Provincial
Email: ministercsf@
franciscans.org.uk

UK Houses:

St Francis House
113 Gillott Road
Birmingham
B16 0ET
Tel: 0121 454 8302
Email:
birminghamcsf
@franciscans.org.uk

St Matthew's House,
25 Kamloops
Crescent,
Leicester LE1 2HX
Tel: 0116 253 9158
Email: leicestercsf
@franciscans.org.uk

San Damiano
38 Drury Street
Metheringham
Lincs LN4 3EZ
Tel: 01526 321115
Email:
metheringhamcsf@
franciscans.org.uk

As Franciscan sisters, an autonomous part of the Society of St Francis, our primary vocation is to live the gospel in our time and in the places to which we are called. The setting for this is our life in community, under vows. Our wide range of backgrounds, abilities and gifts contributes to many ways of expressing the three elements of prayer, study and work. Prayer together and alone, with the Eucharist having a central place, is the heart of each house and each sister's life. Five of our sisters are priests; and three live the solitary life. Study nurtures our spiritual life and enables and enriches our ministries. Work includes the practical running of our houses and a wide range of ministries; currently these include hospitality, spiritual direction, prison chaplaincy, parish work and missions, preaching, leading quiet days and retreats, writing, being a presence in poor urban areas, and work with deaf blind people. Some of this work is salaried, much is voluntary. Each new sister brings her unique gifts, adding a new dimension to our life. As we move on into our second century, we are excited by the challenge of living the Franciscan life in the twenty-first century.

JOYCE CSF
(Minister General, assumed office 8 February 2002)

EUROPEAN PROVINCE

HELEN JULIAN CSF
(Minister Provincial, assumed office 8 February 2002)

Angela Helen	Liz
Beverley	Maureen
Chris	Nan
Christine James	Patricia Clare
Elizabeth	Phyllis
Gina	Sue
Gwenfryd Mary	Teresa
Hilary	
Jannafer	*Sisters resident in Korea:*
Jennifer Chan	Frances
Jenny Tee	Jemma
Judith Ann	

Companions & Third Order

Companions are individual Christians who wish to associate themselves with the Society through prayer, friendship and in seeking to live the spirit of the Gospel in the way of St Francis. For more information about

The Vicarage
11 St Mary's Road
Plaistow
London E13 9AE
Tel: 020 8552 4019
Email: stmaryscssf@
franciscans.org.uk

St Alphege Clergy
House, Pocock St
Southwark
London SE1 0BJ
Tel: 020 7928 8912
Email:
southwarkcsf@
franciscans.org.uk

Box 1003
Gumi Post Office
Gumi
Gyeongbukdo
730-600
REPUBLIC OF KOREA
Tel: (054) 451 2317
Email: koreanfs
@hotmail.com

Website: www.
franciscans.org.uk

Registered Charity
No. 286615

St Francis House,
3743 Cesar Chavez
St, **San Francisco**,
CA 94110, USA
Tel: 415 824 0288
Fax: 415 826 7569
Email: csfsfo@aol.com

Website: www.
communitystfrancis
.org

becoming a Companion contact the Secretary for Companions, Hilfield Friary, Dorchester, Dorset DT2 7BE, UK. For the Third Order SSF, *see separate entry.*

Community Publication
franciscan, three times a year. Subscription: £7.00 per year. Write to the Editor of *franciscan*, The Friary of St Francis, Hilfield, Dorset DT2 7BE, UK.

Community History: Elizabeth CSF, *Corn of Wheat*, Becket Publications, Oxford, 1981.

Guest and Retreat Facilities
METHERINGHAM
Guests are welcome, both men and women, in groups or as individuals. There is one single room for an individual to stay on retreat, for a few days 'away from it all', to have a holiday or a sabbatical, or simply to spend time with God in the peace and tranquillity of the countryside.

The house provides comfortable and friendly space for quiet days and meetings. Two rooms are available: The Sitting Room/Library (max 12 people) furnished with easy chairs, and the Chapel/Conference Room (max 24 people) furnished with moveable padded chairs. Sisters may be available to spend time with individuals or groups for retreats, talks, quiet days, spiritual direction, prayer guidance or simply to offer a listening ear.

The Community also welcomes Working Guests who stay and share our life and work for a period of time. If you are interested in this, please write to the Sisters at Metheringham.

Office Book: Daily Office SSF

Bishop Protector
Rt Revd Michael Perham, Bishop of Gloucester

AMERICAN PROVINCE

The Sisters came to the United States in 1974, and for over thirty years we have engaged in many types of ministry, but with special concern for the poor, the marginalized, and the sick. We can be found in hospitals and nursing homes; among the homeless, immigrants, and people with AIDS; teaching student deacons and serving on diocesan commissions; providing spiritual direction and directing retreats in parishes. In all things we strive to be instruments of God's love.

PAMELA CLARE CSF
(Minister Provincial, assumed office June 2010)

Cecilia	Lynne	Ruth
Jean	Maggie	*Postulants:* 1

Associates
Contact: Mark H Casstevens TSSF, Secretary for Associates, PO Box 4970, Austin, Texas 78765-4870, USA.   *Email: mhcasstevens@hotmail.com*

Community Wares
CSF Office Book, home retreat booklets, Franciscan prayer cards.

Community Publication: The Canticle.

Sister Jean (left of centre) meets the Dalai Lama

Contact St Francis House to subscribe – $5 for two years.
Guest and Retreat Facilities: At the San Francisco house, there is a guest apartment, which has one bedroom (two beds) and a small kitchen. It has its own entrance. The suggested cost is $50 per night.

Most convenient time to telephone: 9.00 am – 5.00 pm, 7.45 pm – 9.00 pm.

Office Book: CSF Office Book

Bishop Protector: Rt Revd Nedi Rivera, Bishop of Eastern Oregon

Community of St John Baptist
(UK)

CSJB

Founded 1852

The Priory
25 Woodstock
Road West,
Begbroke
Oxfordshire
OX5 1RJ
UK
Tel: 01865 855320

Email: csjbteam
@csjb.org.uk

Morning Prayer
7.30 am

Tierce 9.00 am

Eucharist
9.15 am

Midday Office
12 noon

Evening Prayer
5.00 pm

Compline
8.30 pm
(8.15 pm Sun)

Founded by Harriet Monsell and Thomas Thelluson Carter to help women rejected by the rest of society, we are now a Community of women who seek to offer our gifts to God in various ways. These include parish and retreat work, spiritual direction, and ministry to the elderly. Two sisters are ordained to the priesthood: both work in local benefices as well as presiding regularly at the community Eucharist. Sisters are also involved in the ministry of spiritual accompaniment, retreat giving and are available to facilitate quiet days.

We have close links with the sisters of our affiliated community at Mendham, New Jersey, USA *(see separate entry)*; and we also have links with the Justice and Peace Movement.

Daily life centres on the Eucharist and the Divine Office, and we live under the threefold vows of poverty, chastity and obedience. Following the Rule of St Augustine, we are encouraged to grow into 'an ever-deepening commitment of love for God and for each other as we strive to show forth the attractiveness of Christ to the world'.

In 2012, we hope to move to Ripon College, Cuddesdon, and have recently made an interim move from our much- loved Priory to a house in the grounds which is much smaller; so we are no longer able to offer guest accommodation.

SISTER ANN VERENA CJGS
(Leader)

Sister Doreen Aldred   Sister Elizabeth Jane Barrett
Sister Jane Olive Stencil   Sister Mary Stephen Britt
Sister Edna Frances Wilson   Sister Anne Proudley
Sister Monica Amy

Obituaries
21 Aug 2010   Sister Sheila O'Brien,
                        aged 92, professed 52 years

Oblates & Associates
CSJB has women oblates. Men and women may become Associates or members of the Friends of Clewer – these answer to a call to prayer and service while remaining at home and work. This call includes a commitment to their own spiritual life development and to active church membership. Oblates, Associates and Friends support the sisters by prayer and in other ways, and are likewise supported by the Community, and are part of the extended family of CSJB.

Office Book
Common Worship
Daily Prayer,
with our own
plainsong hymns and
antiphons

Bishop Visitor
Rt Revd
John Pritchard
Bishop of Oxford

Registered Charity:
No 236939

Community Publication
Associates' Letter, has been published three times a year,
but this is now under review. Contact the magazine editor
at csjbteam@csjb.org.uk for information.

Community Wares
Anglican prayer beads, holding crosses.

Community History
Books by Valerie Bonham, all published by CSJB:
   A Joyous Service: The Clewer Sisters and their Work (1989)
   – this is being revised with a reprinting.
   A Place in Life: The House of Mercy 1849–1883 (1992),
   The Sisters of the Raj: The Clewer Sisters in India (1997).

Most convenient time to telephone:
10 am–11.45 am; 2.30 pm–4.30 pm, 7 pm–8 pm, Mon to Sat.

Website: www.csjb.org.uk

Community of St John Baptist (USA)
CSJB

Founded 1852 (in UK)
1874 (in USA)

PO Box 240 –
82 W. Main Street
Mendham, NJ
07945
USA
Tel: 973 543 4641
Fax: 973 543 0327

Email:
csjb@csjb.org

The Community of St John Baptist was founded in England in 1852. The spirit of the Community is to "prepare the way of the Lord and make straight in the desert a highway for our God." We follow the call of our patron through a life of worship, community, and service.

Our Community is made up of monastic women, who share life together under the traditional vows of poverty, chastity and obedience. Our life includes daily participation in the Eucharist and the Divine Office, prayer, and ministry to those in need. We also have married or single Oblates, who commit themselves to a Rule of life and service in the Church, and Associates, who make up the wider family of CSJB.

We live by an Augustinian Rule, which emphasizes community spirit. Those who live with us include Oblates and friends, as well as our pony, dog, and cat. Our Retreat House and guest wing are often full of persons seeking spiritual direction and sacred space. Our buildings are set in a beautiful wooded area.

Our work includes spiritual direction, retreats, hospitality, youth ministry and chaplaincy. The Community participates in a mission in Africa, helps the homeless, and works in parishes.

Website: www.csjb.org

Lauds
7.30 am

SISTER ELEANOR FRANCIS CSJB
(Sister Superior, assumed office 14 December 2009)
SISTER LURA GRACE CSJB *(Assistant Superior)*
SISTER BARBARA JEAN CSJB *(Novice Director)*

Eucharist
8.00 am

Sister Suzanne Elizabeth   Sister Margo Elizabeth
Sister Laura Katharine   Sister Deborah Francis
Sister Pamela   Sister Linda Clare

Terce
9.30 am

Sister Mary Lynne

Noonday Office
12 noon

Oblates & Associates
Oblates make promises which are renewed annually.
The Rule of Life includes prayer, study, service, spiritual

Vespers
5.45 pm

direction, retreats. Associates keep a simple Rule.
Membership is ecumenical.

Compline
8.30 pm

Address of other house
St Mary's Mission House, 145 W. 46th Street, New York,
NY 10036, USA.   Tel: 212 869 5830

Community Publication
Michaelmas, Christmas & Easter Newsletters.

Office Book
Our own book based
upon the Book of
Common Prayer of the
Episcopal Church of
the USA

Community History & Books
J Simpson & E. Story, *Stars in His Crown*, Ploughshare
Press, Sea Bright, NJ, 1976.

Books by Valerie Bonham, all published by CSJB:
A Joyous Service: The Clewer Sisters and their Work (1989)
A Place in Life: The House of Mercy 1849–1883 (1992)
The Sisters of the Raj: The Clewer Sisters in India (1997)

P Allan, M Berry, D Hiley, Pamela CSJB & E Warrell, *An English Kyriale.*

**Most convenient time
for guests to
telephone**
between 10 am and
4.45 pm

Guest and Retreat Facilities
ST MARGUERITE'S RETREAT HOUSE
This has twenty-seven rooms. The address is the same as
for the Convent but the telephone number is: 973 543 4582
There is one new room for a disabled person with
disabled-access bathroom.

CONVENT GUEST WING
This has six rooms (for women only). The cost is $75.00
for an overnight stay with three meals. Closed Mon and
Tue.

Bishop Visitor
Rt Revd Prince Singh,
Bishop of Rochester

Community Wares
Tote bags, mugs, cards, jewelry, candles, ornaments,
tapes, prayer beads.

Community of St John the Divine

CSJD

Founded 1848

St John's House
652 Alum Rock Road
Birmingham
B8 3NS
UK

Tel: 0121 327 4174

Email: csjdivine@
btinternet.com

Website
www.csjd.org.uk

Office Book
Theb Daily Office SSF
(new revised edition
2010)

Bishop Visitor
Rt Revd
David Urquhart,
Bishop of Birmingham

Registered Charity
No. 210 254

The last thirty years have been a time of enormous evolutionary change within our Community. In the last five years, we have been studying in greater depth the essence of the Religious Life, so that we have wisdom and courage to go on further developing new patterns for living our life, that fit the culture of our time, and sharing it with others.

Those coming to explore a vocation in CSJD need to be women and men not afraid of the Community's exploration. Whilst the essence of Religious life is safeguarded and its intrinsic values remain the same, our lifestyle is changing significantly. We are praying there will be those who feel God calling them to a possible vocation in the Religious Life, who would be interested and challenged and like to know more. We would be delighted to meet you.

We are a centre of prayer within the diocese reflecting older examples of living the Religious life from earlier centuries, when Religious Houses were generous in sharing their life. We are a small Community living in the heart of a multicultural city here in Birmingham. The core Community forms the welcoming centre for a growing number of Associates, Alongsiders and others who share much of our life. Our Associates have a very close relationship with the Community. The programme for Alongsiders, running for some nine years, continues to be valued by those seriously wanting to deepen their spiritual life, or by those who for a variety of reasons need time and space to consider significant issues in their life.

Together our vision is to be: a growing centre of prayer within the Diocese; to exercise a ministry of hospitality to the many who come, either as individuals or as groups; to offer spiritual accompaniment; and to be more open to new ways in which God might use us here. New ministries are opening up such as building friendships with our Muslim neighbours and in complementary therapies such as reflexology. All of our ministries seek to reflect something of the ethos of our Community, which has broadened to cover all aspects of health, healing, reconciliation and pastoral care in its widest context, ministries that all seek in helping people find wholeness.

The underpinning of our life and work is a spirituality based on St John, the Apostle of love.

SISTER CHRISTINE CSJD & SISTER MARGARET ANGELA CSJD
(Leaders of the Community, assumed office April 2007)

Sister Teresa   Sister Shirley
Sister Elaine   Sister Helen Alison
Sister Ivy

Obituaries
13 Mar 2010   Sister Marie-Clare, aged 90, professed 53 years

Associates
Associates are men and women from all walks of life who desire to have a close link with the life and work of the Community. They make a simple Commitment to God, to the Community and to one another. Together with the Sisters, they form a network of love, prayer and service. (Guidelines available.)

Alongsiders
Alongsiders come to the Community for varying lengths of time, usually six months to one year. The aim is to provide an opportunity of sharing in the worship and life of the Community, and could be useful for a sabbatical, a time of spiritual renewal, study, to respond to a specific need, or to allow time and space to consider the way ahead. (Guidelines available.)

Community Wares: Various hand-crafted cards for different occasions.

Community Publication: *Annual Report*

Community History
The brochure written for the 150th anniversary contains a short history.

Guest and Retreat Facilities: Quiet Days for individuals and groups. Facilities for residential individual private retreats. Openness to be used as a resource.

Most convenient time to telephone: 9 am, 2.30 pm, 6 pm

Some CSJD sisters and friends.

Community of St John the Evangelist

CSJE

Founded 1912

St Mary's Home
Pembroke Park
Ballsbridge
Dublin 4
IRISH REPUBLIC

Tel: 668 3550

Meditation
6.50 am

Lauds
7.30 am

Terce
9.00 am

Mass
10.30 am (Fri only)

Sext: 12 noon

None
after dinner

Vespers
5.00 pm

Compline
7.45 pm

Founded in Dublin in 1912, CSJE was an attempt to establish Religious Life in the Church of Ireland, although it did not receive official recognition. The founder believed that a group of sisters living hidden lives of prayer and service would exercise a powerful influence. When he died in 1939, there were twenty-four professed sisters and six novices.

From the 1930s, the Community had a branch house in Wales, which became the Mother House in 1967. In 1996, however, the Sisters returned to Dublin to the house originally taken over in 1959 from the Community of St Mary the Virgin. (This CSMV was not connected with the CSMV sisters at Wantage, but was a small community founded in the 1890s which had never grown beyond nine members.) The present house was formerly a school and then a home for elderly ladies of the Church of Ireland. It is now a Registered Nursing and Residential Home under the care of the Community but run by lay people.

The remaining Sisters of CSJE continue to live the Religious Life to the best of their ability and leave the future in the hands of God.

SISTER ANN DORA CSJE
(Sister Superior, assumed office February 2000)
Sister Verity Anne
Sister Kathleen Brigid

Associates and Companions
Associates have a simple Rule, Companions a fuller and stricter Rule. Both groups are now much reduced in number.

Community History
A private booklet was produced for Associates in 1962.

Office Book: Hours of Prayer with the Revised Psalter.

Community of St Laurence

CSL

Founded 1874

Convent
of St Laurence
4A West Gate
Southwell
Notts, NG25 0JH
UK
Tel: 01636 819200

Registered Charity:
No. 220282

The Community was founded in 1874. The Sisters cared for the 'Treasures' of the Church – those in need of love and care, including elderly ladies. In 2001 the Community moved to a new purpose-built convent in Southwell, adjacent to Sacrista Prebend Retreat House and the Cathedral.

Sister Dorothea
Sister Margareta Mary

Obituaries
5 Jul 2009   Sister Brenda, aged 89, professed 52 years

Associates
Associates pray regularly for the community, and include priests and lay people. We have over one hundred associates.

Guest & Retreat Facilties
None, but the convent is adjacent to the Sacrista Prebend Retreat House.

Office Book: CSL Office & Common Worship

Bishop Visitor
Bishop of Southwell & Nottingham

Community of St Mary
(Eastern Province)

CSM

Founded 1865

St Mary's Convent
242 Cloister Way
Greenwich
NY 12834-7922
USA

Tel: 518 692 3028
Fax: 518 692 3029

Email: compunun@
stmaryseast.org

The Sisters of St Mary live a vowed life in community, centered around the daily Eucharist and a five-fold Divine Office. Each sister has time daily for private prayer and study. Our way of life is a modern expression of traditional monastic practice including silent meals in common, plainchant in English for much of our corporate worship, a distinctive habit, and a measure of enclosure.

Our ministry is an outward expression of our vowed life of poverty, chastity and obedience. The specific nature of our work has changed over the years since Mother Harriet and our first sisters were asked to take charge of the House of Mercy in New York City in 1865. Being "mindful of the needs of others," as our table blessing says, we have been led in many ways to care for the lost, forgotten and underprivileged. Today our work is primarily hospitality, retreats, and exploration of outreach through the Internet. Sisters also go out from time to time to speak in parishes, lead quiet days and provide a praying community within the Diocese of Albany's Spiritual Life Center and the Diocese of Northern Malawi.

Website
www.
stmaryseast.org

Matins   6.30 am
(7.30 am Sat & Sun)

Mass   7.00 am
(8.00 am Sat & Sun)

Terce   9.30 am

Sext   12 noon

Vespers   5.30 pm

Compline   7.30 pm

Office Book
*The Monastic Diurnal
Revised,*
(The Community of
St Mary, New York,
1989): a modern
English version of
the *Monastic Diurnal*
by Canon Winfred
Douglas with
supplemental texts
based upon the
American 1979 Book
of Common Prayer.
Copies are for sale.

Community Wares
Assorted illuminated
greeting cards.

Bishop Visitor
Rt Revd William Love,
Bishop of Albany

MOTHER MIRIAM CSM
(*Mother Superior, assumed office 31 August 1996*)
SISTER MARY JEAN CSM (*Assistant Superior*)

Sister Mary Angela	*Juniors:*
Sister Catherine Clare	Sister Jane Chifundo
Sister Mary Elizabeth	Sister Silvia
Sister Martha	
Sister Monica	*Novices:* 1

Associates

Associates of the Community of St Mary are Christian men and women who undertake a Rule of life under the direction of the Community, and share in the support and fellowship of the Sisters, and of one another, whilst living dedicated and disciplined lives in the world. Any baptized, practising Christian who feels called to share in the life and prayer of the Community of St Mary as part of our extended family is welcome to inquire about becoming an Associate. Each prospective Associate plans his or her own Rule with the advice of a Sister. An outline is provided covering one's share in the Eucharist and the Divine Office; a rule of private prayer; abstinence and fasting; and charity and witness. Individual vocations and circumstances vary so widely in today's world that a 'one size fits all' Rule is no longer appropriate. We do ask Associates to pray specifically for the Community, as we do for them, and, because the Divine Office is central to our way of life, to undertake some form of Daily Office. An Associate is also expected to keep in touch with us, and to seek to bring others to know the Community.

Address of other house: Sisters of St Mary, St Mary's Convent, PO Box 20280, Luwinga, Mzuzu 2, MALAWI, South Central Africa

Community Publication: St Mary's Messenger. Contact the subscriptions editor. Cost to subscribers in the USA is $5, to those outside the USA $10.

Community History: Sister Mary Hilary CSM, *Ten Decades of Praise,* DeKoven, Racine, WI, 1965. (*out of print*).

Guest and Retreat Facilities

Accommodations for seven in the Convent Guest wing and a further 50 accommodations on first-come, first-serve basis at adjacent Spiritual Life Center, in Greenwich, NY.

Most convenient time to telephone: 10 am – 7 pm ET.

Community of St Mary

(Southern Province)

CSM

Founded 1865

1100 St Mary's Lane
Sewanee
TN 37375
USA
Tel: 931 598 0046
Fax: 931 598 9519
Email: stmsis@
att.net

**Morning Prayer
& Holy Eucharist**
7.00 am
(8.00 am Holy
Eucharist Sat & Sun)

Noonday Prayer
12 noon
(12.30 pm Sun)

Evening Prayer
5.00 pm

Compline   7.00 pm
(not Sat & Sun)

Office Book
BCP of the ECUSA
plus Plainsong Psalter,
Book of Canticles

Bishop Visitor
Rt Revd John
Bauerschmidt, Diocese
of Tennesee

The Community of St Mary began in New York in 1865. It was the first women's monastic community founded in the United States, and now has three provinces. The Southern Province has its mother house in Sewanee, Tennessee, and a branch house in the Mountain Province, Philippines. The primary focus of our life together is prayer and worship. The sisters gather four times a day for corporate prayer. We nourish ourselves spiritually through meditation, spiritual reading, Bible study and retreats. The sisters take the three-fold vows of simplicity, chastity and obedience. We live in community and hold all things in common. We choose to live a simple life and endeavour to treat God's creation with care. Hospitality and mission are important components of our community's life.

SISTER JULIAN HOPE CSM
(Sister-in-charge, assumed office 10 January 2011)

Sister Lucy	Sister Miriam
Sister Elizabeth Grace	Sister Margaret
Sister Madeleine Mary	Sister Mary Hope
Sister Mary Martha	Sister Ines *(Philippines)*
Sister Mary Zita	

Associates and Oblates
ASSOCIATES are a fellowship of men and women who help CSM through friendship, prayer, support and by their dedicated lives in the world. Each associate writes his/her own rule of life, according to guidelines.
We offer associates hospitality, retreats and spiritual companionship.
OBLATES are a fellowship of men and women who pattern their lives on the monastic tradition of prayer and service. Oblates work closely with the sisters.

Other Address: St Mary the Virgin Church, St Mary's Convent, 2619 Sagada, Mountain Province, PHILIPPINES

Community wares: Photo cards, hand-painted note cards, rosaries (Anglican & Dominican)

Community publication: The Messenger

Community history: James Waring, *Saint Mary's, the Sewanee Sisters and their School,* Sewanee Trust, 2010

Guest and Retreat Facilities: St Dorothy's guest house. A one-bedroom unit with small kitchen and bath and a two-bedroom unit with kitchen and bath. All welcome. Contact CSM for the current fees.

Most convenient time to telephone
Mon-Sat, 9.30 am – 11.30 am, 2 pm – 5 pm

Community
of St Mary
(Western Province)

CSM

Founded 1865

Mary's Margin
S83 W27815
BeaverTrail,
Mukwonago
WI 53149
USA
Tel: 262 363 8489
Email: srstmary@
marysmargin.com
or
CSM@
marysmargin.com

Website: www.
marysmargin.com

Meditation   7.00 am

Morning Prayer
7.30 am

Eucharist
8.00 am (Sun)

Meditation   5.00 pm

Evening Prayer
8.00 pm

Office Book
BCP of ECUSA

Bishop Visitor:
to be appointed

The Western Province of the Community of St Mary was set apart as a separate branch of the community in 1904. We share a common Rule, but have separate administration. Our basic orientation is toward a life of prayer, corporate and personal, reaching out to the Church and the world according to the leading of the Holy Spirit. We live singly or in small groups, each sister using her gifts for ministry as she feels led with the support of the whole group. Mary's Margin is the main house of the Western Province. We offer hospitality to individuals for private retreats and to small groups for meetings and quiet days. The sisters are available as spiritual companions on request.

SISTER LETITIA PRENTICE CSM
(President, assumed office January 1992)
SISTER DORCAS BAKER CSM *(Vice President)*
Sister Mary Paula Bush
Sister Mary Grace Rom

Obituaries

27 Aug 2009   Sister Mary Faith Burgess, aged 85, professed 60 years

31 Oct 2010   Sister Jean Hodgkins, aged 88, professed 56 years

Associates
Associates (both men and women) are part of the community family. They follow a Rule of Life and assist the sisters as they are able.

Other address: The Farm, S82 W27570 Johnson Ave, Mukwonago, WI 53149, USA   Tel: 262 363 58

Guest and Retreat Facilities
We welcome both men and women guests. There are 3 single spaces in the main house for overnight guests plus 2 hermitages (with heat, no plumbing). There are also 2 double rooms in the farm house which is a 7-minute walk from Mary's Margin. The cost is $60 per day (3 meals and 1 overnight). Day groups up to 12 can be accommodated at Mary's Margin. The cost is $15 per person. A deposit of $10 per person must accompany group reservations. Day groups up to 20 can be accommodated at the Club House on the farm. No meal service is provided, but there is a full kitchen available or people may bring bag lunches. The cost is $10 per person.

Community of St Mary the Virgin

CSMV

Founded 1848

St Mary's Convent
Challow Road,
Wantage
Oxfordshire
OX12 9DJ
UK
Tel: 01235 763141

Email:
conventsisters
@csmv.co.uk

Website: www.
csmvonline.co.uk

Lauds
7.00 am

Terce   9.45 am
(9.15 am Sun
& principal feasts)

Eucharist   10.00 am
(9.30 am Sun
& principal feasts)

Sext   12.30 pm

Vespers
5.00 pm

Compline
8.30 pm

The Community of St Mary the Virgin was founded in 1848 by William John Butler, then Vicar of Wantage. As Sisters, we are called to respond to our vocation in the spirit of the Blessed Virgin Mary: "Behold, I am the handmaid of the Lord. Let it be to me according to your word." Our common life is centred in the worship of God through the Eucharist, the daily Office and in personal prayer. From this all else flows. For some it will be expressed in outgoing ministry in neighbourhood and parish, or in living alongside those in inner city areas and in pastoral care for the elderly. For others, it will be expressed in spiritual direction, preaching and retreat giving, in creative work in studio and press A recent development has been our website, which has opened up a new field of mission for the Community. In addition to streaming our Offices live, which enables people all over the world to worship with us, we are able to offer weekly meditations, as well as day retreats and three-day individually-guided retreats, all online.

The Community has had a share in the nurturing and training of a small indigenous community in Madagascar *(see entry for FMJK)*. We still keep in touch with the Sisters there through correspondence and occasional visits.

Other Addresses

St Katharine's House, Ormond Road, Wantage, Oxfordshire OX12 8EA, UK   *Tel: 01235 767380*

366 High Street, Smethwick, B66 3PD, UK
                                        Tel: 0121 558 0094

116 Seymour Road, Harringay, London N8 0BG, UK   *Tel & fax: 020 8348 3477*

Community History
A Hundred Years of Blessing, SPCK, London, 1946.

Community Wares
The Printing Press offers a variety of cards and plainchant music. Orders are not received for cards, which may be purchased at the Convent.   *Email: press@csmv.co.uk*
A variety of other items made by sisters are for sale in the Reception Area.

Office Book: CSMV Office

Bishop Visitor: Rt Revd John Pritchard, Bishop of Oxford

Registered Charity: No 240513

MOTHER WINSOME CSMV
(The Reverend Mother, assumed office 8 December 2006)
SISTER DEIRDRE MICHAEL CSMV *(The Assistant)*

Sister Cecily Clare	Sister Helen Philippa	Sister Valerie
Sister Joan Elizabeth	Sister Valeria	Sister Barbara Claire
Sister Christiana	Sister Phoebe Margaret	Sister Mary Clare
Sister Barbara Noreen	Sister Mary Jennifer	Sister Stella
Sister Yvonne Mary	Sister Jean Mary	Sister Francis Honor
Sister Louise	Sister Christine Ann	Sister Patricia Ann
Sister Anne Mary	Sister Rosemary	Sister Anna
Sister Anne Julian	Sister Bridget Mary	Sister Barbara Anne
Sister Catherine Naomi	Sister Eileen	Sister Trudy
Sister Honor Margaret	Sister Rosemary Clare	Sister Rachel
Sister Enid Mary	Sister Sheila Mary	Sister Elizabeth Jane
Sister Jean Frances	Sister Lorna	Sister Pauline

Obituaries

26 Sep 2009	Sister Margaret Verity, aged 99, professed 57 years
10 Feb 2010	Sister Hilda Kathleen, aged 93, professed 65 years
21 Sep 2010	Sister Margaret Jean, aged 95, professed 64 years
21 Dec 2010	Sister Betty, aged 79 years, professed 40 years
30 Dec 2010	Sister Ethne Ancilla, aged 85, professed 55 years

Oblates

The Oblates of the Community respond to their vocation in the same spirit as Mary: "Behold, I am the handmaid of the Lord. Let it be to me according to your word." Oblates may be married or single, women or men, ordained or lay. Most are Anglicans, but members of other denominations are also welcomed. There is a common Rule, based on Scripture and the Rule of St Augustine, and each Oblate also draws up a personal Rule of Life in consultation with the Oblates' Sister. There is a two-year period of testing as a Novice Oblate; the Promise made at Oblation is renewed annually. In addition to a close personal link with the Community, Oblates meet in regional groups and support each other in prayer and fellowship.

Associates

Associates are men and women, ordained and lay, who wish to be united in prayer and fellowship with the Community, sharing in the spirit of Mary's 'Fiat' in their daily lives. Each Associate keeps a personal Rule of Life, undertakes regular prayer for the Community, is expected to keep in touch with the Associates' Sister, and to make an annual retreat. The Community sends out a quarterly letter with an intercession leaflet. Every two years an Associates' Day is held at the Convent.

Guest and Retreat Facilities

ST MARY'S CONVENT GUEST WING

The guest wing is a still place, enabling space and refreshment for all who come. Everyone is welcome at the Eucharist and Daily Office in St Mary's Chapel. Facilities include a sitting room with a library, a dining room, informal quiet room, computer room and art room. For group retreats and group quiet days we offer a spacious room with its own kitchen attached. Those coming for individual quiet days are allocated a room, and are able to share in a meal in the guests' dining room if they so wish.

Online retreats are offered, both day retreats and three-day individually-guided retreats: please see the website, online events section.

Contact: the Guest Wing. Rooms: Fifteen bedrooms, including one double room, one bedroom with sitting room, one small flat with ensuite facilities, one ground-floor bedroom with ensuite shower for the physically challenged.

Tel: 01235 763141   Email: guestwing@csmv.co.uk

Community of St Michael & All Angels

CSM&AA

Founded 1874

Room 23 Serenicare, 51 General Hertzog Avenue, Dan Pienaar, Bloemfontein 9301, SOUTH AFRICA
Tel: 051 436 7188

Mass is celebrated twice a week.

Office Book
Anglican Prayer Book 1989, of the CPSA

Bishop Visitor
Rt Revd E P Glover, Bishop of Bloemfontein

Warden
Rt Revd T S Stanage, retired Bishop of Bloemfontein

The Community of St Michael and All Angels was founded by the second Bishop of Bloemfontein, Allan Becher Webb, for pioneer work in his vast diocese, which included the Orange Free State, Basutoland, Griqualand West and into the Transvaal. The sisters were active in mission, nursing and education. Sister Henrietta Stockdale became the founder of professional nursing in South Africa. The South African Synod of Bishops has placed her on the *CPSA Calendar* for yearly commemoration on 6 October. In 1874, the sisters established St Michael's School for Girls in Bloemfontein, which still exists today as one of the leading schools in South Africa.

Today, one sister remains, Sister Joan, who celebrated her Diamond Jubilee of Life Profession on 16 December 2010.

Sister Joan Marsh CSM&AA

Community Histories
Margaret Leith, *One the Faith*, 1971 & Mary Brewster, *One the Earnest Looking Forward*, 1991.

Booklets by Sister Mary Ruth CSM&AA: *Dust & Diamonds* (on work in Kimberley); *Cave, Cows & Contemplation* (on thirty years of work at Modderpoort Mission); *Ma'Mohau, Mother of Mercy* (on Sister Enid CSM&AA); *Medals for St Michael's* (CSM&AA in Anglo-Boer War); *Uphill all the Way* (on work in Basutoland/Lesotho)

Obtainable from St Michael's School, PO Box 12110, Brandway 9324, SOUTH AFRICA.

Community of St Peter

CSP

Founded 1861

St Peter's Convent
c/o St Columba's
House
Maybury Hill
Woking, Surrey
GU22 8AB
UK

Tel: 01483 750739
(9.30 am – 5 pm
Mon-Thu)
Fax: 01483 766208

Email:
reverendmother@
stpetersconvent.
co.uk

Office Book
Celebrating Common
Prayer

Bishop Visitor:
Rt Revd David Walker,
Bishop of Dudley

Community History
Elizabeth Cuthbert,
In St Peter's Shadow,
CSP, Woking, 1994

Registered Charity:
No. 240675

The Community was founded by Benjamin Lancaster, a Governor of St George's Hospital, Hyde Park, London. He wished his poorer patients to have convalescent care before returning to their homes. The Sisters also nursed cholera and TB patients, and opened orphanages and homes for children and the elderly. They were asked by priests to help in the parish and they were asked to go to Korea in 1892. They have close links with the Society of the Holy Cross in Korea, which was founded by the Community *(see separate entry).*

Since the closure of their Nursing/Care Home, new work is undertaken outside the Community in the way of continued care, using Sisters' abilities, talents and qualifications. The Sisters live in houses located where they can carry out their various works and ministry. They recite their fourfold daily Office either together in their houses or individually.

REVD MOTHER LUCY CLARE CSP
(Mother Superior, assumed office 29 June 2005)
(St Columba's House address)

Sisters Margaret Paul & Rosamond: *St Mary's Convent & Nursing Home, Burlington Lane, Chiswick, London W4 2QE*

Sister Angela: *41 Sandy Lane, Woking, Surrey, GU22 8BA*

Sister Georgina Ruth: *[Flat 1 Block 4], Whitgift Alms Houses, North End, Croydon CR0 1UB*

Sister Caroline Jane: *c/o St Columba's House address*

Associates and Companions
The associates' fellowship meets at St Columba's at Petertide. The associates support the community in prayer and with practical help, as they are able. They have a simple rule and attend the Eucharist in their own Church as their individual commitments permit. Companions have a stricter rule and say the Daily Office.

Guest and Retreat Facilities
St Columba's House *(Retreat & Conference Centre)*, Maybury Hill, Woking, Surrey, GU22 8AB, UK   *Tel: 01483 766498   Fax: 01483 740441   Email: director@stcolumbashouse.org.uk*
Director: Revd Owen Murphy
22 en-suite single bedrooms (2 with disabled facilities), 5 twin bedrooms (four ensuite). Programme of individual and group retreats. Also a conference centre for residential and day use. Completely refurbished in 2009 for retreatants, parish groups, and day/overnight visits. An outstanding

liturgical space with a pastoral, and liturgical programme. A place to retreat and reflect on life's journey.

Most convenient time to telephone: 9.30 am – 5.00 pm.

Community Publication
Associates' newsletter at Petertide and Christmas; a quarterly letter sent by Reverend Mother, spring and autumn.

Community of St Peter, Horbury

CSPH

Founded 1858

St Peter's Convent
Dovecote Lane
Horbury
Wakefield
West Yorkshire
WF4 6BD
UK
Tel: 01924 272181

Email:
stpetersconvent@
btconnect.com

Lauds   7.30 am

Mass   8.00 am

Midday Office
12.00 noon

Vespers   6.00 pm

Compline
8.30 pm

The Community seeks to glorify God by a life of loving dedication to him, by worship and by serving him in others. A variety of pastoral work is undertaken including retreat and mission work, social work and ministry to individuals in need. The spirit of the community is Benedictine and the recitation of the Divine Office central to the life.

MOTHER ROBINA CSPH
(Revd Mother, assumed office 14 Apr 1993)
SISTER ELIZABETH CSPH *(Assistant Superior)*

Sister Gwynneth Mary
Sister Mary Clare *(priest)*
Sister Phyllis
Sister Jean Clare

Sister Margaret Ann,
2 Main Street, Bossall, York YO2 7NT, UK
Tel: 01904 468253

Obituaries
12 Jun 10   Sister Margaret, aged 92, professed 51 years

Oblates and Associates
The Community has both oblates and associates.

Community Publication: Annual Review: *Keynotes*

Guest and Retreat Facilities: A separate guest wing has four single rooms, with shower room and utility room.

Bishop Visitor: Rt Revd Stephen Platten,
Bishop of Wakefield

Community of the Servants of the Cross

CSC

Founded 1877

resident at:

Green Willow
Residential Home
21/23 Vicarage
Lane East Preston
Littlehampton
BN16 2SP

The Community has an Augustinian Rule and for much of its history cared for elderly and infirm women. In 1997, because of decreasing numbers, the Convent at Lindfield (Sussex) was sold and the Mother House transferred to Chichester, where the former Theological College is now a retirement home. From there, the remaining sisters moved to St Katharine's House, Wantage, but have now moved back to Sussex, to live in a home near to their Warden. There are only two members of the Community remaining.

MOTHER ANGELA CSC
(Mother Superior, assumed office October 1995)
Sister Jane

Bishop Visitor
Rt Revd John Hind, Lord Bishop of Chichester

Warden
Father John Lyon, The Vicarage, 33 Vicarage Lane, East Preston, Littlehampton, BN16 2SP   *Tel: 01903 783318*

Community of the Servants of the Will of God

CSWG

Founded 1953

The Monastery of
the Holy Trinity
Crawley Down
Crawley
West Sussex
RH10 4LH
UK

Tel: 01342 712074

This monastery is set in woodland. The Community of men and women lives a contemplative life, uniting silence, work and prayer in a simple life style based on the Rule of St Benedict. The Community is especially concerned with uniting the traditions of East and West, and has developed the Liturgy, Divine Office and use of the Jesus Prayer accordingly.

FATHER COLIN CSWG
(Father Superior, assumed office 3 April 2008)
FATHER PETER CSWG *(Prior)*

Father Brian   Brother Christopher Mark
Brother Martin   Brother John of the Cross
Sister Mary Angela   Brother Andrew

Obituaries
12 Aug 2009   Father Gregory, aged 78,
                 professed 47 years, Father Superior 1973–2008
Associates
The associates keep a rule of life in the spirit of the monastery.

Community Publication
CSWG Journal: *Come to the Father*, issued Pentecost and All Saints. Write to the Monastery of the Holy Trinity.

Email:
(for guests bookings
& enquiries)
brother.andrew@
cswg.org.uk

Vigils 5.00 am

Lauds 7.00 am

Terce 9.30 am

Sext 12.00 noon

None 1.45 pm

Vespers 6.30 pm

Mass
7.00 pm Mon – Fri
11.00 am Sat & Sun

Community History

Father Colin CSWG, *A History of the Community of the Servants of the Will of God*, 2002. Available from Crawley Down.

Guest and Retreat Facilities

Six individual guest rooms; meals in community refectory; Divine Office and Eucharist, all with modal chant; donations c.£20 per day.

Most convenient time to telephone: 9.30 am – 6.00 pm.

Community Wares

Mounted icon prints, Jesus Prayer ropes, candles and vigil lights, booklets on monastic and spiritual life.

Office Book

CSWG Divine Office and Liturgy

Bishop Visitor

Rt Revd John Hind, Bishop of Chichester

The late Father Gregory in the chapel at the Monastery of the Holy Trinity.

Community of the Sisters of the Church

CSC

Founded 1870

for the whole people of God

Worldwide Community
Website: www. sistersofthechurch .org

ENGLAND
Registered Charity No. for CSC:
271790
Registered Charity No. for CEA:
200240

CANADA
Registered Charity No. 130673262RR0001

AUSTRALIA
Tax Exempt – NPO

Founded by Emily Ayckbowm in 1870, the Community of the Sisters of the Church is an international body of lay and ordained women within the Anglican Communion. We are seeking to be faithful to the gospel values of Poverty, Chastity and Obedience, and to the traditions of Religious Life while exploring new ways of expressing them and of living community life and ministry today. By our worship, ministry and life in community, we desire to be channels of the reconciling love and acceptance of Christ, to acknowledge the dignity of every person, and to enable others to encounter the living God whom we seek.

The Community's patrons, St Michael and the Angels, point us to a life both of worship and active ministry, of mingled adoration and action. Our name, Sisters of the Church, reminds us that our particular dedication is to the mystery of the Church as the Body of Christ in the world.

Each house has its own timetable of corporate worship. The Eucharist and Divine Office (usually fourfold) are the heart of our Community life. Community houses provide different expressions of our life and ministry in inner city, suburban, coastal town and village setting.

LINDA MARY SHUTTLE CSC
(Mother Superior, assumed office July 2009)
Email: lindacsc@bigpond.com
29 Lika Drive, Kempsey, NSW 2440, AUSTRALIA

ENGLAND

SUSAN HIRD CSC
(UK Provincial, assumed office September 2008)
Email: susan@sistersofthechurch.org.uk
CATHERINE HEYBOURN CSC *(Assistant Provincial)*

Aileen Taylor	Mary Josephine Thomas
Anita Cook	Rosina Taylor
Ann Mechtilde Baldwin	Ruth Morris
Annaliese Brogden	Ruth White
Beryl Hammond	Scholastica Ferris
Dorothea Roden	Sheila Julian Merryweather
Hilda Mary Baumberg	Sue McCarten
Jennifer Cook	Teresa Mary Wright
Judith Gray	Vivien Atkinson
Lydia Corby	
Marguerite Gillham	*Novices:* 2

Obituaries
1 Jan 2010   Elspeth Rennells, aged 90, professed 46 years

Addresses in the UK
St Michael's Convent, 56 Ham Common, Richmond, Surrey TW10 7JH
Tel: 020 8940 8711 & 020 8948 2502   Fax: 020 8948 5525
   Email for general enquiries: info@sistersofthechurch.org.uk

82 Ashley Road, Bristol BS6 5NT   *Tel: 01179 413268*
   Email: bristol@sistersofthe church.org.uk

St Gabriel's, 27A Dial Hill Road, Clevedon, N. Somerset BS21 7 HL
Tel: 01275 544471   Email: clevedon@sistersofthe church.org.uk

10 Furness Road , West Harrow, Middlesex HA2 0RL   *Tel: 020 8423 3780*
   Email: westharrow@sistersofthe church.org.uk

112 St Andrew's Road North, St Anne's-on-Sea, Lancashire FY8 2JQ
Tel & Fax: 01253 728016

Well Cottage, Upper Street, Kingsdown, near Deal, Kent CT14 8BH
Tel: 01304 361601   Email: wellcottage@sistersofthechurch.org.uk

CANADA
Arrived in Canada 1890.   Established as a separate Province 1965.

MARGARET HAYWARD CSC
(Provincial, assumed office 26 September 2009)
Email: margaretcsc@sympatico.ca

Elizabeth Nicklin	Heather Broadwell	Michael Trott
(Benedetta)	Marguerite Mae Eamon	Rita Dugger

Addresses in Canada
St Michael's House, 1392 Hazelton Boulevard, Burlington, Ontario L7P 4V3
Tel: 905 332 9240   Email: sistersofthechurch@sympatico.ca

AUSTRALIA
Arrived in Australia 1892.   Established as a separate Province 1965.

LINDA MARY SHUTTLE CSC
(Provincial, assumed office November 1999)
Email: lindacsc@bigpond.com

Audrey Floate	Fiona Cooper	Helen Jamieson
Elisa Helen Waterhouse	Frances Murphy	Rosamund Duncan

Addresses in Australia
Sisters of the Church, PO Box 1105, Glebe, NSW 2037
   Email: cscaust@hotmail.com

Sisters of the Church, 29 Lika Drive, Kempsey, NSW 2440
Tel: 2 6562 2313 Fax: 2 6562 2314

PO Box M191, Missenden Road, NSW 2050
Tel: 2 9516 2407   Email: francescsc@bigpond.com

Unit 15/75, St John's Road, Glebe, NSW 2037
103/28-30 Jackson Street, Toorak, Victoria 3142
Tel: 3 9827 1658
PO Box 713, Melton, Victoria 3337
Tel: 3 9743 6028   *Email: elisacsc@tpg.com.au*

SOLOMON ISLANDS
Arrived in Solomon Islands 1970.   Established as a separate Province 2001.

PHYLLIS SAU CSC
(Provincial, assumed office 18 October 2010)
Email: phyllissauu@yahoo.co.uk
ESTHER TEKU CSC *(Assistant Provincial)*
Email: tekuesther@yahoo.com

Agnes Maeusia	Georgina Iteone	Neverlyn Tohe
Anna Caroline Vave	Janet Karane	Patricia Kalali
Anneth Kagoa	Jennifer Clare	Priscilla Iolani
Annie Meke	Jessica Maru	Rachel Teku
Beglyn Tiri	Joan Yape	Rebecca Margaret Sulupi
Caroline Havideni	Joanna Suunorua	Rose Glenda Kimanitoro
Clarine Tekeatu	Kathleen Kapei	Rose Houte'e
Daisy Gaoka	Lillian Mary Manedika	Roselyn Tengo
Doralyn Sulucia	Lorna Rautonu	Roselyn Tengea
Doreen Awaisi	Lucia Sadias	Ruth Hope Sosoke
Eleanor Ataki	Margosa Funu	Sharon Amani
Emily Mary Ikai	Mary Gladys Nunga	Shirley Hestead
Evelyn Yaiyo	Mary Kami	Veronica Vasethe
Faith Mary Maiva	Mary Leingala	Vivian Marie
Florence Mola	May Peleba	Von Amevuvlian
Florence Toata	Muriel Tisafa'a	*Novices:* 18 *Postulants:* 1

Addresses in the Solomon Islands
Tetete ni Kolivuti, Box 510, Honiara
Patteson House, Box 510, Honiara   *Tel: 22413 & 27582*
PO Box A7, Auki, Malaita   *Tel: 40423*
St Gabriel's, c/o Hanuato'o Diocese, Kira Kira, Makira/Ulawa Province
Fax: 677 50128
St Mary's, Luesalo, Diocese of Temotu, Santa Cruz   *Mobile phone: 7440081*
St Scholastica's House, PO Box 510, Honiara

Associates
Associates are men and women who seek to live the Gospel values of Simplicity, Chastity and Obedience within their own circumstances. Each creates his/her own Rule of Life and has a Link Sister or Link House. They are united in spirit with CSC in its life of worship and service, fostering a mutually enriching bond.

The four
Provincials
(l to r):

Phyllis CSC
(Solomon
Islands),

Linda Mary CSC
(Australia),

Margaret CSC
(Canada),

Susan CSC
(England)

Community History
A Valiant Victorian: The Life and Times of Mother Emily Ayckbowm 1836–1900 of the Community of the Sisters of the Church, Mowbray, London, 1964.

Ann M Baldwin CSC, *Now is the Time: a brief survey of the life and times of the Community of the Sisters of the Church,* CSC, 2005.

Community Publication: *Newsletter,* twice a year.
Information can be obtained from any house in the community and by email.

Community Wares
Books by Sister Sheila Julian Merryweather: *Colourful Prayer; Colourful Advent; Colourful Lent.* All published by Kevin Mayhew, Buxhall, Stowmarket.
Some houses sell crafts and cards. Vestments are made in the Solomon Islands.

Guest and Retreat Facilities
Hospitality is offered in most houses. Ham Common and Tetete ni Kolivuti have more accommodation for residential guests as well as day facilities. Programmes are offered at Ham Common: please apply for details. Please contact individual houses for other information.

Office Book used by the Community
The Office varies in the different Provinces. Various combinations of the Community's own Office book, the New Zealand psalter, the UK *Common Worship* and the most recent prayer books of Australia, Canada and Melanesia are used.

Bishops Visitor
UK	Rt Revd Chistopher Chessun, Bishop of Southwark
Australia	Rt Revd Barbara Darling, Bishop of Eastern Region, Melbourne
Canada	Rt Revd Michael Bird, Bishop of Niagara
Solomon Islands	Rt Revd Dr Terry Brown, retired former Bishop of Malaita

Address of Affiliated Community: Community of the Love of God (*Orthodox Syrian*) Nazareth, Kadampanad South 691553, Pathanamthitta District, Kerala, INDIA
Tel: 473 4822146

Community of the Sisters of the Love of God

SLG

Founded 1906

Convent
of the Incarnation
Fairacres
Parker Street
Oxford OX4 1TB
UK
Tel: 01865 721301
Fax: 01865 250798
Email: sisters@slg.
org.uk
Guest Sister:
guests@slg.org.uk

Website
www.slg.org.uk

Matins
6.00 am (6.15 am Sun)

Terce & Mass
9.05 am

Sext 12.15 pm

None
2.05 pm (3.05 pm Sun)

Vespers 5.30 pm

Compline 8.05 pm

Office Book
SLG Office

A contemplative community with a strong monastic tradition founded in 1906, which seeks to witness to the priority of God and to respond to the love of God – God's love for us and our love for God. We believe that we are called to live a substantial degree of withdrawal, in order to give ourselves to a spiritual work of prayer which, beginning and ending in the praise and worship of God, is essential for the peace and well-being of the world. Through offering our lives to God within the Community, and through prayer and daily life together, we seek to deepen our relationship with Jesus Christ and one another. The Community has always drawn upon the spirituality of Carmel; life and prayer in silence and solitude is an important dimension in our vocation. The Community also draws from other traditions; therefore our Rule is not specifically Carmelite. Another important ingredient is an emphasis on the centrality of Divine Office and Eucharist together in choir, inspired partly by the Benedictine way of life.

SISTER MARGARET THERESA SLG
(Revd Mother, assumed office 24 June 2007)
SISTER CATHERINE SLG *(Prioress)*

Sister Josephine	Sister Helen Columba
Sister Mary Magdalene	Sister Julie
Sister Mary Margaret	Sister Shirley Clare
Sister Benedicta	Sister Avis Mary
Sister Isabel	Sister Alison
Sister Adrian	Sister Tessa
Sister Anne	Sister Raphael
Sister Jane Frances	Sister Barbara
Sister Mary Kathleen	Sister Stephanie Thérèse
Sister Edwina	Sister Clare-Louise
Sister Barbara June	*(Novice Guardian)*
Sister Susan	Sister Freda
Sister Edmée	Sister Judith
Sister Christine	Sister Eve
Sister Cynthia	Sister Elizabeth
Sister Rosemary	Sister Helen

Obituaries
19 Aug 2010   Sister Esther Mary, aged 91,
                         professed 42 years

Oblates and associates
The Community includes Oblate Sisters, who are called to the contemplative life in the world rather than within the monastic enclosure. There are three other groups of

associates: Priest Associates, Companions, and the Fellowship of the Love of God. Information about all these may be obtained from the Revd Mother at Fairacres.

Community Publication: Fairacres Chronicle.
Published twice a year by SLG Press (see under Community Wares).

Community Wares
SLG Press publishes the *Fairacres Chronicle* and a range of books and pamphlets on prayer and spirituality. Contact details:
The Editor, SLG Press, Convent of the Incarnation, Fairacres, Parker Street, Oxford OX4 1TB, UK
Tel: 01865 241874 Fax: 01865 241889
Best to telephone: Mon-Fri 10.30 am – 12 noon, & Mon-Thu afternoons. A call answering service is in place for voicemail if there is no-one currently in the office.
Email: General matters: *editor@slgpress.co.uk*
            Orders only: *orders@slgpress.co.uk*   Website: *www.slgpress.co.uk*

Guest and Retreat Facilities
There is limited accommodation for private retreats, for both men and women, at Fairacres. Please write to or email the Guest Sister to make a booking.
Email: guests@slg.org.uk   Tel (for guest sister): 01865 258152 (with voicemail)

Most convenient time to telephone:
10.30 am – 12 noon; 3.30 pm – 4.30 pm; 6.00 pm – 7.00 pm
Sunday and Friday afternoons are ordinarily covered by an answer phone, but messages are cleared after Vespers.

Bishop Visitor: Rt Revd Michael Lewis, Bishop of Cyprus & the Gulf

Registered Charity: No. 261722
            SLG Charitable Trust Ltd: registered in England 990049

Some participants in an ecumenical meeting at SLG.

Community of the Sisters of Melanesia

CSM

Founded 1980

Bishop Visitor
Most Revd David
Vunagi, Archbishop
of Melanesia
KNT/Headquarter
Verana'aso
PO Box 19
Honiara
SOLOMON ISLANDS

**First Office, Mattins
& Mass** 5.45 am

Morning Office
7.45 am

**Mid-day Office &
Intercession**
11.55 am

Afternoon Office
1.30 pm

**Evensong &
Meditation** 5.30 pm

Compline 8.45 pm

Office Book
CSM Office Book
(adapted from
MBH Office book)

The community of the Sisters of Melanesia is a sisterhood of women in Melanesia. It was founded by Nester Tiboe and three young women of Melanesia on 17 November 1980. Nester believed that a Religious community of women in Melanesia was needed for the work of evangelism and mission, similar to the work of the Melanesian Brotherhood, founded by Brother Ini Kopuria.

On 17 November 1980, the four young women made their promises of Poverty, Celibacy, and Obedience to serve in the community. The ceremony took place at St Hilda's Day at Bunana Island and officiated by the Most Reverend Norman Kitchener Palmer, the second Archbishop of the Province of Melanesia.

The community aims to offer young women in Melanesia an opportunity of training for ministry and mission, so that they may serve Christ in the church and society where they live. To provide pastoral care for women and teenage children and uphold the Christian principles of family life. To be in partnership with the Melanesian Brotherhood and other Religious communities by proclaiming the Gospel of Jesus Christ in urban and rural areas in the islands. To give God the honour and glory, and to extend His Kingdom in the world.

Professed. c. 50, Noviciate c. 40

Addresses of other houses in the Solomon Islands
Joe Wate Household, Longa Bay, Waihi Parish,
Southern Region, Malaita
Marau Missionary Household, Guadalcanal
NAT Household, Mbokoniseu, Vutu,
Ghaobata Parish, East Honiara, Guadalcanal
Sir Ellison L. Pogo Household, Honiara

Community Wares
Vestments, altar linen, weaving and crafts.

Associates: The supporters of the Community of the Sisters of Melanesia are called Associates, a group established in 1990. It is an organization for men and women, young and old, and has over one thousand members, including many young boys and girls. All promise to uphold the Sisters in prayer, and they are a great support in many ways. The Associates of the Community of the Sisters of Melanesia are in the Solomon Islands, Australia and Canada.

Community of the Transfiguration

CT

Founded 1898

495 Albion Avenue
Cincinnati
Ohio 45246
USA
Tel: 513 771 5291
Fax: 513 771 0839
Email: ctsisters@aol.com

Website www.ctsisters.org

Lauds, Morning Prayer
6.30 am

Holy Eucharist 7.00 am

Noon Office 12.30 pm

Evensong 5.00 pm

Compline 8.00 pm

Office Book
CT Office Book
& the Book of Common
Prayer

Community Publication
The Quarterly

Bishop Visitor
Rt Revd Christopher Epting

The Community of the Transfiguration, founded in 1898 by Eva Lee Matthews, is a Religious community of women dedicated to the mystery of the Transfiguration. Our life is one of prayer and service, reflecting the spirit of Mary and Martha, shown forth in spiritual, educational and social ministries. The Mother House of the community is located in Cincinnati, Ohio, where our ministries include a retreat and spirituality center, a school and a recreation center. The community also offers a retreat ministry on the West Coast; and in the Dominican Republic, the Sisters minister to malnourished children and their families through medical clinics and a school. The Sisters live their life under the vows of poverty, chastity and obedience. The motto of the community is Benignitas, Simplicitas and Hilaritas – Kindness, Simplicity and Joy.

Associates & Oblates
The Community has Associates and Oblates.

Other addresses
Transfiguration Spirituality Center, 469 Albion Avenue, Cincinnati, Ohio 45246, USA
Website: tscretreats.org
Bethany School, 555 Albion Avenue, Cincinnati, Ohio 45246, USA
Website: www.bethanyschool.org
Sisters of the Transfiguration, 1633 "D" Street, Eureka, California 95501, USA

St Monica's Recreation Center, 10022 Chester Road, Cincinnati, Ohio 45215, USA

Dominican Republic Ministry:
Sister Jean Gabriel CT, DMG # 13174 *or*
Sister Priscilla Jean CT, DMG # 19105
Agape Flights, 100 Airport Avenue, Venice, Florida 34285, USA

Community history and books
Mrs Harlan Cleveland, *Mother Eva Mary CT: The story of a foundation,* Morehouse, Milwaukee, WI, 1929.
Sibyl Harton, *Windfall of Light: a study of the Vocation of Mother Eva Mary CT,* Roessler, Cincinnati, OH, 1968.

Guest and Retreat Facilities
Transfiguration Spirituality Center: 40 beds
Various guest houses and rooms: 16 beds.

Fikambanan'ny Mpanompovavin l Jesoa Kristy

(Society of the Servants of Jesus Christ)

The FMJK sisters were founded by Canon Hall Speers in 1985. They live in the village of Tsinjohasina, on the high plateau above the rice fields, situated some fifteen kilometres from Antananarivo, the capital of Madagascar. The sisters work in the village dispensary and are active in visiting, Christian teaching and pastoral work in the villages around. They are an independent community but have been nurtured by a connection with CSMV, Wantage, in the UK.

FMJK

Founded 1985

Convent Hasina, BP 28
Ambohidratrimo 105
Antananarivo 101
MADAGASCAR

Bishop Visitor
Most Revd Ranarivello
Samoelajaona,
Archbishop of the Indian
Ocean

SISTER JACQUELINE FMJK
(Masera Tonia, assumed office 5 June 2002)
SISTER CHAPITRE FMJK *(Prioress)*

Sister Ernestine   Sister Vololona
Sister Georgette   Sister Fanja
Sister Isabelle
Sister Odette   *Postulants:* 1 (Angeline)
Sister Voahangy

Community Wares: Crafts and embroidery.

Office Book: FMJK Office and Prayer Book

Other house
Antaralava, Soamanandray, BP 28,
Ambohidratrimo 105, Antananarivo 101,
MADAGASCAR

25th anniversary of the Community's foundation, 5 March 2010

Little Brothers of Francis

LBF

Founded 1987

Franciscan
Hermitage
"Eremophilia"
PO Box 162
Tabulam
NSW 2469
AUSTRALIA

Bishop Visitor
Rt Revd
Godfrey Fryar,
Bishop of
Rockhampton, Qld

We are a community of Brothers who desire to deepen our relationship with God through prayer, manual work, community, and times of being alone in our hermitages. We follow the Rule written by Saint Francis for Hermitages in which three or four brothers live in each fraternity. As others join us we envisage a federation of fraternities with three or four brothers in each.

There are four sources of inspiration for the Little Brothers of Francis. They are:

1. The Gospels

The four Gospels (Matthew, Mark, Luke and John) are central to our spirituality, and the main source material for our meditation and prayer life.

2. St Francis

Francis would recall Christ's words and life through persistent meditation on the Gospels, for his deep desire was to love Christ and live a Christ-centred life.

He was a man of prayer and mystic who sought places of solitude, and hermitages played a central role in his life. Significant events, like the initiation of the Christmas Crib tradition, happened at the hermitage at Greccio, and, of course, he received the stigmata while he was at the hermitage at Mount La Verna.

Though the early brothers embraced a mixed life of prayer and ministry, Francis wanted places of seclusion – hermitages, for the primacy of prayer, in which three or four brothers lived, and for which he wrote a rule.

3. St Francis's Rule for Hermitages

In his brief rule for life within the hermitage, Francis avoided a detailed document and set out the principles that are important.

– Liturgy of the Hours is the focus, and sets the rhythm of the daily prayer.

– Each hermitage was to have at the most four Brothers, which meant they would be both 'little' and 'fraternal'.

– Within this framework, Brothers could withdraw for periods of solitude.

– The hermitages were not to be places or centres of ministry.

4. Desert Fathers

The stories and sayings of the Desert Fathers contain a profound wisdom for any who are serious about the inner spiritual journey. This is why they have held such prominence in monastic circles in both East and West down through the centuries, and why they are a priority source for us.

Each Brother has responsibility for certain areas of the

Brothers have times community's life. Decision-making is by consensus.
of Solitude in their
hermitage, which
vary from a day to
weeks or months,
where they have their *Friends:* The Friends of the Little Brothers of Francis are
own personal rhythm those who feel a spiritual affinity with the Brothers and
of prayer and manual desire to deepen their prayer life and to support the
work.

Brother Howard LBF
Brother Wayne LBF
Brother Geoffrey Adam LBF

Friends: The Friends of the Little Brothers of Francis are
those who feel a spiritual affinity with the Brothers and
desire to deepen their prayer life and to support the
Brothers in their life and witness. They have an independent
organisation, with its own office-bearers and requirements
for membership.

Vigil Office   Contact: Australia – Bishop Graeme Rutherford
followed by   *Email: gcruth@bigpond.com*
Lectio Divina   New Zealand – Ian Lothian   *Email: ianlothian@xtra.com.nz*
(private)   Or by post, contact the Brothers.
2.00 am or 4.00 am

Meditation
6.00 am

Angelus and Mattins
7.00 am

Terce   *Brother*
9.00 am   *Howard*
               LBF
Angelus and Sext
12 noon

None (private)
3.00 pm

Vespers
6.00 pm

Compline
8.00 pm

Office Book   ***Community Publication:*** The *Bush Telegraph.*
LBF Office book,   Contact the Brothers for a subscription, which is by donation.
developed to   ***Community Wares:*** Hand-carved holding crosses, jam,
provide for our   marmalade, cards, tea-towels and honey.
needs as a Franciscan
Hermitage   ***Guest and Retreat Facilities:*** There is a hermitage for one
               person. A fee of $60 per night is negotiable.

The Melanesian Brotherhood

MBH

Founded 1925

Email: mbhches @solomon.com.sb

SOLOMON ISLANDS
REGION
The Motherhouse
of the Melanesian
Brotherhood
Tabalia
PO Box 1479
Honiara
SOLOMON ISLANDS
TEL: +677 26355
FAX: +677 23079

PAPUA NEW GUINEA
REGION
Dobuduru Regional
Headquarters
Haruro
PO Box 29
Popondetta
Oro Province
PAPUA NEW GUINEA

SOUTHERN REGION
Tumsisiro Regional
Headquarters
PO Box 05
Lolowai, Ambae
VANUATU

The Melanesian Brotherhood was founded by Ini Kopuria, a native Solomon Islander from Guadalcanal, in 1925. Its main purpose was evangelistic, to take and live the Gospel in the most remote islands and villages throughout the Solomon Islands, among people who had not heard the message of Christ. The Brotherhood's method is to live as brothers to the people, respecting their traditions and customs: planting, harvesting, fishing, house building, eating and sharing with the people in all these things. Kopuria believed that Solomon Islanders should be converted in a Melanesian way.

Today, the work of the Brotherhood has broadened to include work and mission among both Christians and non-Christians. The Melanesian Brotherhood now has three Regions in the Pacific: Solomon Islands (includes Brothers in the Philippines and Vancouver); Papua New Guinea; and Southern (Vanuatu, New Caledonia & the Diocese of Polynesia). There is a Region for Companions and Brothers in Europe.

Following an ethnic conflict in the Solomon Islands 2000–2003, the Melanesian Brotherhood have been increasingly called upon as peace makers and reconcilers, work for which they were awarded the United Nations Pacific Peace Prize in 2004.

The Brotherhood has also led missions in New Zealand, Australia, Philippines and UK; their missionary approach includes music, dance and a powerful use of drama. There is expected to be a further mission in the UK in 2013 to be conducted with members of other Religious communities in Melanesia.

The Brotherhood aims to live the Gospel in a direct and simple way following Christ's example of prayer, mission and service. The Brothers take the vows of poverty, chastity and obedience, but these are not life vows but for a period of three years, which can be renewed. They train for three years as novices and normally make their vows as Brothers at the Feast of St Simon and St Jude. Most of the Brothers are laymen but a few are ordained.

Community Publications

Companions' Newsletter for the Europe Region (once a year) – contact Canon Brian Macdonald-Milne, address under 'Companions' below.

Obituaries

23 Apr 2010   Brother Andrew Wate, aged 29,
                        professed since 2003

Timetable of the Main House

First Office and Mattins
5.50 am
(6.20 am Sun & holidays)

Holy Communion
6.15 am
(7.15 am Sun & holidays)

Morning Office
8.00 am

Midday Office
12 noon
(Angelus on Sun & holidays)

Afternoon Office
1.30 pm
(not Sun & holidays)

Evensong 5.30 pm
(6.00 pm Sun & holidays)

Last Office
9.00 pm

Office Book
Offices and Prayers of the Melanesian Brotherhood 1996 (not for public sale)

Website:
www.orders. anglican.org/mbh

BROTHER ALICK PALUSI MBH
(Head Brother, assumed office July 2009)
(New elections in October 2011)

SOLOMON ISLANDS REGION
THE MOST REVD DAVID VUNAGI, ARCHBISHOP OF MELANESIA
(Regional Father)
BROTHER LEONARD YANGA MBH *(Regional Head Brother)*
Mr Alphonse Garimae *(Brotherhood Secretary)*
Brother Jesse Araiasi MBH *(Regional Secretary)*
Brother Eric Tano MBH *(Companions Secretary)*

SOUTHERN REGION
THE RT REVD JAMES LIGO,
BISHOP OF VANUATU & NEW CALEDONIA
(Regional Father)
BROTHER WILFORD TARI MBH *(Regional Head Brother)*
Brother Fisher Young MBH *(Regional Secretary)*
To be appointed *(Regional Companions Secretary)*

PAPUA NEW GUINEA REGION
THE MOST REVD JOE KOPAPA, ARCHBISHOP OF PNG & BISHOP
OF POPONDOTA *(Regional Father)*
BROTHER MATTHIAS TOVOTASI MBH *(Regional Head Brother)*
Brother Davis Cyprian MBH *(Regional Secretary)*
Brother John Bodger Yawota MBH
(Regional Companions Secretary)

EUROPE REGION *(for Companions)*
THE MOST REVD DR ROWAN WILLIAMS,
ARCHBISHOP OF CANTERBURY *(Regional Father)*

Professed Brothers: 341
(Solomon Islands: 178; PNG: 91: Southern Region: 72)
Novices: 231
(Solomon Islands: 121; PNG: 60: Southern Region: 50)

SOLOMON ISLANDS REGION
The Solomon Islands Region is divided into Sections according to each Diocese. Each Section has its own Section Father.

CENTRAL MELANESIA SECTION
Section Father: The Most Revd David Vunagi, Archbishop of Melanesia

Address for all SI houses in this Section:
PO Box 1479, Honiara, Guadacanal, SOLOMON ISLANDS

BROTHER SIMON PETER MBH *(Section Elder Brother)*
Central Headquarters, Tabalia

BROTHER LOT POMADI MBH *(Brother in charge)*
 St Barnabas Cathedral Working Household, Honiara　　　Tel: 24609　Fax: 23079
BROTHER ROBERT CONIEL KAILOHU MBH *(Brother in charge)*
 Bishopsdale Working Household, Honiara　　　　　　　Tel: 27695　Fax: 23079
BROTHER EZEKIEL TEMA MBH *(Brother in charge)*
 Iglesia Philipino (I.F.I.), De los Reyos Road 2, 5300 Puerto Princesa City, 5300
 Palawan, PHILIPPINES

CENTRAL SOLOMONS DIOCESAN SECTION
Section Father: The Rt Revd Ben Seka, Bishop of Central Solomons

BROTHER DAVID OSSIE MBH *(Section Elder Brother)*
 Thomas Peo Section Headquarters, Koloti,
 c/o Central Solomons Diocesan Office, PO Box 52, Tulagi, Central Province

Address for other houses in this section:
 c/o Central Headquarters, Tabalia, PO Box 1479, Honiara

BROTHER EDWARD POROLOVANA MBH *(Elder Brother)*
 Ini Kopuria Household, Kolina, Gela
BROTHER ROBERT HARRISON MBH *(Elder Brother)*
 Olimauri Household, Mbambanakira, Guadalcanal
BROTHER JEFFREY HAGAMARIA MBH *(Elder Brother)*
 Calvary Household, Surapau, Guadalcanal
(temporarily closed):
 Selwyn Rapu Working Household, Guadalcanal
BROTHER JIMMY URAU MBH *(Brother in charge)*
 Working Household, Bellona Island

MALAITA DIOCESAN SECTION
Section Father: The Rt Revd Sam Sahu, Bishop of Malaita

Address for houses in this section (except Tasman Working Household):
 c/o Malaita Diocesan Office, PO Box 7, Auki, Malaita Province

BROTHER CALWICK HAPI MBH *(Section Elder Brother)*
 Airahu Section Headquarters, Malaita
BROTHER JAMES TOFI MBH *(Brother in charge)*
 New Dawn Range Working Household, West Kwaio, Malaita
BROTHER BRIAN DO'ORO MBH *(Brother in charge)*
 Urutao Working Household, North Malaita
BROTHER DAVID MAEDIANA MBH *(Brother in charge)*
 Kokom Working Household, Auki, Malaita
BROTHER BARNABAS SAVUSI MBH *(Elder Brother)*
 Apalolo Household, South Malaita
BROTHER ALLEN KIKOA MBH *(Brother in charge)*
 Tasman Working Household, Nukumanu Atoll (PNG), PO Box 1479,
 Honiara, Solomon Islands

YSABEL DIOCESAN SECTION
Section Father: The Rt Revd Richard Naramana, Bishop of Ysabel

Address for houses in this section:
c/o Ysabel Diocesan Office, PO Box 6, Buala, Isabel Province

BROTHER NATHANIEL ROU MBH *(Section Elder Brother)*
Welchman Section Headquarters, Sosoilo
BROTHER JOHN MARK SELENI MBH *(Elder Brother)*
Poropeta Household, Kia
BROTHER RUDOLF TEOHEI MBH *(Brother in charge)*
Alfred Hill Working Household, Jejevo
BROTHER STEPHEN NAU MBH *(Brother in charge)*
Hulon Working Household, Yandina, Russell Islands
BROTHER NORMAN PARAKO MBH *(Elder Brother)*
John Pihavaka Household, Gizo
BROTHER ISSACHAR NICHOLSON MBH *(Brother in charge)*
Noro Working Household, New Georgia Island
BROTHER BERNARD WALAKULU MBH *(Brother in charge)*
Pupuku Working Household, Choiseul Province

HANUATO'O DIOCESAN SECTION
Section Father: The Rt Revd Alfred Karibongi, Bishop of Hanuato'o

Address for houses in this section:
c/o Hanuato'o Diocesan Office, Kirakira, Makira Province

BROTHER ROBERT HENRY MBH *(Section Elder Brother)*
BROTHER NELSON GWALI MBH *(Elder Brother)*
Fox Section Headquarters, Poronaohe, Makira
BROTHER FRANK VAKO MBH *(Elder Brother)*
Simon Sigai Household, Makira
BROTHER NAHAM KAONI MBH *(Brother in charge)*
Mumunioa Working Household, Makira

TEMOTU DIOCESAN SECTION
Section Father: The Rt Revd George Tekeli, Bishop of Temotu

Address for houses in this section:
c/o Temotu Diocesan Office, Luesalo, Temotu Province

BROTHER NICHOLAS SUSUVE MBH *(Section Elder Brother)*
Makio Section Headquarters, Santa Cruz Island
BROTHER BELSHAZZAR PAERE MBH *(Brother in charge)*
Utupua Working Household, Utupua
BROTHER ALBERT BUANA MBH *(Brother in charge)*
Lata Working Household, Santa Cruz Island

SOUTHERN REGION

VANUATU SECTION
Section Father: The Rt Revd James Ligo, Bishop of Vanuatu & New Caledonia

BROTHER BADDELEY HANGO MBH *(Section Elder Brother)*
  Tumsisiro Regional Headquarters, Ambae

Saratabulu Household, West Ambae; Canal Household, Santo Town; Hinge Household, Lorevilko, East Santo; Suriau Household, Big Bay, Santo Bush; Surunleo Household, Bwatnapni, Central Pentecost; Noel Seu Working Household, South Ambae; Patterson Household, Port Vila

BANKS & TORRES SECTION
Section Father: The Rt Revd Nathan Tome, Bishop of Banks & Torres

BROTHER FRESHER DIN *(Section Elder Brother)*
  Sarawia Section Headquarters, Vanua Lava Island

PAPUA NEW GUINEA REGION

POPONDOTA SECTION
Section Father: The Most Revd Joseph Kopapa, Archbishop of PNG & Bishop of Popondota

(Section Elder Brother) Dobuduru Regional Headquarters, Popondetta

Berubona Working Household; St Christopher's Workshop; Damara Household, Safia; Wanigela Household; Nindewari Household

PORT MORESBY SECTION
Section Father: The Rt Revd Peter Ramsden, Bishop of Port Moresby

(Section Elder Brother) Port Moresby Section Headquarters, Oro Village

Cape Rodney Household; Morata Working Household; Pivo Household

DOGURA SECTION
Section Father: The Rt Revd Clyde Igara, Bishop of Dogura

(Section Elder Brother) Mawedama Section Headquarters, Sirisiri, Dogura

Iapoa Household; Pumani Household; Samarai Island Working Household; Podagha Project Household

AIPO RONGO SECTION
Section Father: The Rt Revd Nathan Ingen, Bishop of Aipo Rongo

(Section Elder Brother) Aiome Section Headquarters, Aganmakuk

Kinibong Household; Marvol Household, Ilu Mamusi; Aum Household, Tsendiap; Nambayufa Household, Siane Valley

NEW GUINEA ISLANDS SECTION
Section Father: The Rt Revd Allan Migi, Bishop of New Guinea Islands

(Section Elder Brother) Akolong Section Headquarters

Aseke Household, Au, Gasmata; Hosea Sakira Working Household, Ura, Cape Gloucester

Companions
The Melanesian Brotherhood is supported both in prayer, in their work and materially by the Companions of the Melanesian Brotherhood (C.O.M.B.). They have their own Handbook with both Pacific and Europe versions.

For more information about becoming a Companion, please contact:
The Revd Canon Brian Macdonald-Milne, 39 Way Lane, Waterbeach, Cambridge CB25 9NQ, UK   *Email: bj.macdonaldmilne@homecall.co.uk*

or Companions Chief Secretary, PO Box 1479, Honiara, Solomon Islands
or at the same address: Mr Alphonse Garimae, Secretary to the Brotherhood,
          Tel: +677 26377 (8 am – 4 pm)   *Email: agarimae@yahoo.com*

Alongside Companions, the Brotherhood also has associates whose ministry is more closely associated with the community, except that they do not take the threefold vow. They work voluntarily without wages just like the brothers.

Community History and other books
Brian Macdonald-Milne, *The True Way of Service: The Pacific Story of the Melanesian Brotherhood, 1925–2000*, Christians Aware, Leicester, 2003.

Richard Carter, *In Search of the Lost: the death and life of seven peacemakers of the Melanesian Brotherhood*, Canterbury Press, Norwich, 2006.

Charles Montgomery, *The Shark God: Encounters with myth and magic in the South Pacific*, Fourth Estate/Harper Collins, London, 2006.

Guest and Retreat Facilities
The Community offers hospitality ministry through Chester Rest House in Honiara, Solomon Islands. Two Brothers are mandated to welcome guests and offer a Christian welcome to any person who may want accommodation in their Rest House. This Rest House was funded by Chester Diocese in UK. It is an alcohol-free environment and every guest is ensured to be safe and enjoy the environment. It has 8 twin-bedded rooms, self-catering at £20 per room per night, and 8 self-contained single rooms, self-catering at £40 per room per night. A conference room to accommodate 10–15 people is also available at £10 per day, self-catering. Contacts for advance bookings can be made through email: mbhches@solomon.com.sb or telephone +677 26355.

All the Brotherhood's Headquarters and Section Headquarters can provide simple accommodation for visitors. Retreats can be made by prior arrangement with the relevant Chaplain at Central, Regional or Section headquarters. Tabalia Headquarters has a guest house with eight twin-bedded rooms, self-catering, no cost but a contribution is much appreciated. Meetings, workshops and Retreats can be made by prior arrangement with the Section Elder Brother/Elder Brother at Tabalia.

Women are not allowed to enter the Brotherhood square (St Simon & Jude), which usually is outside the chapel of every Brotherhood station (not in Honiara). Women are not allowed to enter Brothers' dormitories.

Advisors to the Brotherhood
The Revd Canon Brian Macdonald-Milne *(retiring in 2011)*

Order of the Holy Cross

OHC

Founded 1884

Holy Cross
Monastery
PO Box 99
(1615 Rt. 9W)
West Park
NY 12493
USA
Tel: 845 384 6660
Fax: 845 384 6031

Email: superior@
hcmnet.org

Website: www.
holycrossmonastery.
com

Mattins   7.00 am

Holy Eucharist
9.00 am

Midday Prayer
12 noon

Vespers   5.00 pm

Compline   8.30 pm

Mondays are observed
as a sabbath day on
which there are no
scheduled liturgies.

The Order of the Holy Cross is a Benedictine monastic community open to both lay and ordained. The principles governing the Order's life are those of *The Rule of St Benedict* and *The Rule of the Order of the Holy Cross,* written by its founder James Otis Sargent Huntington.

The liturgical life of each house centers around the corporate praying of the Divine Office and the celebration of the Holy Eucharist. Members also expected to spend time in private prayer and meditation.

The work of the Order is varied, depending on the nature of the household and the gifts and talents of its members. Houses vary from traditional monastic centers with active retreat ministries to urban houses from which brothers go forth to minister. A small number of brothers live independently as Monks Not In Residence.

Members are engaged in preaching, teaching, counseling and spiritual direction, parish and diocesan support work, the arts, evangelism, hospice care, and ministry with the homeless. The South African community administers educational and scholarship programs for local children and operates a primary school.

Other Addresses

Mount Calvary Community at St Mary's Retreat House, PO Box 1296, Santa Barbara, CA 93102, USA
Tel: 805 682 4117   Website: www.mount-calvary.org

Holy Cross Priory, 204 High Park Avenue, Toronto, Ontario M6P 2S6, CANADA
Tel: 416 767 9081   Fax: 416 767 4692
Website: www.ohc-canada.org

Mariya uMama weThemba Monastery, PO Box 6013, Grahamstown 6141, SOUTH AFRICA
Tel: 46 622 8111   Fax: 46 622 6424
Website: www.umaria.co.za

Community Wares: Incense and Publications (West Park).

Community Publications
Holy Cross News, published annually.
Mundi Medicina (West Park, NY), 3 times a year
Uxolo (Grahamstown, South Africa), 3 times a year
Mount Calvary Community at St Mary's (Santa Barbara, CA),   3 times a year
Holy Cross Priory (Toronto, Ontario), 3 times a year
Cost – by donation

Bishop Visitor: Rt Revd Mark S Sisk

ROBERT LEO SEVENSKY OHC
(Superior, assumed office 2008)
SCOTT WESLEY BORDEN OHC *(Assistant Superior)*

Thomas Schultz	David Bryan Hoopes	Andrew Colquhoun
Christian George Swayne	Adam McCoy	John Forbis
Laurence Harms	Carl Sword	Bernard Jean Delcourt
Samuel DeMerell	William Brown	James Randall Greve
Rafael Campbell-Dixon	Timothy Jolley	Daniel Ludik
Bede Thomas Mudge	James Robert Hagler	Robert Magliula
Ronald Haynes	Leonard Abbah	James Dowd
Brian Youngward	Reginald-Martin	Smache Josias Morobi
Nicholas Radlemiller	Crenshaw	Charles Julian Mizelle
Roy Parker	Richard Paul Vaggione	
Adrian Gill	Lary Pearce	*Novices:* 2

Obituaries

22 Jan 2011   Cecil R Couch, aged 80, professed 21 years

Associates

The Associates of Holy Cross are men and women of many different Christian traditions affliated to the Order through a Rule of Life and annual retreats and reports.

Guest and Retreat Facilities

WEST PARK: 39 rooms at US$70 per night ($90 weekends). Accommodations for couples and individuals. Closed Mondays.

SANTA BARBARA: 24 beds at US$80 per night ($90 weekends). Closed Mondays.

GRAHAMSTOWN: 19 rooms (doubles and singles). Apply to Guestmaster for rates. Closed Mondays.

TORONTO: 2 single rooms. Canadian $40 per night.

Community History

Adam Dunbar McCoy OHC, *Holy Cross: A Century of Anglican Monasticism*, Morehouse-Barlow, Wilton, CT, 1987.

Order of the Holy Paraclete

OHP

Founded 1915

St Hilda's Priory
Sneaton Castle,
Whitby
North Yorkshire
YO21 3QN
UK
Tel: 01947 602079
Fax: 01947 820854
Email:
ohppriorywhitby
@btinternet.com
Website: www.
ohpwhitby.org

Morning Prayer
7.15 am
(7.30 am Sat & Sun)

Eucharist
7.45 am (Mon, Wed
& Fri)
8.00 am (Sat)
9.30 am (Sun)
12.30 pm (Tue & Thu)

Midday Office
12.40 pm
12.15 pm (Tue & Thu)
12 noon (Sat)

Vespers   6.00 pm
(4.30 pm Sun)

Compline   9.00 pm
(8.30 pm Fri)

Founded as an educational order, the sisters have diversified their work in UK to include hospitality, retreats and spiritual direction, hospital chaplaincy, inner city involvement, preaching and mission, and development work overseas.

The Mother House is at St. Hilda's Priory, Whitby. Some sisters work in the adjacent Sneaton Castle Centre, which caters for a wide variety of day and residential groups. Other UK houses are in York, Dormanstown (near Redcar), Bishopsthorpe and Sleights (near Whitby).

Overseas, the Order's long-standing commitment to Africa has been extended in exciting new developments: raising awareness of AIDS and providing a home for abused girls in Swaziland, and fostering vocations to Religious life in Ghana, where, in response to perceived local interest and support, a new convent has been built in Jachie, Ashanti. An eye clinic is also run by OHP. A second house has been opened in Sunyani. The Order withdrew from their work in Johannesburg in May 2008.

Central to the Order's life in all its houses are the Divine Office and Eucharist, and a strong emphasis on corporate activity.

Houses in the UK

Beachcliff, 14 North Promenade, Whitby, North Yorkshire YO21 3JX
Tel: 01947 601968   Email: ohpbeaccliff@hotmail.co.uk

St Oswald's Pastoral Centre, Woodlands Drive, Sleights, Whitby, North Yorkshire YO21 1RY
Tel: 01947 810496   Email: ohpstos@globalnet.co

1A Minster Court, York YO7 2JJ
Tel: 01904 620601   Email: sistersohp@googlemail.com

3 Acaster Lane, Bishopsthorpe, York, YO23 2SA
Tel: 01904 777294
Email: ohpbishopsthorpe@archbishopofyork.org

All Saints House, South Avenue, Dormanstown, TS10 5LL   *Tel: 01642 486424*
Email: sisteranita@btinternet.com

Houses in Africa

Jachie, Convent of the Holy Spirit, PO Box AH 9375, Ahinsan, Kumasi Ashanti, GHANA
Tel: 233 242 or 203432   Email: ohpjac@yahoo.com

Resurrection House, PO Box 596, Sunyani, Brone Ahafo, GHANA   *Tel: 233 243 706840*
Email: nyamebekyere2010@yahoo.com

The Sisters OHP, Box 523, Piggs Peak, SWAZILAND
Tel: 437 1514   Emails: srkaran@bulembu.org & carole@bulembu.org

Sisters Helena & Samantha OHP

SISTER DOROTHY STELLA OHP
(Prioress, assumed office 15 July 2005)
SISTER HEATHER FRANCIS OHP *(Sub-Prioress)*

Sister Ursula	Sister Patricia	Sister Jocelyn
Sister Barbara Maude	Sister Gillian	Sister Carole
Sister Olive	Sister Hilary Joy	Sister Mavis
Sister Marjorie	Sister Grace	Sister Linda
Sister Constance	Sister Janette	Sister Aba
Sister Janet	Sister Janet Elizabeth	Sister Pam
Sister Alison	Sister Betty	Sister Helen
Sister Michelle	Sister Benedicta	Sister Karan
Sister Mary Nina	Sister Caroline	Sister Margaret
Sister Stella Mary	Sister Margaret Elizabeth	Sister Alberta
Sister Heather	Sister Marion Eva	Sister Sabina
Sister Muriel	Sister Judith	Sister Katherine Therese
Sister Mary Margaret	Sister Erika	Sister Helena
Sister Anita	Sister Maureen Ruth	Sister Samantha
Sister Nancye	Sister Margaret Anne	

Obituaries

2 Jul 2009	Sister Rosa, aged 81, professed 56 years
16 Jan 2010	Sister Sophia, aged 86, professed 59 years
8 Oct 2010	Sister Lucy, aged 83, professed 50 years
19 Nov 2010	Sister Kathleen, aged 94, professed 68 years
7 Feb 2011	Sister Margaret Shirley, aged 76, professed 48 years

Tertiaries and Associates

THE OHP TERTIARY ORDER is a fellowship of women and men, united under a common discipline, based on the OHP Rule, and supporting one another in their discipleship. Tertiaries are ordinary Christians seeking to offer their lives in the service of Christ, helping the Church and showing love in action. They value their links with each other and with the Sisters of the Order, at Whitby and elsewhere, and when possible they meet together for mutual support in prayer, discussion and ministry. The Tertiary Order is open to communicant members of any Trinitarian Church.

THE OHP ASSOCIATES are friends of the Order who desire to keep in touch with its life and work while serving God in their various spheres. Many have made initial contact with the Sisters through a visit or parish mission, or via another Associate. All are welcome, married or single, clergy or lay, regardless of religious affiliation.

THE FRIENDS OF OHP is a group open to men and women, of any religious affiliation or none, with an interest in OHP. The annual subscription of £10 includes a copy of the OHP newsletter and an invitation to an annual meeting.

Community Publication: OHP Newsletter, twice a year. Write to The Publications Secretary at St Hilda's Priory. Annual subscription: £4.50 for the UK, £5.50 for the rest of Europe and £7.00 for the rest of the world.

Community History

A Foundation Member, *Fulfilled in Joy*, Hodder & Stoughton, London, 1964. Rosalin Barker, *The Whitby Sisters*, OHP, Whitby, 2001.

Community Wares

Cards and craft items. St Hilda's Priory has a shop selling books, cards, church supplies and religious artefacts. *Email: sneatonshop@btinternet.com*

Guest and Retreat Facilities

ST HILDA'S PRIORY: six rooms (four single; one double; one twin) available in the Priory or nearby houses. Individuals or small groups are welcome for personal quiet or retreat, day or residential. If requested in advance, some guidance can be provided. There is no programme of retreats at the Priory. Contact the Guest Sister with enquiries and bookings.

SNEATON CASTLE CENTRE: seventy-one rooms (one hundred and twenty beds). The Centre has conference, lecture and seminar rooms with full audio-visual equipment, and recreational facilities. There are two spacious dining rooms and an excellent range of menus. Guests are welcome to join the community for worship or to arrange their own services in the Chapel.

Contact the Bookings Secretary, Sneaton Castle Centre, Whitby YO21 3QN.

Tel: 01947 600051   See also the website: *www.sneatoncastle.co.uk*

ST OSWALD'S PASTORAL CENTRE: 13 rooms (16 beds). 3 self-catering units.

Most convenient time to telephone:: 9 am – 5 pm, Mon-Fri; 10 am – 12 noon Sat

Bishop Visitor: Most Revd John Sentamu, Archbishop of York

Office Book: OHP Office

Registered Charity: No. 271117

Order of Julian of Norwich

OJN

Founded 1985

2812 Summit
Avenue
Waukesha
WI 53188-2781
USA
Tel: 262 549 0452

Email: ojn@
orderofjulian.org

Website
www.
orderofjulian.org

Morning Prayer
5.00 am

Mass 7.00 am

Noonday Office
12 noon

Evensong 5.00 pm

Compline 7.50 pm

Office Book
The BCP of ECUSA
for Morning Prayer,
with enrichments

Bishop Visitor
Rt Revd Edwin Leidel,
retired Bishop of
Eastern Michigan

The Order of Julian of Norwich is a contemplative semi-enclosed Religious order of nuns and monks in the Episcopal Church, living together in one house. We profess traditional vows of poverty, chastity, and obedience, with the added vow of prayer 'in the spirit of our Blessed Mother Saint Julian', the fourteenth-century English anchoress and our patron.

The ministry of the Order to the Church is to be a community of prayer and contemplative presence, expressed in communal liturgical worship in chapel and in the silence and solitude of the cell. Gregorian Chant is used for most of the four-fold Divine Office of the Book of Common Prayer. The Eucharist is the centre of our life, the genesis of our work of contemplative and intercessory prayer. This primary apostolate supports a limited exterior apostolate of spiritual direction, writing, and offering retreats.

Founded in 1985 by the Revd John Swanson, the Order was canonically recognized by the Episcopal Church in 1997, and is affiliated with the Conference of Anglican Religious Orders in the Americas. For further information on the Order or its affiliates, please address the Guardian.

REVD MOTHER HILARY CRUPI OJN
(*Guardian, assumed office 30 April 2010*)
SISTER THERESE POLI OJN (*Warden*)

Revd Father John-Julian Swanson
Sister Cornelia Barry
Brother Barnabas Leben

Sister Ignatia Jenks
Brother Dunstan Galliher

Novices: 1

Associates and Oblates

ASSOCIATES
Friends of the Order, desiring a spiritual bond with the Julian Community who keep a simple Rule (one daily Office, Sunday Mass, annual reports to the Warden of Associates) and pledge financial support for the Order.

OBLATES
Persons committed to live the Order's spiritual and contemplative charism in the world under an adaptation of regular vows. They have a Rule of: two BCP Offices daily; three per cent of their tithe to the Order; three hours contemplative prayer a week; a four-day silent retreat annually; Sunday Mass and seven Holy days of Obligation, etc. They make a semi-annual report to the Warden of Oblates.

Community Publication
Julian's Window, quarterly. Subscription free. Contact Sister Cornelia OJN.

Guest and Retreat Facilities
Three guest rooms. There is no charge.

Community History and other books
Teunisje Velthuizen, ObJN, *One-ed into God: The first decade of the Order of St Julian of Norwich*, The Julian Press, 1996.

Gregory Fruehwirth OJN, *Words for Silence*, Paraclete Press, Orleans, MA, 2008.

John Julian Swanson OJN, *The Complete Julian*, Paraclete Press, Orleans, MA, 2009.

Community Wares
The Julian Shop has books, religious articles, many pamphlets written by members. *Email: julianshop@orderofjulian.org*

Order of St Anne at Bethany

OSA

Founded 1910

25 Hillside Avenue
Arlington
MA 02476-5818
USA

Tel: 781 643 0921
Fax: 781 648 4547

Email: bethany
convent@aol.com

Community Wares:
Communion
altar bread.

We are a small multi-cultural community of women committed to witnessing to the truth that, as Christians, it is here and now that we demonstrate to the Church and the world that the Religious Life lived in community is relevant, interesting, fulfilling and needed in our world and our times.

We strive to recognize and value the diversity of persons and gifts. We believe that God has a vision for each one of us and that opportunities to serve the Church and the world are abundant. For this to become real, we know that our spirits and hearts must be enlarged to fit the dimensions of our Church in today's world and the great vision that God has prepared for our Order. We are especially grateful for our continuing ministry within the Diocese of Massachusetts.

The Rule of the Order of St Anne says our houses may be small, but our hearts are larger than houses. Our community has always been 'people-oriented' and we derive a sense of joy and satisfaction in offering hospitality at our Convent, at the Bethany House of Prayer and in our beautiful chapel.

Always constant in our lives are our personal prayer and our corporate worship, our vows of Poverty, Celibacy and Obedience, our commitment to spiritual growth and development of mind and talents, and our fellowship with one another and other Religious communities, as friends and sisters.

Bishop Visitor: Rt Revd M. Thomas Shaw SSJE, Bishop of Massachusetts

Sister Ana Clara OSA
(Superior, assumed office 1992)

Morning Prayer
7.00 am

Sister Olga   Sister Maria Agnes
Sister Felicitas   Sister Maria Teresa

Eucharist
8.00 am (Tue-Fri)
7.30 am (Sun)

Associates
We have an associate program and continue to receive men and women into this part of our life.

Midday prayers
12 noon

Community History
Sister Johanna OSA (editor), *A Theme for Four Voices*, privately printed, Arlington, Mass., 1985

Evensong
5.00 pm

Revd Charles C Hefling & Sister Ana Clara OSA, *Catch the Vision: celebrating a century of the Order of St Anne*, Order of St Anne-Bethany, Arlington, Mass., 2010

Compline
7.30 pm

Guest and Retreat Facilities
The Bethany House of Prayer, 181 Appleton Street, on the grounds of the Convent and Chapel, sponsors, coordinates and offers a variety of programs and events including Quiet Days, Special Liturgies, contemplative prayer, spiritual direction, day-retreats, hospitality and workshops. For more information call 781 648 2433

Office Book
SSJE Office Book

The five OSA sisters at Bethany with Sister Judith OSA (far left), from the separate OSA community in Chicago, at the launch of Catch the Vision.

Order of St Benedict

Busan

OSB

Founded 1993

810-1 Baekrok-ri
Habuk-myon
Yangsan-shi
Kyungnam 626-860
SOUTH KOREA
Tel: 55 384 1560
Mobile: 010 9335 1560
Email: bundo1993
@hanmail.net

Morning Prayer
6.20 am

Eucharist
7.00 am (Wed only)

**Day Office
(Intercessions)** 12 noon

Evening Prayer 5.30 pm

Compline 8.00 pm

There has been an Anglican community in Seoul for many years, but it was the wish of Bishop Bundo Kim to establish a community in Busan – in the south of Korea. Thus it was that in 1993, the Order of St Benedict was founded in Busan City. In four years, sufficient money was raised by the Diocese to buy a more spacious, rural accommodation in Yangsan (to the north of Busan), offering more room for retreats, and for community and parish work.

SISTER MARTHA HAN OSB
(Senior Sister, assumed office 1998)
Sister Michaela

Associates
There is an informal group of Associates.

Community Publication
Summer and Christmas Newsletters. Contact Sister Martha re donations.

Guest and Retreat Facilities
There are three guest rooms for private retreats, with good kitchen and bathroom facilities. For larger groups, Korean-style accommodation is used. There are no restrictions on length of stay, and both men and women are welcome. There is no set charge but by donation only.
Most convenient time to telephone: 9.30 am – 7.00 pm

Office Book: Korean Common Prayer Book

Bishop Visitor
Rt Revd Solomon Yoon, Bishop of Busan

Order of St Benedict

Camperdown

OSB

Founded 1975
Benedictine

The community was founded in the parish of St Mark, Fitzroy, in the archdiocese of Melbourne on 8 November 1975, when the first two monks were clothed. In 1980, after working in this inner city parish for five years, and after adopting the *Rule of Saint Benedict*, they moved to the country town of Camperdown in the Western District of Victoria. Here the community lives a contemplative monastic life with the emphasis on the balanced life of prayer and work that forms the Benedictine ethos.

In 1993, the Chapter decided to admit women and to endeavour to establish a mixed community of monks and nuns. To this end, two nuns came from Malling Abbey (UK) and one has transferred her stability to Camperdown.

Monastery
PO Box 111
Camperdown
Victoria 3260
AUSTRALIA
Tel: 3 5593 2348
Fax: 3 5593 2887
Email: benabbey@
dodo.com.au

Website
www.
benedictineabbey
.com.au

Vigils 4.30 am

Lauds 6.30 am

Terce &
Conventual Mass
8.15 am

Sext 11.45 am

None 2.10 pm

Vespers 5.00 pm

Compline 7.30 pm

Office Book
Camperdown breviary
with a two-week cycle
of the Psalter and
seasonal and sanctoral
variations.

Abbot Visitor
Rt Revd Dom
Bruno Marin OSB

Confessor
Very Revd Graeme
Lawrence OAM

Diocesan Bishop
Vacancy

The community supports itself through the operation of a printery, icon reproduction, manufacture of incense, crafts and a small guest house. A permanent monastery has now been built and the monastery church was consecrated by the diocesan bishop in February 1995. On July 11th 2002, the community elected the founder, Dom Michael King, as the first Abbot and he was blessed by the Bishop Visitor in the Abbey Church on the Feast of the Transfiguration, August 6th 2002.

In 2005, the Chapter petitioned the Subiaco Congregation of the Benedictine Confederation for aggregation to the Congregation. After a period of probation this was granted on the Feast of SS Peter and Paul 2007. This is an historic step for our community, giving us the opportunity to live our life in association with the Subiaco Congregation, thereby receiving the benefits of such a world-wide body but retaining our Anglican ethos – a great step in ecumenism. Abbot Michael was able to attend the General Chapter of the Congregation held at Subiaco in September 2008 and the Abbot President, assisted by the Abbot of Pluscarden, conducted a Visitation in January 2009. The fruits of our association are already being shown forth.

THE RT REVD DOM MICHAEL KING OSB
(*Abbot, elected 11 July 2002*)

Dom Placid Lawson   Brother Anselm Johns
Sister Mary Philip Bloore   *Novices:* 1
Sister Raphael Stone

Oblates
There is a small group of clerics and lay people who form the Oblates of St Benedict attached to the community. The group numbers ninety persons from Australia, New Zealand and Canada following the Benedictine life according to their individual situations. Oblates usually visit the monastery once a year and keep in regular contact with the parent community.

Guest and Retreat Facilities
There is a small guest house (St Joseph's), which can accommodate six people, open to men and women, for private retreats and spiritual direction. Guests eat with the community and are welcome to attend the services in the church. A donation of $50.00 per day is suggested.

Community Publication
The Community produces a newsletter yearly in December.

Community Wares: Printing, icons, cards, incense, devotional items.

Order of St Benedict

Community of St Mary at the Cross, Edgware

OSB

Founded 1866

Website: www. edgwareabbey.org.uk

Living under the Rule of St Benedict, and dedicated to St Mary at the Cross, this community has a special vocation to stand with Christ's Mother beside those who suffer; its heart in prayer, the Divine Office & the Eucharist are central to its life.

Beginning in Shoreditch, Mother Monnica Skinner and Revd Henry Nihill worked together, drawn to the desperate poverty and sickness around them. Awareness of the needs, especially of 'incurable children', led to the building of a hospital, marking the beginning of the community's life work, developing to meet the needs of its time. This work continues today in the provision of care and nursing for elderly frail people in a 30-bed Care Home, Henry Nihill House, adjacent to Edgware Abbey.

In 2010, the decision was made to close the large convent building, to take effect during 2011, Henry Nihill House, the Chapel, cloisters and gardens remaining in the Edgware Charitable Trust. Buildings near the Chapel are being converted into accommodation for the Sisters, and for guests. Edgware Abbey, with its good transport links from the M1 and A1 will continue in a smaller setting, and the Sisters will maintain their ministry of hospitality and service to the churches.

Edgware Abbey
94A Priory Field
Drive, Edgware
Middlesex HA8 9PU
UK
Tel: 020 8958 7868
Fax: 020 8958 1920
Email: info
@edgwareabbey.org.
uk

Vigils (private)

Lauds 8.00 am

Midday Office
11.55 am (not Sun)

Vespers 5.30 pm
4.40pm Fri

Compline 8.00 pm

Mass
7.45 am or 11.00 am
(weekdays)
11.00 am
(Sun & feast days)

RT REVD DAME MARY THÉRÈSE ZELENT OSB
(Abbess, elected 30 March 1993)
Dame (Mary Eanfleda) Barbara Johnson

Oblates: Our Oblates are part of our extended Community family: living outside the cloister; following the spirit of the Holy Rule of St Benedict; bonded with the Community in prayer and commitment to service.

Community Publication: Abbey Newsletter, published yearly. There is no charge but donations are welcome. Obtainable from the Convent.

Community Wares: Small Convent shop. Goods available include printed and hand-crafted cards for many occasions, devotional items, attractive hand-crafted goods, a good range of books, including new publications.

Guest and Retreat Facilities
The Abbey guest and retreat facilities will be opening for Lent 2012: 3 en-suite bedrooms, B & B accommodation; guest reception area with kitchenette; space for small day groups & clergy groups, parish quiet day groups etc.; use of Chapel and garden; limited parking space.

Bishop Visitor
Rt Revd Peter Wheatley, Bishop of Edmonton

Office Book: Divine Office with own form of Compline

Registered Charity: No. 209261

---

*Order of
St Benedict

Malling
Abbey

OSB*

Founded 1891

Christians are called to seek and serve God in many different ways. The *Rule of St. Benedict* provides a way of life for those whose vocation is to seek God through prayer and life in community. We express this Benedictine tradition in our daily Eucharist and seven-fold sung Office, in personal prayer and *lectio divina*. These are complemented by work in the house and large gardens and hospitality to our many guests. Times for recreation, study, literary and artistic work and various crafts complete a full and satisfying day. A newcomer who wishes to explore her vocation to the enclosed Benedictine life is welcomed, first for several weeks as an aspirant, then for at least six years of training and discernment before she makes her solemn life vows. Each novice is encouraged to make her own unique contribution to the common life, while also entering into the community's heritage and traditions. These include our concern for God's creation, our work for Christian unity and interfaith dialogue, and the practical care of the Abbey's Norman and medieval buildings.

St Mary's Abbey
52 Swan Street
West Malling, Kent
ME19 6JX
UK
Tel: 01732 843309
Fax: 01732 849016

Website: www.
mallingabbey.org

Vigils 4.30 am (5.00
     am Sun)

Lauds 6.50 am (8.10
     am Sun)

Eucharist 7.30 am
     (9.00 am Sun)

Terce 8.45 am

Sext 12.00 noon

None 3.00 pm

Vespers 4.45 pm
     (5.00 pm Sun)

Compline 7.30 pm

Office Book
Malling Abbey Office

MOTHER MARY DAVID BEST OSB
(Abbess, elected 16 September 2008)
SISTER MARY STEPHEN PACKWOOD OSB *(Prioress)*

Sister Macrina Banner   Sister Mary Michael Wilson
Sr Mary Mark Brooksbank   Sister Miriam Noke
Sister Mary John Marshall   Sister Mary Owen
Sister Ruth Blackmore   DeSimone
Sister Mary Cuthbert Archer Sister Margaret Joy Harris
Sister Mary Gundulf Wood   *Sub-Prioress*
Sister Felicity Spencer
Sister Bartimaeus Ives   *Novices:* 2

Obituaries

7 Dec 2009   Sister Mary Ignatius Conklin,
                       aged 92, professed 44 years
7 Jun 2010   Sister Mary Simon Corbett,
                       aged 69, professed 42 years
27 Nov 2010   Sister Jean CHF, aged 92, professed 64 years

Oblates

Oblates are men and women who feel called by God
to follow the Benedictine way in their lives outside the
cloister. After a two-and-a-half-year period of training
and discernment they make a promise of the conversion
of their life during the Eucharist and are then welcomed
into the oblate family. Their commitment is expressed
in a personal Benedictine rule of life, which balances
their personal prayer, worship and *lectio divina* with their
responsibility to family and work.

Community Wares

Cards and booklets printed and painted at the abbey are
on sale at the Guest House.

In the Abbey gardens (photo courtesy of Greenwich Youth for Christ)

Guest and Retreat Facilities
At the Abbey Guest House we can welcome ten residential guests in single rooms as well as a limited number of day guests. Our guests come to share in the worship and God-centred quiet, and to have the space and time for spiritual reflection and refreshment. There is no charge, though donations are welcome.
MONASTIC EXPERIENCE We welcome enquiries from women who wish to deepen their spiritual lives by spending several months living alongside the community within the enclosure. This enables them to experience something of the common life according to the Rule of St. Benedict and the traditions of our community. There is no charge nor is there any wage. Further details from the Mother Abbess.

Most convenient time to telephone: 9.30 am – 11.00 am

Bishop Visitor: Rt Revd John Waine

Order of St Benedict

Mucknell Abbey

OSB

Founded 1941

Mucknell Abbey
Mucknell Farm
Lane
Stoulton
Worcestershire
WR7 4RB
Email:
information@
mucknellabbey.
org.uk

Website: www.
mucknellabbey.
org.uk

Registered Charity:
No. 221617

After sixty years at Burford, the contemplative community of monks and nuns sold their monastery in 2008 and bought a derelict farm near Worcester. This has been transformed into a monastery incorporating as many 'sustainable' features as possible. Having moved into their new home in November 2010, the Community is now trying to establish an atmosphere of stillness and silence in which the Community and its guests are enabled to be open and receptive to the presence of God. While the recitation of the Divine Office and the celebration of the Eucharist constitute the principal work of the Community, the ministry of hospitality, the development of the surrounding 40 acres of land (which comprises a large kitchen garden, orchard, newly-planted woodland and wild flower meadows), the production of incense for a world-wide market, and various income-generating crafts provide a variety of manual work for members of the Community and those guests who wish to share in it. The monastery seeks to be a place of encounter and reconciliation, celebrating the wonder and richness of Creation and modelling a responsible stewardship of it. The Community's concern has always been to pray for Christian Unity, and it now rejoices in having a Methodist presbyter in its number. Dialogue with people of other faiths and those seeking a spiritual way, either within or outside an established religious tradition, is a priority.

Community Wares
Incense: *incense@mucknellabbey.org.uk*
Hand-written icons, using traditional materials, and block mounted icon prints: *icons@mucknellabbey.org.uk*
Chinese brush painted cards: *cards@mucknellabbey.org.uk*

Office of Readings
6 am

Lauds 7 am

Terce 8.45 am

Eucharist
Noon (11 am Sun &
solemnities)

None 2.15 pm

Vespers 5.30 pm

Compline 8.30 pm

RT REVD BROTHER STUART BURNS OSB
(Abbot, elected 14 October 1996)

Sister Scholastica Newman   Brother Philip Dulson
Sister Mary Bernard Taylor   Sister Mary Kenchington
Sister Sue Allatt   Brother Ian Mead
Brother Thomas Quin   *Novices:* 2
Brother Anthony Hare   *Vocational alongsiders:* 3

Friends: There is a Friends' Association.
Contact: *friends@mucknellabbey.org.uk*

Office Book: Mucknell Abbey Office

Bishop Visitor: Rt Revd John Inge, Bishop of Worcester

Order of St Benedict

Servants of Christ Priory

OSB

Founded 1968

28 West Pasadena
Avenue
Phoenix
AZ 85013 2002
USA
Tel: 602 248 9321
Email:
cderijk@cox.net

Morning Prayer
6.00 am

Mass 6.30 am

Midday Prayer
12 noon

Evening Prayer
4.30 pm

Compline 8.00 pm

A community united in love for God and one another following the Benedictine balance of prayer, study and work reflects the life of the monks. Outside engagements are accepted as long as they do not interfere with the monastic routine.

THE VERY REVD CORNELIS J. DE RIJK OSB
(Prior, assumed office November 1985)
The Revd Lewis H. Long

Oblates
Oblates follow a rule of life consistent with the *Rule of St Benedict* adapted to their lifestyle. Those in the metropolitan Phoenix area meet once a month at the monastery.

Community Wares: We have a gift shop which stocks prayer books, Bibles, hymnals, religious books and jewelry. We also supply altar bread and candles to numerous parishes. Through the sale of home-made bread, marmalade and jam, we raise funds for Navajo Indians, especially the seniors on the Reservations.

Guest and Retreat Facilities: We have two single rooms and two double rooms for individuals who wish to come and participate in our life. Day guests are also welcome. Guests have use of the grounds, the library, and share meals with the community. We are closed in August. there is a separate guest house with two double beds, sitting room, fireplace, kitchen and bahroom.

Office Book: The BCP of ECUSA

Bishop Visitor: Rt Revd Kirk Stevan Smith, Bp of Arizona

Order of St Benedict

Salisbury

(formerly Elmore)

OSB

Founded 1914

St Benedict's Priory
19A The Close
Salisbury SP1 2EB
UK
Tel: 01722 335868
Email:
salisbury.priory@
virginmedia.com

Vigils 5.30 am

Morning Worship
at Cathedral 7.30 am
Lauds (at Priory)
8.00 am Sun & Thu

Terce 10.00 am

Midday Prayer
12.45 pm
(at Sarum College)
12.15pm Sat & Sun
(at Priory)

Evensong
at Cathedral (times
vary)
Compline 8.30 pm

Eucharist
7.30 am with Morning
Worship at Cathedral;
10.30 am Sun
Choral Eucharist at
Cathedral;
8.00 am Thu with
Lauds at Priory

The monastery aims to provide an environment within which the traditional monastic balance between worship, study and work may be maintained with a characteristic Benedictine stress upon corporate worship and community life. To this end, outside commitments are kept to a minimum.

VERY REVD DOM SIMON JARRATT OSB
(Conventual Prior, elected 13 December 2005)
(RT REVD) DOM KENNETH NEWING OSB *(Sub-Prior)*
Dom Francis Hutchison
Dom Bruce De Walt

Obituaries
8 Mar 2010 Brother Hugh Kelly, aged 81,
49 years in community

Oblates
An extended confraternity of oblates, numbering over 250 men and women, married and single, seek to live according to a rule of life inspired by Benedictine principles. From the start, the community has believed in the importance of prayer for Christian unity and the fostering of ecumenism. Details can be obtained from the Oblate Master.

Community History
Petà Dunstan, *The Labour of Obedience*, Canterbury Press, Norwich, 2009

Community Publications
Books:
Augustine Morris, *Oblates: Life with Saint Benedict* £4.25.
Simon Bailey, *A Tactful God: Gregory Dix*, £12.99.

Guest and Retreat Facilities
The Community is currently seeking planning permission to extend the Priory to enable us to receive retreatants. There is currently a single parlour to receive visitors.

Most convenient time to telephone
9.00 am – 9.50 am; 10.30 am – 12.15 pm; 3.00 pm – 4.45 pm
Tel: 01722 335868

Office Book: Own Office books at the Priory

Bishop Visitor
Rt Revd Dominic Walker OGS, Bishop of Monmouth

Registered Charity
Pershore Nashdom & Elmore Trust – No. 220012

St Gregory's Abbey Three Rivers OSB

Founded 1939

St Gregory's Abbey
56500 Abbey Road
Three Rivers
Michigan 49093-9595
USA
Tel: 269 244 5893
Fax: 269 244 8712
Email: abbot@
saintgregorys
threerivers.org

Website
saintgregorys
threerivers.org

Matins 4.00 am
(5.30 am Sun &
solemnities, with
Lauds)

Lauds 6.00 am

Terce & Mass
8.15 am (8.30 am Sun &
solemnities)

Sext 11.30 am
(12 noon Sun &
solemnities, with
None)

None 2.00 pm

Vespers 5.00 pm

Compline 7.45 pm

St Gregory's Abbey is the home of a community of men living under the Rule of St Benedict within the Episcopal Church. The center of the monastery's life is the Abbey Church, where God is worshipped in the daily round of Eucharist, Divine Office, and private prayer. Also offered to God are the monks' daily manual work, study and correspondence, ministry to guests, and occasional outside engagements.

RIGHT REVD ANDREW MARR OSB
(*Abbot, elected 2 March 1989*)
VERY REVD AELRED GLIDDEN OSB (*Prior*)

Father Benedict Reid*   Brother Martin Dally
Father Jude Bell   Brother Abraham Newsom
Father William Forest   *Postulants:* 1

*resident elsewhere

Community Publications and History
Abbey Newsletter, published four times a year.
A subscription is free. To be added to the mailing list, write to the Abbey Business office.

The book *Singing God's Praises* was published in the Fall of 1998. It includes articles from community newsletters over the past sixty years and also includes a history of St Gregory's. Copies can be bought from the Abbey, price $20 a copy, postpaid.

Community Wares: The Abbey sells a calendar each year featuring photographs taken by one of the monks.

Guest and Retreat Facilities
Both men and women are welcome as guests. There is no charge, but $40 per day is 'fair value for services rendered' that is not tax-deductible. For further information and arrangements, contact the guest master by mail, telephone or e-mail at *guestmaster@saintgregorysthreerivers.org*

Associates
We have a Confraternity which offers an official connection to the Abbey and is open to anyone who wishes to join for the purpose of incorporating Benedictine principles into their lives. For further information and an application form, please write the Father Abbot.

Office Book: The community uses home-made books based on the Roman Thesaurus for the Benedictine Office.

Bishop Visitor: Rt Revd Arthur Williams,
suffragan Bishop of Ohio (retired)

Order of St Helena

OSH

Founded 1945

Convent of
St Helena
3042 Eagle Drive,
Augusta
GA 30906
USA
Tel: 706 798 5201
Fax: 706 796 0079

Email:
augofficemgr
@comcast.net

Website
www.osh.org

Matins
7.30 am

Eucharist
8.00 am

**Diurnum
and intercessions**
noon

Vespers
5.00 pm

Compline
7.00 pm

The Order of St Helena witnesses to a contemporary version of traditional monasticism, taking a threefold vow of Poverty, Celibate Chastity and Obedience. Our life in community is shaped by the daily Eucharist and fourfold Office, plus hours of personal prayer and study, and from this radiates a wide range of ministries.

As an Order, we are not restricted to any single area of work but witness and respond to the Gospel, with individual sisters engaging in different ministries as they feel called by God and affirmed by the community. Our work is thus wonderfully varied: sisters work in parishes as priests or as pastoral assistants; they lead retreats, quiet days and conferences; work with the national Church and various organizations; offer spiritual direction; are psychotherapists; teach; serve in hospital chaplaincies and community service programs. Seven sisters are ordained priests.

In 1997, the Order adopted a new style of governance and no longer has a superior or single sister as head. Instead, the Order was led by a four-member Leadership Council, with responsibility and ultimate authority vested equally in all four members. Since 2007, the Council has had three members.

In 2008, the sisters closed both their New York convents and consolidated into one house in Augusta, Georgia.

Leadership Council:
SISTER MARY LOIS OSH *(Administrator)*
REVD SISTER CAROL ANDREW *(Pastoral)*
REVD DR ELLEN FRANCIS POISSON *(Vocations)*

Revd Sister	Sister Linda Julian
Mary Michael Simpson	Sister June Thomas
Sister Ruth Juchter	Sister Ann Prentice
Sister Cornelia	Sister Veronica Aryeequaye
Sister Ellen Stephen	Sister Linda Elston
Sister Barbara Lee	Sister Faith Anthony
Sister Benedicta	Sister Grace
Sister Cintra Pemberton	
Sister Elsie Reid	*Novices:* 2
Revd Sister Rosina Ampah	

Associates
ASSOCIATES – open to all women and men. Write to the Secretary for Associates at the Augusta Convent.

Community Publication: *saint helena*, published quarterly, free of charge. Write to the Convent of St Helena for a subscription. Also available online at www.osh.org.

Community Wares and Books

Hand-made rosaries – *write to* Sister Mary Lois.

Sister Cintra Pemberton OSH, *Soulfaring: Celtic Pilgrimage then and now,*
        SPCK, London, & Morehouse, Harrisburg, PA, 1999.

Doug Shadel and Sister Ellen Stephen OSH, *Vessel of Peace: The voyage toward*
        spiritual freedom, Three Tree Press, 1999.

Sister Ellen Stephen OSH, *Together and Apart: a memoir of the Religious Life,*
        Morehouse, Harrisburg, PA, 2008.

Office Book: *The Saint Helena Breviary, Monastic Edition*, which includes all the music in plainchant notation, is now published. It follows closely the BCP of the Episcopal Church of the USA. The focus is on inclusive language and expanded imagery for God, following principles set forth by the Standing Commission for Liturgy and Music of the Episcopal Church, USA. The *Saint Helena Psalter*, extracted from the Breviary, was published in November 2004, *The Saint Helena Breviary, Personal edition*, in July 2006, both by Church Publishing Co., Inc.

Bishop Visitor: Rt Revd Neil Alexander, Bishop of Atlanta

Registered Charity No: US Government 501 (c)(3)

Sisterhood of the Holy Nativity

SHN

Founded 1882

Bethlehem-by-the-Lake
W1484
Spring Grove Road
Ripon
WI 54971-8655
USA
Tel: 920 748 5332

Email: abizac50
@hotmail.com

Matins   7.30 am

Eucharist   8.00 am

Diurnum
(Noonday Prayer)
12 noon

Vespers   5.30 pm
(6.30 pm Sun)

Compline
8.00 pm

Office Book
The Monastic Breviary,
published by the Order
of the Holy Cross

Ours is a mixed life, which means that we combine an apostolic ministry with a contemplative lifestyle. The Rule of the Sisterhood of the Holy Nativity follows the model of the Rule of St Augustine of Hippo. As such, we strive to make the love of God the motive of all our actions. The 'charisms', which undergird our life, are Charity, Humility, Prayer, and Missionary Zeal. Our work involves us with children's ministries such as Sunday School, Summer Camp and Vacation Bible School, as well as ministry to those we meet in everyday life.

TO BE ELECTED *(Revd Mother)*
SISTER ABIGAIL SHN *(Assistant Superior)*

Sister Margaretta   Sister Kathleen Marie
Sister Columba   Sister Charis

Obituaries
10 Feb 2011   Sister Elsbeth, aged 96, professed 60 years
29 Mar 2011   Sister Boniface, aged 83, professed 49 years,
                        Revd Mother 1986–96, 2007–2011

Associates and Oblates
ASSOCIATES are men and women who connect themselves to the prayer life and ministry of the community, and keep a Rule of Life.
OBLATES can be men or women who desire a closer connection with the Community and are able to commit to spending at least three weeks each year living and working with the Sisters at one of our Houses. We have fourteen Oblates and have seven Novice Oblates.

Other Addresses
St. Mary's Retreat House, 505 East Los Olivos Street, Santa Barbara, CA 93105 USA   *Tel: 805 682 4117*

Guest and Retreat Facilities
St Mary's Retreat House in Santa Barbara, CA, is open for retreats by reservation. At this time, St Mary's is staffed by members of the Order of the Holy Cross, while we travel there to give occasional retreats. You may contact the Brothers at 805 682 4117 or by mail at Mount Calvary Community of OHC.

Community Publication
We put out a newsletter occasionally. There is no charge. Anyone interested may contact us at the address above or by email.

Bishop Visitor
Rt Revd Russell E Jacobus, Bishop of Fond du Lac

Sisterhood of St John the Divine

SSJD

Founded 1884

St John's Convent
233 Cummer Ave
Toronto
Ontario M2M 2E8
Canada
Tel: 416 226 2201
ext. 301
Fax: 416 222 4442
Emails: convent@
ssjd.ca
guesthouse@ssjd.ca

Website www.ssjd.
ca

Morning Prayer
8.30 am

Holy Eucharist
12 noon (8.00 am Sun)

Mid-day Office
12 noon (when
Eucharist not at noon)

Evening Prayer
5.00 pm

Compline   8.10 pm
(Tue, Wed, Thu & Sat)

Office Book
Book of Alternative
Services 1985

The Sisterhood of St John the Divine is a contemporary expression of the Religious life for women within the Anglican Church of Canada. Founded in Toronto, we are a prayer- and gospel-centred monastic community, bound together by the call to live out our baptismal covenant through the vows of poverty, chastity and obedience. These vows anchor us in Jesus' life and the transforming experience of the Gospel. Nurtured by our founding vision of prayer, community and ministry, we are open and responsive to the needs of the Church and the contemporary world, continually seeking the guidance of the Holy Spirit in our life and ministry.

St John's Convent nurtures and supports the life of the whole Sisterhood. Our guest house welcomes individuals and groups who share in the community's prayer and liturgy; offers regularly scheduled retreats and quiet days, spiritual direction, and discernment programs for those seeking guidance in their life and work; and provides Sisters to preach, teach, speak, lead retreats and quiet days. Our programs help people build bridges between our secular culture, the Church, and the monastic tradition; we offer music and liturgical leadership for the Church; work in ecumenical outreach.

The Sisterhood supports St John's Rehab Hospital through membership in the Hospital Corporation and Board of Directors, and through its presence on the Hospital staff. The Sisters advocate for a vision of health care which expresses SSJD's mission and values in a multi-faith, multi-cultural setting, and provides spiritual and pastoral support for patients, staff and volunteers.

Other address
ST JOHN'S HOUSE, BC,
3937 St Peter's Rd, Victoria, British Columbia V8P 2J9
Tel: 250 920 7787   Fax: 250 920 7709
E-mail: bchouse@ssjd.ca

A community of Sisters committed to being a praying presence in the Diocese of British Columbia. Prayer, intentional community, hospitality, and mission are at the heart of our life in the Diocese and beyond.

Community Wares
A variety of cards made by Sisters or Associates. Good selection of books on spiritual growth for sale at the Convent (not by mail) and a few CDs. Anglican rosaries made by the sisters and some knitted items.

Bishop Visitor: Most Revd Colin Johnson

SISTER ELIZABETH ANN ECKERT SSJD
(*Reverend Mother, assumed office 13 April 2005, re-elected 13 April 2010*)
SISTER ELIZABETH ROLFE-THOMAS SSJD *(Assistant to the Reverend Mother)*

Sister Constance Murphy	Sister Anitra Hansen
Sister Joyce Bodley	Sister Margaret Mary Watson
Sister Wilma Grazier	Sister Jessica Kennedy
Sister Jean Marston	Sister Constance Joanna Gefvert *(priest)*
Sister Beryl Stone	Sister Brenda Jenner
Sister Merle Milligan	Sister Anne Norman
Sister Doreen McGuff	Sister Helen Claire Gunter
Sister Patricia Forler	Sister Susan Elwyn
Sister Madeleine Mary Salter	Sister Louise Manson
Sister Jocelyn Mortimore	Sister Dorothy Handrigan
Sister Margaret Ruth Steele	Sister Amy Hamilton
Sister Sarah Jean Thompson	*Novices:* 2

Obituaries

17 May 2009   Sister Peta-Ann Jackson, aged 73, professed 6 years
9 Apr 2011   Sister Helena Ward, aged 93, professed 61 years
30 Apr 2011   Sister Thelma-Anne McLeod, aged 82, professed 50 years

Associates and Oblates

Our approximately nine hundred associates are women and men who follow a Rule of Life and share in the ministry of the Sisterhood. The Sisterhood of St John the Divine owes its founding to the vision and dedication of the clergy and lay people who became the first Associates of SSJD. A year of discernment is required before being admitted as an Associate to see if the Associate Rule helps the person in what she/he is seeking; and to provide the opportunity to develop a relationship with the Sisters and to deepen the understanding and practice of prayer. The Associate Rule provides a framework for the journey of faith. There are three basic commitments: belonging in a parish; the practice of prayer, retreat, study of scripture, and spiritual reading; and the relationship with SSJD. Write to the house nearest you for further information.

We have a small but growing number of Oblates. Oblates are women who wish to make a promise of prayer and service in partnership with the Sisterhood. Each Oblate develops her own Rule of Life in partnership with the Oblate Director, her spiritual director, and a support group. A year of discernment is also required, as well as an annual residency program. Write to Sister Constance Joanna at the Convent in Toronto for more information.

Community Publication: The Eagle (newsletter). Contact the Convent Secretary. Published quarterly. $10.00 suggested annual donation.

Community History and Books

Sister Eleonora SSJD, *A Memoir of the Life and Work of Hannah Grier Coome, Mother-Foundress of SSJD, Toronto, Canada,* OUP, London, 1933 (out of print).

The Sisterhood of St John the Divine 1884–1984, published 1931 as *A Brief History;* 4th revision 1984, (out of print).

Sister Constance Joanna SSJD, *From Creation to Resurrection: A Spiritual Journey,* Anglican Book Centre, Toronto, 1990.

Sister Constance SSJD, *Other Little Ships: The memoirs of Sister Constance SSJD*, Patmos Press, Toronto, 1997.

Sister Thelma-Anne McLeod SSJD, *In Age Reborn, By Grace Sustained*, Path Books, Toronto, 2007.

Dr Gerald D Hart, *St John's Rehab Hospital, 1885–2010, the Road to Recovery*,York Region Printing, Autora, ON, 2010

Guest and Retreat Facilities

Guest House has 37 rooms (42 people) used for rest, quiet time and retreats. Contact the Guest Sister at the Convent for details about private accommodation, scheduled retreats, quiet days and other programs.

The Sisters in Victoria also lead quiet days and retreats and have room for one guest. Please contact St John's House, BC, for detailed information.

At a clothing of a novice.

Sisterhood
of St Mary

SSM

Founded 1929

St Andrew's Mission
PO Haluaghat
Mymensingh
BANGLADESH

The community is located on the northern border of Bangladesh at the foot of the Garo hills in India. The community was formed in Barisal at the Sisterhood of the Epiphany, and was sent here to work among the indigenous tribal people, side by side with St Andrew's Brotherhood already working in the area. The membership of the Sisterhood has always been entirely indigenous. The first sisters were Bengalis. The present sisters are the fruit of their work – four are Garo, one is Bengali. They take the vows of Poverty, Purity and Obedience and live a very simple life. They lead a life of prayer and formation of girls. They also look after the Church and do pastoral work among women and children in the Parish.

Prayer 6.30 am

Meditation 8.00 am

Prayers
9.00 am, 11.30 am,
3.00 pm, 6.00 pm

Compline 8.00 pm

SISTER MIRA MANKHIN SSM
(Sister Superior, assumed office 2002)
Sister Anita Raksam
Sister Bregita Doffo
Sister Mala Chicham
Sister Sobha Choudhury

Community Wares: Some handicrafts and vestments for church use and sale.

Office Book: Church of Bangladesh BCP & own book for lesser Offices

Bishop Visitor: Rt Revd Paul Sarker, Bishop of Dhaka

Sisters of Charity

SC

Founded 1869

237 Ridgeway
Plympton
Plymouth
PL7 2HP
UK
Tel: 01752 336112
Email:
plymptonsisters
@tiscali.com.uk

Morning Prayer
8.00 am

Vespers 5.00 pm

Compline 7.00 pm

Office Book
Daily Prayer

Registered Charity:
No. X33170

A Community following the Rule of St Vincent de Paul and so committed to the service of those in need. The Sisters are involved in parish work and the Community also has a nursing home in Plympton.

MOTHER ELIZABETH MARY SC
(Revd Mother, assumed office 21 April 2003)
SISTER CLARE SC *(priest)* *(Assistant)*

Sister Theresa
Sister Angela Mary
Sister Rosamund
Sister Hilda Mary

Sister Mary Joseph
Sister Gabriel Margaret
Sister Mary Patrick

Obituaries
6 Feb 2010   Sister Faith Mary, aged 95, professed 68 years

Oblates and Associate Members
The Community has a group of Oblates and Associate Members, formed as a mutual supportive link. We do not provide a rule of life; instead we ask our Oblates and Associate Members to add to their existing rule the daily use of the Vincentian Prayer. Oblates are also asked to use the Holy Paraclete hymn and one of the Daily Offices, thereby joining in spirit in the Divine Office of the Community. Oblates are encouraged to make an annual retreat. Associate Members support us by their prayers and annual subscription.

Other addresses
Saint Vincent's Nursing Home, Fore Street, Plympton, Plymouth PL7 1NE   *Tel: 01752 336205*

Guest and Retreat Facilities
We welcome individuals for Quiet Days.
Most convenient time to telephone: 4.00 pm – 6.30 pm

Bishop Visitor: Rt Revd Robert Evens, Bishop of Crediton

Sisters of the Incarnation SI

Founded 1981

The House of the
Incarnation
6 Sherbourne Terrace
Dover Gardens
SA 5048
AUSTRALIA
Tel: 08 8296 2166
Email: sisincar
@bigpond.com

Office Book
A Prayer Book for
Australia (1995 edition)
for
Morning and Evening
Prayer, and Compline;
Midday Prayer is from
another source.

The sisters live under vows of poverty, chastity and obedience in a simple life style, and seek to maintain a balance between prayer, community life and work for each member and to worship and serve within the church. They combine the monastic and apostolic aspects of the Religious Life. The monastic aspects include prayer, domestic work at home, community life and hospitality. The sisters are engaged in parish ministry.

The community was founded in the diocese of Adelaide in 1981 as a contemporary expression of the Religious Life for women in the Anglican Church. In 1988, the two original sisters made their Profession of Life Intention within the Sisters of the Incarnation, before the Archbishop of Adelaide, the Visitor of the community. One member was ordained to the diaconate in 1990 and the priesthood in 1993. The governing body of the community is its chapter of professed sisters, which elects the Guardian, and appoints an Episcopal Visitor and a Community Advisor.

SISTER PATRICIA SI
(*Guardian, assumed office 1981*)
Sister Juliana (*priest*)

Friends
The community has a group of Friends who share special celebrations and significant events, many of whom have supported the community from the beginning, while others become Friends as we touch their lives. There is no formal structure.

Bishop Visitor: Rt Revd Dr K Rayner

The Sisters of Jesus Way – see opposite page

Sisters of Jesus Way

Founded 1979

Redacre
24 Abbey Road
West Kirby
Wirral
CH48 7EP
UK
Tel: 0151 6258775
Email:
sistersofjesusway
@redacre.org.uk

Website: www.
redacre.org.uk

Morning Prayer
8.00 am

Intercessory prayer
(community only)
2.00 pm

Evening Prayer
7.00 pm

Registered Charity
No 509284

Two Wesley deaconesses founded the Sisters of Jesus Way. There have been many strands that have been instrumental in the formation of the community but primarily these have been the Gospels, the Charismatic Renewal, the teaching and example of the Pietists of the 17th and early 18th centuries as practised in some German communities and the lives of saints from many denominations.

Our calling is to love the Lord Jesus with a first love, to trust the heavenly Father as his dear children for all our needs both spiritual and material and to allow the Holy Spirit to guide and lead us. Prayer, either using the framework of a simple liturgy or informal, is central to all that we do. We make life promises of simplicity, fidelity and chastity. Our work for the Lord varies as the Holy Spirit opens or closes doors. We welcome guests, trusting that as the Lord Jesus lives with us, they will meet with him and experience his grace. Music, some of which has been composed by the sisters, is very much part of our life. We work together, learning from the Lord to live together as a family in love, forgiveness and harmony.

SISTER MARIE
(Little Sister, assumed office 1991)
SISTER SYLVIA *(Companion Sister)*

Sister Hazel	Sister Susan
Sister Florence	Sister Louise
Sister Beatrice	

Obituaries
13 May 2011   Sister Lynda, aged 47, professed 20 years

Associates
The Followers of the Lamb are a small group of women following a simple Rule of Life and committed to assisting the Sisters.

Bishop Guardian
Rt Revd Dr Peter Forster, Bishop of Chester

Guest and Retreat Facilities
8 single rooms, 4 double rooms. Several rooms for day visitors and small groups.

Most convenient time to telephone: 9.30am–12.30pm; 2.30pm–6pm; 7.30pm–9pm

Community Publication
Twice-yearly teaching and newsletter. Contact Sister Louise.

Community History
Published by the Sisters of Jesus Way and available from the Community:
The Beloved Community – Beginnings; A Time to Build;
Circles of Love – the Life and Work of the Sisters of Jesus Way

Society of the Holy Cross

SHC

Founded 1925

3 Jeong-dong
Jung-ku
Seoul 100-120
KOREA
Tel: 2 735 7832
or 2 735 3478
Fax: 2 736 5028
Email: holycross25
@yahoo.com

Website
www.sister.or.kr

Morning Prayer
6.15 am

Holy Eucharist
6.45 am

Midday Prayer
12.30 pm
(12 noon Sun & great feast days)

Evening Prayer
5.00 pm

Compline 8.00 pm

Office Book
Revised Common
Prayer for MP & EP
and Compline; & SHC
material for Midday
Office

The community was founded on the feast day of the Exaltation of the Holy Cross in 1925 by the Rt Revd Mark Trollope, the third bishop of the Anglican Church in Korea, admitting Postulant Phoebe Lee and blessing a small traditional Korean-style house in the present site of Seoul. The Community of St Peter, a nursing order in Woking, Surrey, England, sent eighteen Sisters as missionaries to Korea between 1892 and 1950, who nourished this young community for a few decades. Sister Mary Clare CSP, who was the first Mother Superior of this community, was persecuted by the North Korean communists and died during the 'death march' in the Korean War in 1950. This martyrdom especially has been a strong influence and encouragement for the growth of the community.

Our spirituality is based on a modified form of the Augustinian Rule harmonized with the Benedictine one. Bishop Mark Trollope, the first Visitor, and Sister Mary Clare CSP compiled the Divine Office Book and the Constitution and Rule of the Community. The activities that are being continuously practised even now include pastoral care in parishes, running homes for the elderly and those with learning difficulties, teaching English, and counselling people.

We run a programme for vocation one weekend each month, and a spiritual prayer meeting and workshop monthly with people who want to improve their spiritual life. We also conduct Quiet Hours and Retreats individually or in groups. We lead contemplation based on Ignatian Spirituality or Lexio Divina.

SISTER ALMA SHC
(Reverend Mother, assumed office 1 Jan 2010)
SISTER HELEN ELIZABETH SHC *(priest) (Assistant Superior)*

Sister Monica	Sister Pauline
Sister Phoebe Anne	Sister Angela
Sister Edith	Sister Theresa
Sister Cecilia	Sister Grace
Sister Maria Helen	Sister Helen Juliana
Sister Etheldreda	Sister Lucy Edward
Sister Catherine *(priest)*	Sister Martha
Sister Maria Clara	Sister Prisca

Friends and Associates

FRIENDS are mostly Anglicans who desire to have a close link with the community. They follow a simple Rule of Life, which includes praying for the Sisters and their work. Friends also form a network of prayer, fellowship and mutual support within Christ's ministry of wholeness and reconciliation. About one hundred members come together for the annual meeting in October at the Motherhouse. The committee members meet bi-monthly at the convent.

ASSOCIATES: forty-five friends have been trained for admission and vow-taking for full membership between 2005 and 2011.

Other Addresses
St Anne's Nursing Home for Elderly People,
619-28 Onsuri, Kilsang, Kangwha, Inch'on, 417-840 South Korea
Tel: 32 937 1935 Fax: 32 937 0696   Email: anna1981@kornet.net
Website: www.oldanna.or.kr
St Bona House for Intellectually Handicapped People,
2–4 Neamni, Kadok, Chongwon, Chungbuk 363-853, South Korea
Tel: 82 43 297 8348   Fax: 82 43 298 3156   Email: sralma@naver.com
Website: www.bona.or.kr

Community Publication
Holy Cross Newsletter, published occasionally, in Korean.
Sister Catherine SHC, *Holy Vocation* (booklet for the SHC 75th anniversary, 2000)

Community History
Jae Joung Lee, *Society of the Holy Cross 1925–1995*, Seoul, 1995 (in Korean).
Sisters Maria Helen & Catherine, *The SHC: the First 80 Years*, 2005
Sister Helen Elizabeth (ed), *Fragrance of the Holy Cross,* 2010 (story of Sister Mary Clare in Korean)

Guest and Retreat Facilities
The Community organizes retreats and quiet days monthly for Associates and groups and individuals.

Community Wares
Wafers and wine for Holy Eucharist.

Bishop Visitor
Rt Revd Paul Kim,
Bishop of Seoul

Sister Catherine
baptises a baby.

Society of the Precious Blood
(UK)

SPB

Founded 1905

Burnham Abbey
Lake End Road
Taplow, Maidenhead
Berkshire SL6 OPW
UK
Tel & Fax:
01628 604080
Email:
burnhamabbey@
btinternet.com

Website: www.
burnhamabbey.org

Lauds   7.30 am
Eucharist   9.30 am
Angelus & Sext
12.00 noon
Vespers   5.30 pm
Compline   8.30 pm

Office Book
SPB Office Book

Bishop Visitor
Rt Revd
Stephen Cottrell,
Bishop of Chelmsford

Registered Charity
No. 900512

We are a contemplative community whose particular work within the whole body of Christ is worship, thanksgiving and intercession. Within these ancient Abbey walls, which date back to 1266, we continue to live the Augustinian monastic tradition of prayer, silence, fellowship and solitude. The Eucharist is the centre of our life, where we find ourselves most deeply united with Christ, one another and all for whom we pray. The work of prayer is continued in the Divine Office, in the Watch before the Blessed Sacrament and in our whole life of work, reading, creating, and learning to live together. This life of prayer finds an outward expression in welcoming guests, who come seeking an opportunity for quiet and reflection in which to deepen their own spiritual lives, or to explore the possibility of a religious vocation.

SISTER MARY BERNARD SPB
(Reverend Mother, assumed office 30 January 2003)

Sister Margaret Mary   Sister Mary Benedict
Sister Dorothy Mary   Sister Victoria Mary
Sister Jane Mary   Sister Miriam Mary
Sister Mary Laurence   Sister Elizabeth Mary
Sister Mary Philip   Sister Grace Mary

Companions and Oblates: Oblates are men and women who feel drawn by God to express the spirit of the Society, united with the Sisters in their life of worship, thanksgiving and intercession. They live out their dedication in their own situation and make a yearly Promise. Men and women who desire to share in the prayer and work of the Society but cannot make as full a commitment to saying the Office may be admitted as Companions.

Community History
Sister Felicity Mary SPB, *Mother Millicent Mary,* 1968.
   Booklets and leaflets on the history and life of the Abbey.
Community Wares: We have a small shop for cards.
Community Publications: Newsletter, yearly at Christmas.
Companions/Oblates Letter, quarterly.
Guest and Retreat Facilities: We have a small guest wing with three single rooms for individual (unconducted) retreats. We also have rooms available for Quiet Days or Groups. We do not make a charge but are grateful for a donation if you can afford it. The usual amount seems to be £30 a night, £5 for a Quiet Day and £5 per person for a group.
Most convenient time to telephone: 10.30 am – 12 noon, 3.00 pm – 4.30 pm, 7.00 pm – 8.00 pm

Society of the Precious Blood

(Lesotho)

SPB

Founded 1905

Priory of Our Lady
Mother of Mercy
PO Box 7192
Maseru 100
LESOTHO
Tel: 00266 58859585
00266 270002605
Email: spbmasite@
leo.co.ls

Morning Prayer
7.00 am

Eucharist 7.30 am

Terce 10.00 am

Midday Office
12 noon

Evening Prayer
5.30 pm

Compline 8.00 pm

Office Book
Daily Prayer & An
Anglican Prayer Book
1989, CPSA

St Monica's
House of Prayer
46 Green St, West End
Kimberley, 8301
SOUTH AFRICA
Tel: 00275 38 331161

Five Sisters of the Society of the Precious Blood at Burnham Abbey came to Masite in Lesotho in 1957 to join with a community of African women, with the intention of forming a multi-cultural contemplative community dedicated to intercession. In 1966, this community at Masite became autonomous, although still maintaining strong ties of friendship with Burnham Abbey. In 1980, a House of Prayer was established in Kimberley in South Africa, which has developed a more active branch of the Society.

SISTER ELAINE MARY SPB
(*Prioress, assumed office 24 September 1997*)

Sister Josephine Mary
Sister Theresia Mary
Sister Lucia Mary
Sister Diana Mary

Sister Cicily Mary
Sister Camilla Mary

Intern Oblates: 2

Obituaries
7 Dec 2010   Sister Magdalen Mary, aged 97,
                              professed 48 years

Oblates and Companions
The Community has thirteen oblates (in Lesotho, South Africa, Zambia, New Zealand and the UK), and eighty-six Companions and Associates (in Lesotho, South Africa and the UK). All renew their promises annually. Oblates are sent prayer material regularly. Companions and Associates receive quarterly letters and attend occasional quiet days.

Community History and books
Sister Theresia Mary SPB, *Father Patrick Maekane MBK*, CPSA, 1987
Evelyn Cresswell (Oblate SPB), *Keeping the Hours*, Cluster Pubs, Pietermaritzburg, 2007

Community Publication
Annual *Newsletter*; apply to the Prioress. No charge.

Community Wares: Cards, crafts, religious booklets.

Guest and Retreat Facilities
Small guest house with three bedrooms. There is no fixed charge. It is closed in winter (June to mid-August). Both men and women are welcome for retreats, which may be private or accompanied by a Sister. We also welcome anyone who wishes to share our life for a few months, to live with us in the Priory.

Bishop Visitor
Rt Revd Adam Taaso, Bishop of Lesotho

Society of the Sacred Advent

SSA

Founded 1892

Community House
34 Lapraik Street
Albion
QLD 4010
AUSTRALIA
Tel: 07 3262 5511
Fax: 07 3862 3296

Email:
sistersofssa@
stmarg.qld.edu.au

eunice@
stmarg.qld.edu.au

Quiet time
6.00 am

Morning Prayer
6.30 am
(7.00 am Sun & Mon)

Eucharist 7.00 am
(7.30 am Sun)

Midday Prayer
12 noon

Evensong 5.30 pm

Compline 7.30 pm
(8.00 pm Wed & Sat)

The Society of the Sacred Advent exists for the glory of God and for the service of His Church in preparation for the second coming of our Lord and Saviour Jesus Christ.

Members devote themselves to God in community under vows of poverty, chastity and obedience. Our life is a round of worship, prayer, silence and work. Our Patron Saint is John the Baptist who, by his life and death, pointed the way to Jesus. We would hope also to point the way to Jesus in our own time, to a world which has largely lost touch with spiritual realities and is caught up in despair, loneliness and fear.

As part of our ministry, Sisters may be called to give addresses, conduct Retreats or Quiet Days, or to make themselves available for spiritual direction, hospital chaplaincy and parish work. The aim of the Community is to grow in the mind of Christ so as to manifest Him to others. The Society has two Schools, St Margaret's and St Aidan's and two Sisters are on each of the School Councils.

SISTER EUNICE SSA
(*Revd Mother, assumed office 21 March 2007*)

Sister June Ruth   Sister Beverley
Sister Sandra   Sister Gillian

Obituaries
8 Oct 2010   Sister Dorothy, aged 88, professed 65 years

Fellowship and Company
THE FELLOWSHIP OF THE SACRED ADVENT
Since 1925, the work of the Community has been helped by the prayers and work of a group of friends known as the Fellowship of the Sacred Advent. They have a simple Rule of Life.

THE COMPANY OF THE SACRED ADVENT began in 1987.
This is a group of men and women, clergy and lay, bound together in love for Jesus Christ and His Church in the spirit of St John the Baptist. It seeks to proclaim the Advent challenge: 'Prepare the Way of the Lord.' Members have a Rule of Life and renew their promises annually.

Members of the Fellowship and Company are part of our extended Community family. The Sisters arrange Retreats and Quiet Days and support them with their prayers, help, or spiritual guidance, as required.

Other address
Society of the Sacred Advent, 261 Anduramba Road, Crows Nest, Queensland 4355, AUSTRALIA

Community Publication
There is a Newsletter, twice yearly. For a subscription, write to Sister Sandra SSA. The cost is A$5 per year.

Community History: Elizabeth Moores, *One Hundred Years of Ministry,*
published for SSA, 1992.

Community Wares: Cards and crafts.

Bishop Visitor: Rt Revd Godfrey Fryar, Bishop of Rockhampton

Guest and Retreat Facilities
There are twenty single rooms. Both men and women are welcome. The facilities are closed over Christmas and in January.

Office Book
A Prayer Book for Australia; *The Daily Office SSF* is used for Midday Prayer.

Society of the Sacred Cross SSC

Founded 1914
(Chichester);
to Wales in 1923

Tymawr Convent
Lydart
Monmouth
Gwent NP25 4RN
UK

Tel: 01600 860244

Email:
tymawrconvent
@btinternet.com

The community, part of the Anglican Church in Wales, lives a monastic, contemplative life of prayer based on silence, solitude and learning to live together, under vows of poverty, chastity and obedience, with a modern rule, Cistercian in spirit. At the heart of our corporate life is the Eucharist with the daily Office and other times of shared prayer spanning the day. All services are open to the public and we are often joined by members of the neighbourhood in addition to our visitors. Our common life includes study, recreation and work in the house and extensive grounds.

It is possible for women and men, married or single, to experience our life of prayer by living alongside the community for periods longer than the usual guest stay. Hospitality is an important part of our life at Tymawr and guests are most welcome. We also organise and sponsor occasional lectures and programmes of study for those who wish to find or develop the life of the spirit in their own circumstances.

The community is dedicated to the crucified and risen Lord as the focus of its life and the source of the power to live it.

Community Wares
Colour photographs cards of Tymawr available at 60p each (including envelope).

Community Publication: Tymawr Newsletter, yearly at Advent. Write to the above address.

Website
www.
churchinwales.org.
uk/tymawr/index.
html

Morning Prayer
7.15 am

Terce
8.45 am

Eucharist
12.00 noon

Evening Prayer
5.15 pm

**Silent Corporate
Prayer**
7.45 pm

Compline
8.15 pm

Office Book
CCP, with additional
SSC material.

Bishop Visitor
Rt Revd Dominic
Walker OGS, Bishop
of Monmouth

Registered Charity:
No. 1047614

SISTER GILLIAN MARY SSC
(Revd Mother, assumed office 2010)
SISTER VERONICA ANNE SSC *(Assistant)*

Sister Lorna Francis*
Sister Heylin Columba*
Sister Rosalind Mary
Sister Elizabeth

Novices: 1

* *Living the contemplative life away from Tymawr*

Obituaries
18 Feb 2010   Sister Mary Jean, aged 86, professed 49 years,
Revd Mother 1998–2010
7 May 2010   Sister Anne, aged 92, professed 57 years

Oblates and Associates
There are forty-eight Oblates, living in their own homes,
each having a personal Rule sustaining their life of prayer.
One hundred and sixteen Associates, women and men,
have a simple commitment. Three Companion Brothers,
who are priests, live a life of prayer as a 'cell' under a Rule
inspired by SSC's Rule. One Companion Sister lives a
solitary life of prayer under vow. Three months are spent
annually with SSC.

Guest and Retreat Facilities
The community offers facilities for individual guests and
small groups. There are five rooms (one double) in the
guest wing of the Main House for full board. Michaelgarth,
the self-catering guest house offers facilities for individuals
or groups (five singles and two doubles), and also for day
groups. The Old Print House offers full facilities for day
groups of up to eight. Individuals may have private retreats
with guidance from a member of the community. The
community occasionally organises retreats and study days.
Pilgrimages round the grounds, on a variety of themes,
can be arranged. Please write with a stamped addressed
envelope for details.

Most convenient time to telephone:
6.45 pm – 8.00 pm only, except Mondays, Fridays and
Sundays.

Community History
Sister Jeanne SSC, *A Continuous Miracle,*
(privately printed)

Society of the Sacred Mission

SSM

Founded 1893

Office Book
Celebrating
Common Prayer

Bishops Visitor
Rt Revd
John Pritchard,
Bishop of Oxford
(PROVINCE OF
EUROPE)

Most Revd
Philip Freier,
Archbishop of
Melbourne
(SOUTHERN
PROVINCE)

Most Revd
Thabo Makgoba,
Archbishop of Cape
Town
(SOUTHERN AFRICAN
PROVINCE)

Founded in 1893 by Father Herbert Kelly, the Society is a means of uniting the devotion of ordinary people, using it in the service of the Church. Members of the Society share a common life of prayer and fellowship in a variety of educational, pastoral and community activities in England, Australia, Japan, Lesotho, and South Africa.

PROVINCE OF EUROPE
COLIN GRIFFITHS SSM
(Provincial, assumed office April 2010)

Frank Green	*Associates:*
Ralph Martin	Margaret Moakes
Andrew Muramatsu	Paul Golightly
Jonathan Ewer	Elizabeth Baker
Edmund Wheat	Robin Baker
Mary Hartwell	Marcus Armstrong
Elizabeth Macey	Joan Golightly
Michael Maasdorp	Karen Walker

Associates and Companions (applicable to all provinces)
ASSOCIATES: are men and women who share the life and work of a priory of the Society.
COMPANIONS: are men and women who support the aims of the Society without being closely related to any of its work. They consecrate their lives in loving response to a vocation to deepen their understanding of God's will, and to persevere more devotedly in commitments already made: baptism, marriage or ordination.

Addresses
Provincial & Administrator:
The Well, Newport Road, Willen MK15 9AA, UK
Tel: 01908 241974   Email: ssmlondon@yahoo.co.uk

St Antony's Priory, Claypath, Durham DH1 1QT, UK
Tel: 0191 384 3747   Email: durham.ssm@which.net

1 Linford Lane, Milton Keynes, Bucks MK15 9DL, UK   *Tel: 01908 663749*

Community History
Herbert H Kelly SSM, *An Idea in the Working*, SSM Press, Kelham, 1908.
Alistair Mason, *SSM: History of the Society of the Sacred Mission*, Canterbury Press, Norwich, 1993.

Community Publication: *SSM News* (newsletter of the Province of Europe) The Secretary, SSM Newsletter, The Well, Newport Road, Willen MK15 9AA, UK

SOUTHERN PROVINCE
CHRISTOPHER MYERS SSM
(Provincial, assumed office November 2009)

Laurence Eyers	*lay members:*
Henry Arkell	Geoff Pridham
David Wells	Stuart Smith
Dunstan McKee	Lynne Rokkas
Matthew Dowsey	Joy Freier
Margaret Dewey	John Lewis
Steven de Kleer	Des Benfield
Gregory Stephens	Joyce Bleby Lewis
	Judith Nurton Smith
	Iris Trengrove

Addresses
St John's Priory, 14 St John's Street, Adelaide, SOUTH AUSTRALIA 5000
Tel: 8 8223 1014   Fax: 8 8223 2764   Email: ssm.adelaide@bigpond.com
St Michael's Priory, 75 Watson's Road, Diggers Rest, Victoria 3427,
AUSTRALIA
Tel: 03 9740 1618   Fax: 03 9740 0007   Email: ssm.melbourne@bigpond.com

Community Publication:
Sacred Mission (newsletter of the Southern Province): Editor, St John's Priory, 14 St John's Street, Adelaide, SOUTH AUSTRALIA 5000

SOUTHERN AFRICAN PROVINCE
(re-founded September 2004)
MICHAEL LAPSLEY SSM
(Provincial, assumed office September 2004)

William Nkomo	Moiloa Mokheseng	Sello Moholisa
Robert Stretton	Keketso Sebotsa	Ishmael Mothibi
Tanki Mofana	Samuel Monyamane	
Mosia Sello	Mosuoe Rahuoane	*Novices: 2*
Moeketsi Motojane	Barry Roberts	
Moeketsi Khomongoe	Nkoenyane Moroka	

Addresses
33 Elgin Road, Sybrand Park, Cape Town, SOUTH AFRICA, 7708
Tel: 21 696 4866 Email: michael.lapsley@attglobal.net

SSM Priory, PO Box 1579, Maseru 100, LESOTHO
Tel: 22315979   Fax: 22310161   Email: priorssm@ilesotho.com

Society of St Francis

SSF

Founded 1919 (USA)
1921 (UK)

Minister General
Email: clark.berge@
s-s-f.org
**Minister Provincial
(European
Province)**
Email: ministerssf
@franciscans.org.uk

**European Province
Website:** www.
franciscans.org.uk

Office Book
The Daily Office SSF
(revised edition 2010)

Bishop Protector
Rt Revd
Michael Perham,
Bishop of Gloucester

**European Province
SSF
Registered Charity:**
No. 236464

Community History
Petà Dunstan
This Poor Sort
DLT, London, 1997
£19.95 + £2 p&p

The Society of St Francis has diverse origins in a number of Franciscan groups which drew together during the 1930s to found one Franciscan Society. SSF in its widest definition includes First Order Brothers, First Order Sisters (CSF), Second Order Sisters (OSC) and a Third Order. The First Order shares a common life of prayer, fraternity and a commitment to issues of justice, peace and the integrity of creation. In its larger houses, this includes accommodation for short-term guests; in the city houses, the Brothers are engaged in a variety of ministries, chaplaincies and care for poor people. The Brothers are also available for retreat work, for counselling and for sharing in the task of mission in parishes and schools. They also undertake work in Europe and there are houses in America, Australasia and the Pacific, and are supportive to incipient communities in Zimbabwe and Korea.

CLARK BERGE SSF
(Minister General, assumed office 1 November 2007)

EUROPEAN PROVINCE
SAMUEL SSF
(Minister Provincial, assumed office 1 July 2002)
BENEDICT SSF *(Assistant Minister)*

Alan Michael	Jason Robert
Amos	John
Andrew	Julian
Angelo	Kentigern John
Anselm	Kevin
Arnold	Malcolm
Austin	Martin
Bart	Martin John
Benjamin	Nathanael
Christian	Nicholas Alan
Colin Wilfred	Peter
Damian	Philip Bartholomew
David Jardine	Raphael
Desmond Alban	Raymond Christian
Donald	Reginald
Edmund	Ronald
Giles	Thomas Anthony
Hugh	Vincent
James Anthony	Wilfrid
James William	*Novices: 5*

Obituaries
26 Feb 2010   Edward, aged 88, professed 53 years
24 Dec 2010   Paul Anthony, aged 51, professed 23 years

Companions: Companions are individual Christians who wish to associate themselves with the Society through prayer, friendship and in seeking to live the spirit of the Gospel in the way of St Francis. For more information about becoming a Companion contact: The Secretary for Companions at Hilfield Friary.

Third Order: See separate entry.

Addresses   **All email addresses are @franciscans.org.uk**
The Friary, **Alnmouth**, Alnwick, Northumberland NE66 3NJ
     Tel: 01665 830213   Fax: 01665 830580   Email: alnmouthssf
Bentley Vicarage, 3a High Street, **Bentley**, Doncaster DN5 0AA
     Tel: 01302 872240
St Matthias's Vicarage, 45 Mafeking Rd, **Canning Town**, London E16 4NS
     Tel: 020 7511 7848
The Master's Lodge, 58 St Peter's Street, **Canterbury**, Kent CT1 2BE
     Tel: 01227 479364   Email: canterburyssf
St Mary-at-the-Cross, **Glasshampton**, Shrawley, Worcestershire WR6 6TQ
     Tel: 01299 896345   Fax: 01299 896083   Email: glasshamptonssf
The Friary of St Francis, **Hilfield**, Dorchester, Dorset DT2 7BE
     Tel: 01300 341345   Fax: 01300 341293   Email: hilfieldssf
25 Karnac Road, **Leeds** LS8 5BL *Tel: 0113 226 0647   Email: leedsssf*
St Peter's Vicarage, Druridge Drive, Cowgate, **Newcastle upon Tyne**, NE5 3LP   *Tel: 0191 286 9913*
House of the Divine Compassion, 42 Balaam St, **Plaistow**, London E13 8AQ
     Tel: 020 7476 5189   Email: plaistowssf
The Vicarage, 11 St Mary's Road, **Plaistow**, London E13 8AQ
     Tel: 020 8552 4019   Email: stmarycssf

Community Publications: franciscan, three times a year – annual subscription is £7.00. Write to the Subscriptions Secretary at Hilfield Friary. Books available from Hilfield Friary book shop include: *The Daily Office SSF,* £10 + £2 p&p.

Community Wares: Hilfield Friary shop has on sale 'Freeland' cards, SSF publications and books of Franciscan spirituality and theology, as well as traidcraft goods.

Guest and Retreat Facilities

HILFIELD   The friary guest house has eight bedrooms (two twin-bedded) for men and women guests and two self-catering houses of six bedrooms each for the use of families and groups. Individually-guided retreats are available on request. There are facilities for day guests and for groups of up to forty. The seven brothers living at Hilfield are now joined by lay people, men and women, including two families, who together comprise the Hilfield Friary Community, an intentional Franciscan community focussing on peace, justice and the integrity of creation. The Hilfield Peace and Environment Programme is an annual programme of courses and events which shares Franciscan insights on the care of creation and reconciliation. *(www. hilfieldfriary.org.uk).* The Friary is normally closed from Sunday afternoon until Tuesday morning.

ALNMOUTH   The Friary has twelve rooms (including one twin-bedded) for men or women guests. Some conducted retreats are held each year and individually-guided

Little Portion Friary
PO Box 399
Mount Sinai
NY 11766/0399, USA
Tel: 631 473 0533
Fax: 631 473 9434
Email: mtsinaifriary
@s-s-f.org

San Damiano
573 Dolores Street
San Francisco
CA 94110, USA
Tel: 415 861 1372
Fax: 415 861 7952
Email: judehillssf
@aol.com

St Clare's House
1601 Oxford Street
Berkeley
CA 94709, USA
Tel: 510 705 1591

St Francis Friary
2449 Sichel Street
Los Angeles
CA 90031, USA
Tel: 323 222 7495

Divine Providence
Friary
Rua José Pedro de
Carvalho Lima 180
333 Morumbi
São Paulo-SP 05712-
080
BRAZIL
Tel: (11) 3672 5454

Minister Provincial
Tel: 415 861 7951
Fax: 415 861 7952
Email: judehillssf
@aol.com

Province Website
www.s-s-f.org

retreats are available on request. The recently -innovated chalet is available for families and groups in particular need referred by churches and social services. The Friary is closed for twenty-four hours from Sunday afternoon.

GLASSHAMPTON The guest accommodation, available to both men and women, comprises five rooms. Groups can visit for the day, but may not exceed fifteen people. The friary is closed from noon on Mondays for twenty-four hours.

PROVINCE OF THE AMERICAS

The Province of the Americas of SSF was founded as the Order of St Francis in 1919 by Father Claude Crookston, who took the name Father Joseph. Under his leadership the community developed, based first in Wisconsin and then on Long Island, New York.

The Order originally combined a monastic spirituality with a commitment to missions and evangelizing. In 1967, the OSF friars amalgamated with the Society in the UK and became the American Province of SSF.

Our lives are structured around our times together of formal prayer and the Eucharist, which give our lives a focus. Brothers engage in a wide variety of ministries: community organizing, missions, work in parishes and institutions, counselling and spiritual direction, study, the arts, serving the sick and infirm and people with AIDS, the homeless, workers in the sex industry, political work for the rights of people who are rejected by society. We come from a wide variety of backgrounds and cultural traditions. Living with each other can be difficult, but we work hard to find common ground and to communicate honestly with each other. God takes our imperfections and, in the mystery of Christ's body, makes us whole.

JUDE SSF
(Minister Provincial, assumed office May 2005)
THOMAS SSF *(Assistant Minister)*

Ambrose-Christobal	James
Antonio Sato	Jonathan Guthlac
Clark Berge	Leo-Anthony
(Minister General)	Maximilian Kolbe
Derek	Richard Jonathan
Dunstan	Robert Hugh
Eric Michael	Simon
Ivanildo	

Novices: 5   *Postulants:* 2

Addresses for Province of Divine Compassion

The Hermitage
PO Box 46
Stroud
NSW 2425
AUSTRALIA
Tel: 2 4994 5372
Fax: 2 4994 5527

Email: ssfstrd@
bigpond.com

The Friary
PO Box 6134
Buranda
Brisbane
QLD 4102
AUSTRALIA
Tel: 7 3391 3915
Fax: 7 3391 3916

Email: BrDonald@
franciscan.org.au

Website: www.
franciscan.org.au

Friary of the Divine
Compassion
PO Box 13-117
Hillcrest
Hamilton
AOTEOROA NEW
ZEALAND
Tel: 7 856 6701

Email: friary
@franciscan.org.nz

Website: www.
franciscan.org.nz

Community Publication: *The Little Chronicle*, electronic now. Write to: The Editor TLC, PO Box 399, NY 11766/0399, USA.   Email: kendrick05@aol.com

Guest and Retreat Facilities: There is a guest house at Little Portion Friary (Mount Sinai address), with twelve rooms, accommodating a maximum of sixteen guests. It is closed on Mondays. If there is no answer when telephoning, please leave a message on the answering machine.
San Damiano & St Clare's House have two rooms for guests: contact by email or telephone.

Office Book: SSF Office Book

Bishop Protector: Rt Revd Jon Bruno, Bp of Los Angeles

THE PROVINCE OF DIVINE COMPASSION

SSF friars went from England to Papua New Guinea in the late 1950s and the first Australian house was established in 1964. The first New Zealand house followed in 1970. In 1981, the Pacific Province was divided into two: Australia/New Zealand and the Pacific Islands. The latter was divided again in 2008 into Papua New Guinea and the Solomon Islands. Since 1993 when the first Korean novices were admitted to form the Korean Franciscan brotherhood, they were linked by covenant to SSF and became part of SSF at our Provincial Chapter in 2010. We have reached a consensus to change the name of the province to the Divine Compassion.

ALFRED BOONKONG SSF
(Minister Provincial, assumed office 1 May 2003)
CHRISTOPHER JOHN SSF *(Assistant Minister)*

Bart	Gabriel Maelesi	Stephen
Brian	James Andrew	William
Bruce-Paul	Lawrence	*Novices:* 3
Damian Kenneth	Lionel	
Daniel	Nathan-James	
Donald Campbell	Noel-Thomas	

Guest and Retreat Facilities
There is limited accommodation for short stay guests in the Brisbane, Stroud, Hamilton and Korea houses. In all cases, payment is by donation.
   Additionally, in Korea larger numbers can be accommodated at the nearby Diocesan Retreat House managed by the Brothers.

The Friary
156 Balsan-Ri
Nam-Myeon
Chuncheon 200-922
Republic of Korea
Tel: 33 262 4662
Fax: 33 262 4068

Email:
kfb1993@kornet.net

Website:
www.francis.or.kr

Community Wares
Holding Crosses
(Stroud and Brisbane)

Office Book
The Daily Office SSF

At Stroud, the old monastery of the Community of St Clare is also available for accommodation. The booking telephone number is: 2 4960 7100.

Community Publication
New Zealand: *Franciscan Angles (3 per year)*
Australia: *Franciscan Angles, (3 per year)*
Korea: *Friary Notes* (in English – bi-annual) & *Pyeonghwaui Hwanggi* (in Korean – quarterly)
All are available on the relevant websites. To subscribe to printed copies, please contact the Hamilton, Brisbane or Korea address as appropriate. In all cases, subscription is by donation.

Bishops Protector
Most Revd Roger Herft, Archbishop of Perth
(Protector General)
Most Revd David Moxon, Archbishop of the New Zealand Dioceses & Bishop of Waikato
(Deputy Protector for New Zealand)
Most Revd Paul Kim, Bishop of Seoul
(Deputy Protector for Korea)

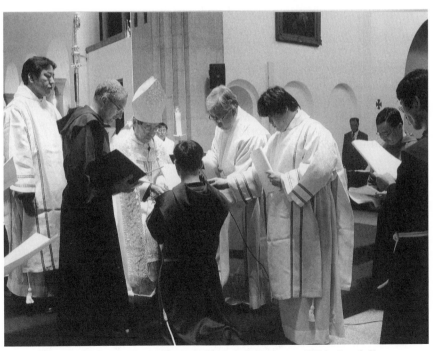

The 2010 life profession of Brothers Stephen & Lawrence SSF in Seoul, Korea

PROVINCE OF THE SOLOMON ISLANDS

GEORGE SSF
(Minister, assumed office October 2008)

Athanasius Faifu	Hartman Dena	Matthew Sikoboki
Andrew Manu	Hilcliff Tahani	Nathanael Volohi
Benjamin Tabugau	Hilton Togara	Patrick Paoni
Caspar Gu'urou	Ini Mumua	Patteson Kwa'ai
Christopher Gegeo	Isom Waisi	Samson Amoni
Clifton Henry	John Kogudi	Samson Siho
Comins Romano	John Mark Ofu	Selwyn Tione
Elliott Faga	John Rare	Stephen Watson Hovu
Ellison Ho'asepepe	Jonas Balugna	Thomas Hereward Peleba
Ellison Sero	Judah Kea	Winston Paoni
Ezekiel Kelly	Lent Fugui	
Francis Ngofia	Luke Manitara	*Novices:* 8
Gabriel Maelasi	Manasseh Birahu	
George Dau	Martin Tawea	
Ham Kavaja	Matthew Melake	

Obituaries
13 Nov 2009   Colin Baura, aged 73, professed 42 years

Bishop Protector: Rt Revd Richard Naramana, Bishop of Ysabel

Addresses

Patteson House
PO Box 519
Honiara
Guadalcanal
SOLOMON ISLANDS
Tel: 22386
Regional Office
          tel & fax: 25810

St Bonaventure Friary
Kohimarama
          Theological College
PO Box 519
Honiara, Guadalcanal
SOLOMON ISLANDS
Tel: 50128

Saint Francis Friary
PO Box 7
Auki, Malaita Province
SOLOMON ISLANDS
Tel: 40054

San Damiano Friary
Diocese of Hanuato'o
Kira Kira
Makira Ulawa Province
SOLOMON ISLANDS

Michael Davis Friary
PO Box 519
Honiara
Guadalcanal
SOLOMON ISLANDS

La Verna Friary/
          Little Portion
Hautambu
PO Box 519
Honiara
Guadalcanal
SOLOMON ISLANDS

Holy Martyrs Friary
Luisalo
PO Box 50
Lata
Temotu Province
SOLOMON ISLANDS

PAPUA NEW GUINEA PROVINCE

LAURENCE HAUJE SSF
(Minister Provincial, assumed office October 2008)
Email: *lhauje@gmail.com*

Anthony Kambua	Lucas Kuyang	Selwyn Suma
Charles Iada	Nathaniel Gari	Wallace Yovero
Colin Velei	Oswald Dumbari	Wilbert Bebena
Dominic Ombeda	Peter Kevin	Worrick
John Gai	Reuben Arthur	
Lester Meso	Rhoy Wadidika	*Novices:* 3
Lindsay Ijiba	Samuel Pokia	

Bishop Protector
Most Revd Joseph Kopapa, Archbishop of PNG & Bishop of Popondota

Addresses
Saint Mary of the Angels Friary, Haruro, PO Box 78, Popondetta 241, Oro
Province, PNG   *Tel: 329 7060*

Geoffrey's Friary, Katerada, PO Box 78, Popondetta 241, Oro Province, PNG

Saint Francis Friary, Koki, PO Box 1103, Port Moresby, NCD, PNG
Tel & fax: 320 1499   Email: ssfpng@daltron.com.pg

Martyrs' House, PO Box 35, Popondetta, Oro Province, PNG
Tel & fax: 3297 491

Philip Beawa Friary, Ukaka, PO Box 22, Alotau, Milne Bay Province, PNG

Geoffrey's Friary, Katerada in PNG

Society of St John the Divine

SSJD

Founded 1887

Cottage 252
Umdoni Retirement
Village
PO Box 300
Pennington 4184,
Natal
South Africa

Tel: 039 975 9552

Emails:

maryevelyn
@polka.co.za

hil777
@telkomsa.net

**Angelus
& Morning Prayer**
8.15 am

**Angelus
& Midday Office**
12.15 pm

**Angelus
& Evening Office**
5.00 pm

Compline
7.30 pm

Prayer Time
8.30 – 9.00 pm

The Society has never been a large community, with just sixty professions over a century, and has always worked in Natal. Originally the community ran schools and orphanages. In 1994, after the death of the older Sisters, the four of us who remained moved to a house that was more central in Durban.

We moved to Umdoni Retirement Village in Pennington in 2003. Our involvement outside the village involves being on the Board of Governors of our school, St John's Diocesan Scool for Girls in Pietermaritzburg, and all our Associates, Friends and Oblates worldwide. Both Sisters Hilary and Mary Evelyn are Layministers and exercise their ministry within Umdoni.

Sister Mary Evelyn   Sister Margaret Anne
Sister Sophia   Sister Hilary

Oblates and Associates
These are people who are linked with us and support us in prayer.
Oblates: There is one, non-resident, and she renews her oblation annually.
Associates: There are over a hundred, some overseas. They have a Rule of Life and renew their promises annually.
Friends: They have a Rule of Life and like the Associates and Oblates meet with the Sisters quarterly, and they renew their promises annually.

Community Publication
One newsletter is sent out each year to Oblates, Associates and friends at Advent.

Community History and books
Sister Margaret Anne SSJD, *What the World Counts Weakness*, privately published 1987.
  Sister Margaret Anne SSJD, *They Even Brought Babies*, privately published.

Community Wares
Crocheted girdles for clergy and lay ministers.

Bishop Visitor
Bishop Rubin Phillip, Bishop of Natal

Office Book
An Anglican Prayer Book 1989 (South African) for Morning & Evening Prayer.
Our own SSJD book for Midday Office & Compline.

Society of St John the Evangelist

(UK)

SSJE

Founded 1866

St Edward's House
22 Great College St
Westminster
London SW1P 3QA
UK
Tel: 020 7222 9234
Fax: 020 7799 2641

Emailu: superior@
ssje.org.uk

Website www.ssje.
org.uk

Mattins
7.00 am
(7.30 am Sun)

Eucharist
7.30 am
(8.00 am Sun)

Terce 9.00 am

Sext 12 noon

Evensong 6.30 pm

Compline 9.30 pm

A Registered Charity.

The Society of Saint John the Evangelist is the oldest of the Anglican orders for men, out of which the North American Congregation (and others worldwide) grew. We have been at the forefront of the Religious life since then, and have pioneered a new and more flexible way into the Community for the twenty-first century. New members first of all become 'Seekers' and then take simple annual vows as 'Internal Oblates' and live alongside us for a period of years before coming into First Vows. In this way, we escape the rigidity of the old system as people these days come from a much wider background than was formerly the case.

We seek to make use of their individual God-given talents as they seek to become what our Founder, Father Benson, envisaged: mission priests and lay brothers, based on their Community and its prayer life, but proclaiming Christ to the world. So we are engaged in running quiet days and retreats, both within and outside the House, counselling and spiritual direction. We look to befriend people whose English is limited and teach then as well as helping with students from overseas. We work in liturgics and preach and run parish missions. St Edward's House is a centre for private retreats and hospitality and is used by many religious and charitable groups for meetings, prayer etc.

FATHER PETER HUCKLE SSJE
(Superior, assumed office 7 March 2002)
BROTHER JAMES SIMON SSJE
(Assistant Superior and Novice Guardian)
Father Peter Palmer

Obituaries
23 Jun 2009   Father Alan Bean,
aged 95, professed 61 years
11 Jun 2010   Father David Campbell, aged 95,
professed 53 years, Superior-General 1976–91

The Fellowship of St John
The Fellowship was completely revamped in 1998 and this is an on-going process. It seeks to become a group of members, lay and ordained, who, through the connection with SSJE, seek to deepen their own spiritual life through a number of simple obligations. It has its own committee and the Father Superior is the Warden.

There are members throughout the country: those in London and the South East meet regularly in St Edward's House. The Newsletter is sent out to some five hundred subscribers and organisations every month, including people in Australia, Canada, Europe, South Africa and New Zealand.

People wanting to be associated with SSJE in this way serve a year's probation and are then admitted. Further details may be obtained from the Contacts' Officer, Brother James Simon.

Community Publication: *Newsletter,* published monthly, editor c/o St Edward's House. All enquiries to Brother James Simon (*Contacts Officer*). £6 per annum.

Guest and Retreat Facilities

There are Quarterly Quiet Days. Individual retreatants are welcomed and there are also facilities for Quiet Days. There are nineteen single rooms.

Email for guest master: guestmaster@ssje.org.uk

Most convenient time to telephone: 9.30 am – 8.30 pm

Bishop Visitor: Rt Revd Dominic Walker OGS, Bishop of Monmouth

---

Society of St John the Evangelist

(North American Congregation)

SSJE

Founded 1866

The Monastery
980 Memorial Drive
Cambridge
MA 02138
USA
Tel: 617 876 3037

Email: monastery@
ssje.org

Website www.ssje.
org

The Society of St John the Evangelist was founded in the parish of Cowley in Oxford, England, by Richard Meux Benson in 1866. A branch house was established in Boston in 1870. The brothers of the North American Congregation live at the monastery in Cambridge, Massachusetts, near Harvard Square, and at Emery House, a rural retreat sanctuary in West Newbury, Massachusetts. They gather throughout the day to pray the Divine Office, and live under a modern Rule of Life, adopted in 1997, which is available online at www.ssje.org. At profession, brothers take vows of poverty, celibacy and obedience.

SSJE's guesthouses offer hospitality to many. Young adults may serve for year as Monastic Interns. Guests may come individually or in groups for times of silent reflection and retreat. SSJE brothers lead retreats and programs in their own houses and in parishes, dioceses throughout North America. SSJE brothers also serve as preachers, teachers, spiritual directors and confessors. One of the brothers, Thomas Shaw, is Bishop of Massachusetts. Each year, SSJE brothers serve as chaplains for pilgrimages in Israel/Palestine sponsored by St George's College, Jerusalem. In recent years, brothers have been leading retreats and teaching in Anglican churches and seminaries in Kenya and Tanzania. Nearer to home, they are engaged in part-time in ministries with students and young adults, the Deaf, Asian-Americans, and those in Twelve-step Programs.

Other address

Emery House, 21 Emery Lane, West Newbury, MA 01985, USA   *Tel: 978 462 7940*

Morning Prayer
6.00 am

Eucharist
7.45 am

Midday Prayer
12.30 pm

Evening Prayer
6.00 pm

Compline
8.30 pm

(The schedule varies slightly during the week. The complete schedule can be found on the community's website.)

Office Book
BCP of ECUSA, and the Book of Alternate Services of the Anglican Church of Canada

Cowley Publications
Website:
www.cowley.org

Community History
This is now being written.

Bishop Visitor
Rt Revd
Frank T. Griswold, III

BROTHER GEOFFREY TRISTRAM SSJE
(*Superior, assumed office 4 May 2010*)
BROTHER JAMES KOESTER SSJE (*Deputy Superior*)
BROTHER DAVID VRYHOF SSJE (*Assistant Superior*)

David Allen   John Mathis
John Oyama (*in Japan*)   Mark Brown
Bernard Russell   Kevin Hackett
Thomas Shaw   Robert L'Esperance
John Goldring (*in Canada*)
Jonathan Maury   *Novices:* 1
Eldridge Pendleton   Luke Witewig
Curtis Almquist

Obituaries
22 May 2009 Paul Wessinger, aged 94, professed 65 years

Associates
The Fellowship of Saint John is composed of men and women throughout the world who desire to live their Christian life in special association with the Society of Saint John the Evangelist. They have a vital interest in the life and work of the community and support its life and ministries with their prayers, encouragement and gifts. The brothers of the Society welcome members of the Fellowship as partners in the gospel life, and pray for them by name during the Daily Office, following a regular cycle. Together they form an extended family, a company of friends abiding in Christ and seeking to bear a united witness to him as "the Way, the Truth and the Life", following the example of the beloved Disciple. For further information, or to join the Fellowship, visit the Society's website: www.ssje.org.

Community Publication
Cowley: a quarterly newsletter. Available online (www.ssje.org) or in printed form (contact monastery@ssje.org). For a subscription, write to SSJE at the Cambridge, Massachusetts, address. The suggested donation is US$20 annually.

Guest and Retreat Facilities
MONASTERY GUESTHOUSE in Cambridge, MA – sixteen rooms.
EMERY HOUSE in West Newbury, MA – six hermitages, three rooms in main house.
At both houses: US$75 per night/ US$40 for full-time students (closed in August).

Society of St Margaret

(Duxbury)

SSM

Founded 1855
(US Convent founded 1873)

St Margaret's Convent
50 Harden Hill Road
PO Box C
Duxbury
MA 02331-0605
USA
Tel: 781 934 9477
Email: convent@
ssmbos.org

Website
www.ssmbos.org

Morning Prayer
6.00 am

Eucharist 7.30 am

Noon Office
12 noon

Evening Prayer
5.30 pm

Compline 8.30 pm

Office Book
BCP
of the Episcopal
Church of the USA

The Sisters of St Margaret are an Episcopal Religious Order of women called to glorify God and proclaim the gospel of Jesus Christ through our worship and work, prayer and common life. Our commitment to God and to one another is expressed through vows of poverty, celibate chastity and obedience.

The Eucharist is central to our lives. From the center we go forth to celebrate the diversity, fullness and creativity of the people of God. We reverence all, seeking the living Christ in one another and in all creation. We strive for a spirit of fearlessness in Christian service, encouraged and empowered by the presence of the Spirit.

Our Sisters minister in many places: schools, prisons, parishes, nursing homes and homeless shelters. Our Houses offer hospitality to guests, retreatants, parish and civic groups, and all who long for a contemplative space in their lives. As a Community we will deepen our commitment to prayer, inviting others to join us in seeking greater intimacy with God. We live out our values in ministry with the poorest of the poor in Haiti; at the crossroads of urban life in lower Manhattan; and in Boston and its suburbs.

SISTER ADELE MARIE SSM *(priest)*
(Mother Superior, assumed office March 2011)
SISTER CAROLYN SSM *(Assistant Superior)*

Sister Bernardine	Sister Mary Gabriel
Sister Lucy Mary	Sister Adele
Sr Catherine Louise *(priest)*	Sister Julian
Sister Jane Margaret	Sister Christine
Sister Marjorie Raphael	Sister Marie Thérèse
Sister Marion	Sister Brigid
Sister Mary Michael	Sister Promise
Sister Emily Louise	Sister Grace
Sister Gloria	Sr Sarah Margaret *(priest)*
Sister Marie Margaret	Sister Kristina Frances
Sister Ann	Sister Kethia
Sister Claire Marie	

Obituaries
23 May 2010   Sister Rosemary, aged 91,
                                        professed 60 years

Associates: Associates of one Convent of the Society of St Margaret are Associates of all. They have a common Rule, which is flexible to circumstances. They include men and women, lay and ordained. No Associate of the Society may be an Associate of any other community.

Addresses of other houses
Sisters of St Margaret, 375 Mount Vernon Street, Apt 611, Boston, MA 02125, USA
St Margaret's Convent, Port-au-Prince, HAITI   *Tel: 509 3443 3683*
Mailing address: St Margaret's Convent, Port-au-Prince, c/o Agape Flights, Inc., 100 Airport Avenue, Venice, FL 34285-3901, USA
Email: mariemargaretssm@yahoo.com

Neale House, 50 Fulton Street, New York, NY 10038-1800, USA
Tel: 212 619 2672Email: nealehouse@gmail.com

Community Publication: St Margaret's Quarterly. For information, contact the Editor at the Boston Convent. *Email: communications@ssmbos.com.* The subscription rate is $8.

Community History
Sister Catherine Louise SSM, *The House of my Pilgrimage: a History of the American House of the Society of Saint Margaret,* privately published, 1973.
Sister Catherine Louise SSM, *The Planting of the Lord: The History of the Society of Saint Margaret in England, Scotland & the USA;* privately published, 1995.

Community Wares: Haitian Gift Shop, with cards, crafts and altar linens for sale for the benefit of the Scholarship Fund for schools in Port-au-Prince is temporarily suspended. For further information, email *convent@ssmbos.org.*

Guest and Retreat Facilities: All our houses have facilities for guests and retreatants. For costs and details of facilities, contact the house you are interested in.

Bishop Visitor: Rt Rev David Joslin, Assisting Bishop of Rhode Island

---

Society of St Margaret

(Hackney)

SSM

Founded 1855
(St Saviour's Priory 1866)

St Saviour's Priory is one of the autonomous Houses which constitute the Society of St Margaret founded by John Mason Neale. Exploring contemporary ways of living the Religious life, the community seeks, through a balance of prayer and ministry, to respond to some of the needs that arise amongst the marginalised in East London. The Office is four-fold and the Eucharist is offered daily. The Sisters' outreach to the local community includes: working as staff members (lay or ordained) in various parishes; supporting issues of justice and racial equality; supporting the gay community; Sunday Stall and Drop in Centre; Dunloe Centre for the homeless and alcoholics; complementary therapy; individual spiritual direction and retreats; dance workshops; art work and design. The Sisters also share their community building and resources of worship and space with individuals and groups.

St Saviour's Priory
18 Queensbridge
Road
London E2 8NS
UK
Tel: 020 7739 9976
Email: ssmpriory@
aol.com

**Leader of the
community**
020 7613 1464

Guest Bookings
020 7739 6775
Fax: 020 7739 1248

*(Sisters are not
available on Mondays)*

Website: www.
stsaviourspriory.
org.uk

Morning Prayer
7.15 am
(7.30 am Sun)
followed by
Eucharist
(12.15 pm on major
feasts)

Midday Office
12.45 pm

Evening Prayer
5.00 pm

Night Prayer   8.30 pm

Office Book
Celebrating Common
Prayer

Registered Charity
No 230927

THE REVD SISTER HELEN LODER SSM *(priest)*
(Leader of the Community, assumed office 17 February 2001)
THE REVD SISTER JUDITH BLACKBURN SSM *(priest)*
& SISTER ANNA HUSTON SSM *(Assistant Leaders)*
Sister June Atkinson
Sister Frances (Claire) Carter
Sister Elizabeth Crawford
Sister Pauline (Mary) Hardcastle
Sister Enid Margaret Jealous
Sister Moira Jones
Sister Sue Makin
Sister Pamela Radford

Obituaries
21 Aug 2009   Sister Mary Michael (Lilian) Stokes
                         aged 91, professed 39 years

Associates and Friends
Associates make a long term commitment to the Society
of St Margaret, following a Rule of Life and helping the
Community where possible. An Associate of one SSM
house is an Associate of all the houses. There are regular
quiet days for Associates who are kept in touch with
community developments.
Friends of St Saviour's Priory commit themselves to a year of
mutual support and friendship and are invited to regular
events throughout the year.

Community Publication: The Orient, yearly. Write to The
Orient Secretary at St Saviour's Priory. Brochures about
the Community are available at any time on request.

Community Wares: Traidcraft, South American Toybox,
cards, books and religious items for sale.

Community History
Memories of a Sister of S. Saviour's Priory, Mowbray, 1904.
A Hundred Years in Haggerston, published by St Saviour's
Priory, 1966.
Sister Catherine Louise SSM, *The Planting of the Lord: The
History of the Society of Saint Margaret in England, Scotland &
the USA;* privately published, 1995.

Guest and Retreat Facilities
Six single rooms for individual guests. Excellent facilities
for non-residential group meetings.
Most convenient time to telephone: 10.30 am – 1.00 pm (Not
Mondays).

Bishop Visitor
Rt Revd Dominic Walker OGS, Bishop of Monmouth

Society of St Margaret
(Uckfield)
SSM

Founded 1855

St Margaret's
Convent
Hooke Hall
250 High Street
Uckfield
East Sussex
TN22 1EN
UK
Tel: 01825 766808

Emails:
uckfieldssm
@hotmail.co.uk

egmotherssm
@hotmail.com

Eucharist 8.00 am
(9.30 am Sun & 11
am Wed in the parish
church)

Matins 9.00 am
(8.00 am Sun & Wed)

**Midday Office & Litany
of the Holy Name**
12.30 pm

Vespers
5.00 pm (4.45 pm Sun)

Compline 8.00 pm

Office Book
'A Community Office'
printed for St
Margaret's Convent,
East Grinstead

The Convent at Hooke Hall is one of the autonomous Convents which constitute the Society of St Margaret, founded by John Mason Neale. The Sisters' work is the worship of God, expressed in their life of prayer and service. They welcome visitors as guests and retreatants, and are involved in spiritual direction and parish work. At Chiswick they care for elderly people in a nursing home and have guests. There is a semi-autonomous house and a branch house in Sri Lanka.

MOTHER CYNTHIA CLARE SSM
(Mother Superior, assumed office 2 March 2000)
SISTER MARY PAUL SSM *(Assistant Superior)*

Sister Raphael Mary	Sister Lucy
Sister Mary Michael	Sister Barbara
Sister Rita Margaret	Sister Elizabeth
Sister Jennifer Anne	Sister Sarah

Associates: Associates observe a simple Rule, share in the life of prayer and dedication of the community, and are welcomed at all SSM convents.

Other address: St Mary's Convent & Nursing Home, Burlington Lane, Chiswick, London W4 2QF, UK
Tel: 020 8 994 4641   Fax: 020 8995 9796

Community Publication: St Margaret's Chronicle, Newsletter twice a year. Write to the Editor at St Margaret's Convent. £4.00 per annum, including postage and packing.

Community History
Sister Catherine Louise SSM, *The Planting of the Lord: The History of the Society of Saint Margaret in England, Scotland & the USA;* privately published, 1995.
Pamela Myers & Sheila White, *A Legacy of Care: St Mary's Convent and Nursing Home, Chiswick, 1896 to 2010,* St Mary's Convent, Chiswick, 2010.
Doing the Impossible: a short sketch of St Margaret's Convent, East Grinstead 1855–1980, privately published, 1984. Postscript 2000.

Guest and Retreat Facilities
Day retreatants are welcome: both individuals and groups of up to twelve people. Some Sisters are available for support in these retreats. Donations are appreciated. Quiet afternoons are arranged on a regular basis.

Bishop Visitor
Rt Revd John Hind,
Bishop of Chichester

Registered Charity:
No. 231926

St Margaret's
Convent
157 St Michael's
Road
Polwatte
Colombo 3
SRI LANKA

Bishop Visitor
awaiting appoitnment

Most convenient time to telephone:
10.00 am – 12 noon, 7.00 pm – 8.00 pm.

SEMI-AUTONOMOUS HOUSES OVERSEAS

The Sisters run a Retreat House, a Hostel for young
women, a Home for elderly people, and are involved in
parish work and church embroidery.

SISTER CHANDRANI SSM
(Sister Superior, assumed office 2006)
Sister Lucy Agnes
Sister Jane Margaret
Sister Mary Christine

Other address
A children's home:
St John's Home, 133 Galle Rd, Moratuwa, SRI LANKA

Society of
St Margaret

(Walsingham)

SSM

Founded 1855
(Walsingham Priory
founded 1955)

The Priory of Our
Lady
Bridewell Street
Walsingham
Norfolk
NR22 6ED
UK

Tel: 01328 820340
(Revd Mother)
Tel: 01328 820901
(Sisters & guests)

In January 1994, the Priory of Our Lady at Walsingham
reverted to being an autonomous house of the Society
of St Margaret. The Sisters are a Traditional Community
whose daily life is centred on the Eucharist and the daily
Office, from which flows their growing involvement in
the ministry of healing, and reconciliation in the Shrine,
the local parishes and the wider Church. They welcome
guests for short periods of rest, relaxation and retreat, and
are available to pilgrims and visitors. They also work in the
Shrine shop and the Welcome Centre.

SISTER MARY TERESA SSM
(Reverend Mother, installed 30 May 2011)

Sister Christina Mary	Sister Mary Clare
Sister Alma Mary	*(at Uckfield)*
Sister Francis Anne	Sister Caroline Jane CSP
Sister Columba	*(exploring transfer)*
Sister Phyllis *(in care)*	
Sister Mary Joan *(in care)*	*Postulants:* 1

Obituaries
7 Dec 2010   Sister Joan Michael, aged 77,
professed 53 years

Emails:
Mother: teresa@prioryofourlady.uk.com
Bursar: bursar@prioryofourlady.uk.com

Bishop Visitor: Rt Revd Peter Wheatley, Bp of Edmonton

**Readings
& Morning Prayer**
7.00 am

Mass 9.30 am
(9.15 am Thu, followed
by Exposition to 10.15
am) (No Mass on Sun
in Sisters' Chapel)
**Exposition of the
Blessed Sacrament**
10.30am–12.30pm
(except Sun & Thu)

Midday Prayer
12.45 pm

Evening Prayer
5.00 pm

Night Prayer
8.45 pm
(7.00 pm Sun)

Associates
There are Associates, and Affiliated Parishes and Groups.

Community Publication: Community booklet, *Wellspring*, published annually in the autumn. Write to the Priory for information. £3.50, including postage.

Community History:
Sister Catherine Louise SSM, *The Planting of the Lord: The History of the Society of Saint Margaret in England, Scotland & the USA;* privately published, 1995.

Community Wares: Cards (re-cycled) and embroidered; books; Religious objects (statues, pictures, rosary purses etc).

Guest and Retreat Facilities: St Margaret's Cottage, (self-catering) for women and men, families and small groups. One single room (bed sit, ensuite) on the ground floor, suitable for a retreatant, and three twin rooms upstairs.

Most convenient time to telephone: 10.30 am – 12.30 pm; 2.30 pm – 4.30 pm; 6.30 pm – 8.30 pm.

Office Book: The Divine Office

Registered Charity: No. 25515

Society of St Paul

SSP

Founded 1958

2728 Sixth Avenue
San Diego
CA 92103-6397
USA
Tel: 619 542 8660
Email: anbssp@
earthlink.net

Bishop Visitor
Rt Revd
James R Mathes,
Bishop of San Diego

The Society of St Paul began in Gresham, Oregon in 1958. Early ministry included nursing homes, a school, and commissary work in the Mid-East and Africa. In 1959, SSP was the first community for men to be recognized by the canons of ECUSA. The brothers live a life of prayer and are dedicated to works of mercy, charity and evangelism. In 1976, the order moved to Palm Desert, California, providing a retreat and conference center until 1996. In 2001, the brothers moved to St Paul's Cathedral in San Diego. In particular, we are involved at St Paul's Senior Homes and Services, the Uptown Faith Community Services, Inc., Dorcas House, a foster home for children whose parents are in prison in Tijuana, Mexico, and St Paul's Cathedral ministries.

THE REVD CANON BARNABAS HUNT SSP
(Rector, assumed office 1989)
THE REVD CANON ANDREW RANK SSP *(Associate Rector)*

Fellowship of St Paul
The Fellowship of St Paul, our extended family, is an association of Friends, Associates and Companions of the Society of St Paul, who live a Rule of Life centered on the Glory of God.

Society of the Sisters of Bethany

SSB

Founded 1866

7 Nelson Road
Southsea
Hampshire
PO5 2AR
UK
Tel: 02392 833498
Email: ssb@
sistersofbethany.
org.uk

Website: www.
sistersofbethany.
org.uk

Mattins   7.00 am

Mass   7.45 am
(8.00 am Sun; 9.30 am
Wed & alternate Sats)

Terce   9.15 am

Midday Office
12.00 noon

Vespers   5.00 pm

Compline   8.00 pm

Office Book
Anglican Office book
with adaptations

Registered Charity:
No. 226582

By prayer and activity, the Sisters seek to share in the work of reconciling the divided Churches of Christendom and the whole world. At the heart of each Sister's vocation is a call to prayer. Praying in the Spirit which unites us all to Christ and in Christ, for the wholeness of broken humanity, for the integrity of creation, for the peace of the world and for the Kingdom of God.

The Community prays daily for the unity of Christians. The intention of the Eucharist every Thursday is for Unity and is followed by their Office for Unity. On Fridays a three-hour Prayer Watch is kept in Chapel, and in addition each Sister has her own special intentions.

Each Sister makes the offering of herself in the hidden life of prayer within the Community, in the belief that God desires and accepts that offering. They are encouraged to persevere by some words of Abbé Paul Couturier with which he concluded one of his letters to the Community: "In Christ let us pray, pray, pray for Unity."

By simplicity of life-style, the Sisters try to identify with those for whom they share in Christ's work of intercession in the power of the Holy Spirit. The work of the Sisters includes giving hospitality for those seeking spiritual or physical refreshment and arranging retreats and quiet days. Some Sisters also give spiritual direction, lead quiet days and help in parishes. From time to time they are engaged in missions and cathedral chaplaincy work.

The Community motto is: 'Silentium et Spes' – In Quietness and Confidence – Let us pray to the Lord [Isaiah 30:15].

MOTHER RITA-ELIZABETH SSB
(Reverend Mother, assumed office 22 October 2009)
SISTER MARY JOY SSB *(Assistant Superior)*

Sister Katherine Maryel	Sister Gwyneth
Sister Ruth Etheldreda	Sister Joanna Elizabeth
Sister Florence May	Sister Elizabeth Pio
Sister Ann Patricia	

Postulants: 1

Obituaries

11 Aug 2010	Sister Christina Mary, aged 90, professed 61 years, Mother Superior 1984–94
12 Oct 2010	Sister Constance Mary, aged 90, professed 45 years

Associates

The Associates are a body of close friends who unite their life of prayer to that of the Community and who are accepted as members of an extended Community family.

They live in their own homes and accept a simple rule of life which is the expression of a shared concern to love and serve God and one another after the example of Martha, Mary and Lazarus.

Community Wares: Cards.

Community Publication: Associates' magazine, July and December

Guest and Retreat Facilities: Six guest rooms (1 twin-bedded). Individual retreatants can be accommodated. Closed at Christmas.

Most convenient time to telephone: 9.30 am – 11.45 am, 1 pm – 4 pm, 6 pm – 7.45 pm

Bishop Visitor: Rt Revd Trevor Willmott, Bishop of Dover & Bishop in Canterbury

Some other Communities
AFRICA

Benedictine Sisters of Bethany (EBSB)   Bamenda , CAMEROON

The EBSB sprang fom the Emmanuel Sisterhood, a community of sisters that was founded in 1971 in Makak, among members of the Eglise Presbyterienne du Cameroon (EPC). The sisters moved to Bafut in 1975, a year after they had transferred to the Presbyterian Church in Cameroon (PCC). Their foundress, Sister Madeleine Marie Handy, was the first women ordained in the PCC (in 1978). She died in 1999 and was succeeded by Sister Judith Ngo Nyemb.

One of the Emmanuel sisters, Sister Jane Manka'a, who had joined the community aged just 16, had a vision of working with the many homeless and orphaned street children found in Bamenda. To this end, she left the Emmanuels and became an Anglican. She started the Good Shepherd Home in Bamenda, which cares for 35 children, who would otherwise have nowhere to go and no one to look after them. The new community is called the Benedictine Sisters of Bethany.

Community of St Paul (CSP)   Maciene, MOZAMBIQUE

ASIA

The Order of Women, Church of South India

Soon after the inauguration of the CSI in 1948, a Religious Order for women was organized under the initiative and leadership of Sister Carol Graham, a deaconess in the Anglican Church before 1948. The Order has both active and associate members. The former take a vow of celibacy, observe a rule of life and are engaged in some form of full-time Christian service. The Order is a member of the Diakonia World Federation. The Sisters are dispersed among the twenty-one dioceses of the CSI.

Sisters of St Francis (SSF)

206 Eoamri, Miwonmyeon, Cheongwongun, Chungcheonbukdo 363-872, REPUBLIC OF KOREA   *Tel: (043) 225 6856*

AUSTRALASIA AND THE PACIFIC

Congregation of the Sisters of the Visitation of Our Lady (CVL)

Convent of the Visitation, Hetune, Box 18 , Popondetta,

Oro Province, PAPUA NEW GUINEA

EUROPE

Society of the Franciscan Servants of Jesus and Mary (FSJM)
Posbury St Francis, Crediton, Devon EX17 3QG, UK

Society of Our Lady of the Isles   (SOLI)
Lark's Hame, Aithness, Isle of Fetlar, Shetland ZE2 9DJ, UK   *Tel: 01957 733303*

NORTH AMERICA & THE CARIBBEAN

Order of St Anne   (OSA)
Convent of St Anne, 1125 North LaSalle Boulevard, Chicago, IL 60610-2601, USA
        Tel: 312 642 3638

Order of the Teachers of the Children of God   (TCG)
5870 East 14th Street, Tucson, AZ 85711, USA
                Tel: 520 747 5280   Fax: 520 747 5236   Email: smltcg@aol.com

Society of Our Lady St Mary   (SLSM)
Bethany Place, PO Box 762, Digby, Nova Scotia BOV 1AO, CANADA

SINGLE CONSECRATED LIFE

One of the earliest ways of living the Religious life is for single people to take a vow of consecrated celibacy and to live in their own homes. This ancient form of commitment is also a contemporary one with people once again embracing this form of Religious life. Some may have an active ministry whilst others follow a contemplative lifestyle. In 2002, the Advisory Council (for Religious communities in the Church of England) set up a Personal Vows group in response to enquiries from bishops and others to advise those who wish to take a vow of consecrated celibacy. The Sub Group now provides support for those who have professed this vow and arranges an annual gathering. In the Roman Catholic Church, this form of living the consecrated life was affirmed by Vatican II, which re-established the order of consecrated Virgins (OCV) and now an order of Widows is also emerging.

People exploring this call should be single, mature Christians (men or women) already committed to a life of prayer and willing to undertake a period of discernment before taking a temporary vow which may precede a life vow. An appropriate spiritual director and support from a Religious community or through the single consecrated life network is important to ensure adequate formation.

The vow is received by a person's bishop. The bishop (or his appointee) becomes the 'guardian of the vow' and the act of consecration is registered with the Advisory Council.

Persons in Life Vows: 14
Persons in Temporary Vows: 12

For further information the contact is: Revd Sue Hartley SCL, 272 New North Road,
Ilford IG6 3BT   *Tel: 020 8500 4592   Email: suehartley@internet.co*

Directory of dispersed Communities

In this section are communities that from their foundation have lived as dispersed communities. In other words, their members do not necessarily live a common life in community, although they do come together for chapter meetings and other occasions each year.
Like traditional communities, they do take vows that include celibacy.

Oratory of the Good Shepherd

OGS

Founded 1913

Website
www.ogs.net

Bishop Visitor
Rt Revd Jack Nicholls

The Oratory of the Good Shepherd is a society of priests and laymen founded at Cambridge (UK), which now has provinces in North America, Australia, Southern Africa and Europe.

Oratorians are bound together by a common Rule and discipline; members do not generally live together in community. The brethren are grouped in 'colleges' and meet regularly for prayer and support, and each province meets annually for retreat and chapter. Every three years, the General Chapter meets, presided over by the Superior of the whole Oratory, whose responsibility is to maintain the unity of the provinces.

Consecration of life in the Oratory has the twin purpose of fostering the individual brother's personal search for God in union with his brethren, and as a sign of the Kingdom. So through the apostolic work of the brethren, the Oratory seeks to make a contribution to the life and witness of the whole Church.

In common with traditional communities, the Oratory requires celibacy. Brothers are accountable to their brethren for their spending and are expected to live simply and with generosity. The ideal spiritual pattern includes daily Eucharist, Offices, and an hour of prayer. Study is also regarded as important in the life. During the time of probation which lasts one or two years, the new brother is cared for and nurtured in the Oratory life by another brother of his College. The brother may then, with the consent of the province, make his first profession, which is renewed annually for at least five years, though with the hope of intention and perseverance for life. After five years, profession can be made for a longer period, and after ten years a brother may, with the consent of the whole Oratory, make his profession for life.

Companions and Associates
The Oratory has an extended family of Companions, with their own rule of life, and Associates. Companionship is open to men and women, lay or ordained, married or single.

Community History
George Tibbatts, *The Oratory of the Good Shepherd: The First Seventy-five Years*, The Almoner OGS, Windsor, 1988.

Obituaries
3 Jan 2010	John Thorold, aged 94, professed 57 years
27 Apr 2010	John Ruston, aged 81, professed 55 years

CARLSON GERDAU OGS
(Superior, assumed office August 2005)
Apt 19 A/N, 60 Sutton Place South, New York, NY 10022, USA
Tel: 212 421 6942   Email: cgerdau@ogs.net

The Community in Australia
TREVOR BULLED OGS   *(Provincial, assumed office 2002)*
Holy Trinity Rectory, Box 1220, Fortitude Valley, Brisbane,
Queensland 4006, AUSTRALIA
Tel: 73852 1635   Email: tbulled@ogs.net

Michael Boyle	Barry Greaves	Kenneth Mason
Robert Braun	Charles Helms	Geoffrey Tisdall
Michael Chiplin	Ronald Henderson	
Keith Dean-Jones	Roger Kelly	*Probationers:* 1

The Community in North America
PHILIP HOBSON OGS   *(Provincial, assumed office August 2005)*
151 Glenlake Ave, Toronto, Ontario, M6P 1E8, CANADA
Tel: 416 604 4438   Email: phobson@ogs.net

Troy Beecham	William Derby	Edward Simonton
David Brinton	Robert MacSwain	
Gregory Bufkin	Walter Raymond	*Probationers:* 1

The Community in Southern Africa
JOHN SALT OGS   *(Provincial, assumed office 2010)*
Bishopsholme, PO Box 62, ST HELENA
Email: jsalt@ogs.net

Tammy Masikani	Jabulani Ngidi	Mark Vandayar
James Mvuba	Douglas Price	*Probationers:* 5
Thanda Ngcobo	Thami Shange	

The Community in Europe
DOMINIC WALKER OGS   *(Acting Provincial, assumed office December 2010)*
Bishopstow, Stow Hill, Newport NP20 4EA, UK
Tel: 01633 263510   Email: dwalker@ogs.net

Peter Baldwin	Peter Ford	Michael Longstaffe
Michael Bartlett	Nicholas Gandy	Robert Pipes
Alexander Bennett	Peter Hibbert	Christopher Powell
Michael Bootes	David Johnson	Lindsay Urwin
Michael Bullock	David Jowitt	Peter Walker
Malcolm Crook	Brian Lee	

Directory of acknowledged Communities

In this section are communities that are 'acknowledged' by the Church as living out a valid Christian witness, but whose members do not all take traditional Religious vows. Some communities expect their members to remain single whilst others may include members who are married: some have both members who remain celibate and those who do not. The specific vows they take therefore will vary according to their own particular Rule. However, communities in this section have an Episcopal Visitor or Protector. Some are linked to communities listed in section 1, others were founded without ties to traditional celibate orders. This section also includes some ashrams in dioceses in Asia.

In the Episcopal Church of the USA, these communities are referred to in the canons as 'Religious communities' – as distinct from those in section 1 of this *Year Book*, which are referred to as 'Religious orders'. However, this distinction is not used in other parts of the Anglican Communion where 'communities' is also used for those who take traditional vows.

Brotherhood of Saint Gregory

BSG

Founded 1969

Brotherhood of
Saint Gregory
PO Box 57
White Plains
NY 10602
USA

Email:
Servant@
gregorians.org

Website
www.
gregorians.org

Office Book
The Book of Common
Prayer (1979)

The Brotherhood of Saint Gregory was founded on Holy Cross Day 1969, by Richard Thomas Biernacki, after consultation with many Episcopal and Roman Catholic Religious.

The first brothers made their profession of vows in the New York monastery of the Visitation Sisters. Later that year, Bishop Horace Donegan of New York recognized the Brotherhood as a Religious Community of the Episcopal Church.

The community is open to clergy and laity, without regard to marital status. Gregorian Friars follow a common Rule, living individually, in small groups, or with their families, supporting themselves and the community through secular or church-related employment.

The Rule requires the Holy Eucharist, the four Offices of the Book of Common Prayer, meditation, theological study, Embertide reports, the tithe, and participation in Annual Convocation and Chapter.

The postulancy program takes a minimum of one year; novitiate at least two years, after which a novice may make first profession of annual vows. Members are eligible for life profession after five years in annual vows.

Gregorian Friars minister in parishes as liturgists, musicians, clergy, artists, visitors to the sick, administrators, sextons, and teachers. A number serve the diocesan and national church. For those in secular work the 'servant theme' continues, and many are teachers, nurses, or administrators.

Community Publications & Wares

The Brotherhood produces a quarterly newsletter titled *The Servant*. Subscription is US$8.00 per year. An order blank is available by mail or via our website.

There are a number of Brotherhood publications – please write or visit our website for further details regarding placing an order.

Community History

Karekin Madteos Yarian BSG, *In Love and Service Bound: The First 40 years of the Brotherhood of Saint Gregory*, BSG, 2009.

Bishop Visitor

Rt Revd Rodney R Michel,
                    assisting Bishop of Pennsylvania

Brother Richard Thomas Biernacki, BSG
(Minister General and founder, assumed office 14 September 1969)

Brother James Teets
Brother Luke Antony Nowicki
Brother William Francis Jones
Brother Stephen Storen
Brother Tobias Stanislas Haller *(priest)*
Brother Edward Munro *(deacon)*
Brother Donovan Aidan Bowley
Brother Christopher Stephen Jenks
Brother Ciarán Anthony DellaFera
Brother Richard John Lorino
Brother Ronald Augustine Fox
Brother Maurice John Grove
Brother Charles Edward LeClerc *(deacon)*
Brother Virgilio Fortuna
Brother Gordon John Stanley *(deacon)*
Brother Karekin Madteos Yarian
Brother William David Everett
Brother Thomas Bushnell
Brother Thomas Mark Liotta *(deacon)*
Brother James Mahoney
Brother Robert James McLaughlin

Brother Peter Budde
Brother John Henry Ernestine
Brother Francis Sebastian Medina
Brother Aelred Bernard Dean
Brother Joseph Basil Gauss
Brother Mark Andrew Jones *(priest)*
Brother Richard Matthias
Brother William Henry Benefield
Brother Nathanael Deward Rahm
Brother Thomas Lawrence Greer
Brother Enoch John Valentine
Brother Ron Fender
Brother Michael Elliott *(priest)*
Brother David Luke Henton
Brother David John Battrick *(priest)*
Brother Will Harpest
Brother Bo Alexander Armstrong
Brother Francis Jonathan Bullock

Novices: 4
Postulants: 1

BETHEL ASHRAM
Warickadu, Kuttapuzha P.O., Tiruvalla, Pathanamthitta District, Kerala, INDIA
Tel: 09562 335401

The Ashram is a part of Madhya (Central) Kerala Diocese, CSI. Located in Warickad, since 1926 the Ashram has run a school, looked after orphans and run a dispensary. Today its ministry includes a small geriatric care ward, a retirement home for monastic sisters of the Church of South India, and a boarding school. It is also used as a place of retreat for the diocese.

Achamma George *(Mother)*

CHRISTA KULU ASHRAM
Tirupattur, Vellore, Tamil Nadu 635602, INDIA

The Christu Kula Ashram was among the earliest Christian Ashrams, starting in 1921. This was one of the first Protestant Ashrams and it aimed to promote equality between Europeans and Indians, and to give an Indian presentation of Christian life and worship. It is in Vellore Diocese, CSI, and is linked to the National Missionary Society of India.

CHRISTA PREMA SEVA ASHRAM
Shivajinagar, Pune – 411 005, INDIA   *Tel: 20 553 9276*

Founded as the Ashram for the Christa Seva Sangha in 1922 by Jack Winslow to create a community of Indian and British members living in equality, the original community ceased in the early 1960s. Some members of this group were influential in the formation of the Third Order SSF (see entry elsewhere). A decade later, a multi-denominational group of Religious began to reside here. This group too did not continue and the Ashram is now the focus of a non-celibate community.

Revd B L Sojawal *(Acharya)*

CHRISTA SEVAKEE ASHRAM
Karkala, Karnataka, INDIA

Started in 1950 in Karnataka (Southern) Diocese, CSI, this Ashram runs a home for aged men and two homes for aged women, altogether caring for fifty elderly people, who are deserted, poor or without relatives. The institution has completed its Golden Jubilee of service. This Ashram is also functioning as a self-employment training centre, a centre for retreats and conferecnes, and as a short-term stay home for deserted women or women in distress.

COMMUNITY OF ST STEPHEN
4 Rajput Road, Delhi 110 054, INDIA   *Tel: 11 2396 5437*

Mrs S M Rao *(Head)*

CHRISTAVASHRAM
Manganam P.O., Kottyam District, Kerala 686 018, INDIA
Email: christavashram@gmail.com
Website: manganam.tripod.com/ashram/index.html

Christavashram (Society of St Thomas) is an active Christian community for service, founded in 1934, based on Christian principles with the motto "Thy Kingdom Come". It is in Madhya (Central) Kerala Diocese, CSI.

The Community consists of 120 people, including members, staff and children of the Kerala Balagram, staff and trainees of the Gurukul Ecumenical Institute and Peace Centre staying in the campus, and 30 Associate members living outside.

The sources of income for the Community are its agricultural and dairy farms, and contributions from Associate members and friends. All members are committed to contributing "Bread labour", and all earnings go to a common pool from where the needs of members are met. Any honorarium received either from the Ashram's own institutions or from outside goes to the "Common purse".

Chapel: It is an open and ecumenical chapel, welcoming people for meditation and prayers, besides daily common prayers in the morning and noon, Sunday communion services are held in different denominations' rites at 7.30 am.

Guests
The Ashram welcomes visitors from India and abroad. participants from abroad for the Gurukal ccourses, peace studies and seminars are welcome. As a simple life style is followed with vegetarian food, the cost of food and accommodation is kept to a minimum. Yoga practice is offered at the Ashram. Smoking and consumption of alcohol is not permitted in the Ashram premises.

Please contact the Ashram if you have any questions or would like more information about them.

DEVASEVIKARAMAYA
Devasevikaramaya 31, Kandy Road, Kurunegala, SRI LANKA
Tel: 0094 372 221803

Community of St Aidan & St Hilda
The Lifeboat House, Marygate, Holy Island,
Berwick-upon-Tweed TD15 2SQ

The Community of St Aidan & St Hilda is a dispersed ecumenical body, drawing inspiration from the lives of the Celtic saints.

Revd Ray Simpson *(Founding Guardian)*
Revd Graham Booth, Revd Simon Reed, Mrs Penny Warren *(Guardians)*

Church Mission Society

CMS

CMS is a community of people in mission obeying the call of God to proclaim the Gospel in all places and to draw all people into fellowship with the Lord Jesus Christ. Its founders' vision grew out of the experience of mission community, from which grew a commitment to cross-cultural mission. Most of the founders of CMS were members of the Clapham Sect, an informal community living around Clapham Common, also known as The Saints. Their most famous member was William Wilberforce MP. The Saints formed Wilberforce's core base of support for his campaign against the international slave trade. But this was not their concern; they also wanted social reform at home and a missionary movement to take the Gospel beyond the boundaries of Europe.

CMS has always had a significant community feel about it, being a membership Society, whose members associated together in order to promote and support evangelistic mission. Some members even refer to CMS as their "family". A transforming community life was also part of CMS mission service, in mission compounds, mission schools and hospitals and the various CMS training colleges.

CMS had a major influence in forming what today is called the Anglican Communion. About two-thirds of the Churches of the Anglican Communion trace their origins to the missionary movement fostered by CMS or have had CMS contributions to their early growth and development. Over its 200-year existence, CMS has sent out about 10,000 people in mission.

CMS has always been a membership society. Under a new constitution, approved in 2009, community members affirm seven promises, including a commitment to participating in mission service, regular prayer, bible reading, study, reflection, supporting the Church's mission, and mutual encouragement.

CMS supports people in mission in over thirty-five countries in Africa, Asia, Europe (including the UK), the Middle East and Latin America.

John Ripley *(Chair of Trustees)*
The Reverend Canon Tim Dakin
(Community Leader/Executive Director)
Membership: 2,500+

Community Publications: CMS produces a community newsletter, titled *Connect*, three times a year, distributed free to members. It publishes occasional monographs on mission themes through the CMS Crowther Centre for Mission Education. See the CMS website (www.cms-uk.org) for news and information about its mission work and regular printed publications.

Community Wares: Free resources for prayer, group study and seasons of the Christian year are available on www.cms-uk.org and books, resources and craft products from CMS-connected projects around the world are for sale on the CMS shop: www.shop.org.uk.

Conference Facilities
CMS in Oxford has excellent modern conference facilities for meetings from two to 150 people. See www.cms-uk.org/conferencing for details.

Community of St Denys CSD

Founded 1879

contact address
- as for leader

Community History
CSD: The Life & Work of St Denys', Warminster to 1979, published by CSD, 1979. *(out of print)*

Most convenient time to telephone
9am–1pm

Website
www.ivyhouse.org

Bishop Visitor
vacancy

Registered Charity
No 233026

The Community was founded for mission work at home and overseas. The remaining Sisters live in individual accommodation. The present dispersed community of men and women live with a Rule of Life based on the monastic virtues and a particular ministry towards encouragement in the practice of prayer and active service. The Retreat centre at Ivy House, Warminster, continues actively under a secular Warden and staff, providing hospitality for retreats and conferences for groups and individuals. There is a Board of Trustees responsible for financial matters.

MRS JUNE WATT
(Leader, assumed office October 2010)
57 Archers Court, Castle St, Salisbury SP1 3WE, UK
Email: junewatt@internet.com

Committed members: 33

among whom the professed sisters are:
Sister Margaret Mary Powell
Sister Phyllis Urwin
Sister Frances Anne Cocker *(priest)*
Sister Elizabeth Mary Noller *(priest)*

Fellowship: CSD has a fellowship (friends)
Community Publication: Annual *Newsletter* and quarterly prayer leaflet. Write to the Leader (address above). A suggested donation of £5.00 is welcome.

Guest and Retreat Facilities
St Denys Retreat Centre, Ivy House, is available for various types of retreat and conferences. Guests are also welcome. It has 22 rooms, 6 of which are double. (Closed during the Christmas period.) Bookings to the Warden, Ivy House, 2/3 Church Street, Warminster BA12 8PG
Tel: 01985 214824   Email: stdenys@ivyhouse.org

Companions of St Luke, OSB

Founded 1992

Abbey of
St Benedict
2288 220th Street
Donnellson
Iowa 52625
USA

Tel: 319 837 8421
Email:
abbotmichael
johnaustin
@yahoo.com

Website:www.
holythoughts.org

Matins
7.00 am
followed immediately
by the Mass

Noonday Prayer
12 noon

Vespers
5.00 pm

Compline
8.00 pm

Bishop Visitor
Rt Revd Dean Wolfe,
Episcopal Diocesan
of Kansas

The Companions of St Luke is a Benedictine community founded on the Rule of St Benedict incorporating both traditional and contemporary aspects of Religious life. The Companions of St Luke is a community who honours the rich tradition and wisdom that has been passed down to us through the ages, yet knows that if Religious life is to prosper into the 21st century that it must be open to the movement of the Holy Spirit and the windows of opportunity that it might bring. The Companions are a hybrid reflecting the best of what 'Orders and Christian communities' offer.

The Companions of St Luke is about making choices. Members are given choices of living at the Abbey or living their life in mission in the larger community. Members may choose to follow the traditional model of living as a single person or in a married state, both requiring a chaste life. The Community is a blend of male and female.

Vowed members take vows of: obedience, conversion of life, and stability; Oblates take corresponding promises of the same.

Michael-John Austin was consecrated Abbot at Conception Abbey (Roman), Missouri, in 2004. Since then, the Abbot Primate of the Roman Catholic Church has invited Michael-John to participate in the gathering of the Abbots of the Americas, representing Anglican tradition. Michael-John is also a member of the National Association of Episcopal Christian Communities.

MICHAEL-JOHN AUSTIN
(Abbot, founder 1992)

Brother Thomas Ferrell
Brother Raymond Owens
Brother Matthias Smith
Sister Monica Ruth Mullen
Brother Chad-Anselm Gerns
Sister Anna Grace Madden
Sister Catherine Unterseher
Sister Clare Benedicta Myers
Brother Paul Howard
Sister Vincent-Marie Rittenhouse
Brother David-Vincent Cotton
Sister Cecilia Lamoy
Brother Luke Doucette

Sister Mary Catherine Christopher
Sister Hannah Sophia Korver
Sister Mary Francis Deulen
Sister Sophia Stevenson Holt
Brother Aidan Maguire
Brother Bede Leach
Brother Timothy Titus Lunt
Brother Gregory Kingsley
Sister Bernadette Barrett
Brother Simon DiNapoli

Novices: 6
Postulants: 6

Oblates and Companions
The Companions of St Luke has an Oblate program. Oblates are considered by this community to have a 'full and authentic' vocation deserving its own formation. Oblates sit with their vowed counterparts in the Office, have voice and seat in Chapter.
The Companions of St Luke also offers a 'Companion Associate' affiliation. These are individuals who desire to be affiliated with the Community and grow in their own understanding of what it means to live an intentional life grounded in baptism.

Office Book
The Office Prayer Book. This prayer book is unique to the charism of the community and incorporates part of the Rule of St Benedict, as well as antiphons taken from the Gospel of Luke and Acts. The prayer book also includes the Eucharist, Rite II setting from the BCP.

Community Publication
The Community has a quarterly newsletter called 'The Bridge'. This may be mailed, or downloaded from the website: www.holythoughts.org.

Guest and Retreat Facilities
The Abbey of St Benedict dedicated Phase One of its building projects in August 2008. The three buildings are able to accommodate fifteen individuals, all with private bathrooms and independent heating and air-conditioning. Each building has common areas and hospitality.

Most convenient time to telephone
The Abbey welcomes calls at all times. If someone is not near the phone, an answering system will take the message.

(Society of the) Community of Celebration

SCC

Founded 1973

The Community of Celebration is a life-vowed, contemporary residential community whose roots stretch back to the renewal of the Church of the Redeemer, Houston, Texas, in the 1960s. Today the Community resides in Aliquippa (near Pittsburgh), Pennsylvania. Members are women and men, single and married, adults and children, lay and ordained. Following the Rule of St Benedict, members live a rhythm of prayer, work, study, and recreation.

Our ministry is to be a Christian presence among the poor, responding to the needs around us by offering safe, affordable housing; wellness programs to women in the county jail; serving with neighborhood organizations concerned with the revitalization of Aliquippa, and providing hospitality, retreats, sabbaticals, and conferences. We provide various chaplaincies, supply clergy, liturgical consultants, worship leadership and speakers for conferences.

809 Franklin Avenue
Aliquippa
PA 15001-3302,
USA
Tel: 724 375 1510
Fax: 724 375 1138

Email: mail@
communityof
celebration.com

Website
communityof
celebration.com

Morning Prayer
8.00 am

Noonday Prayer
12.30 pm

Evening Prayer
5.30 pm

Compline
9.00 pm

Conventual **Eucharist**
is celebrated on
Saturday evenings at
5.30 pm, and Saints'
days as applicable.
Monthly service Taizé
worship.

Office Book
Book of Common
Prayer

Bishop Visitor
Rt Revd
C. Christopher Epting

BILL FARRA
(Primary Guardian, assumed office 1995)
MAY MCKEOWN *(Guardian for Vocations)*

Mimi Farra   Joe Beckey
Revd Steven McKeown   Revd Phil Bradshaw
James von Minden   Margaret Bradshaw

Associates
Companions of the Community of Celebration follow the
Rule of Life for Companions.

Other address: Celebration UK Branch house, c/o Revd
Phil Bradshaw, 35 Cavendish Road, Redhill, Surrey RH1
4AL, UK

Community Publication
News from Celebration – twice a year. Contact Bill Farra for
a free subscription.

Community books
Phil Bradshaw, *Following the Spirit*, O Books, 2010
W Graham Pulkingham, *Gathered for Power*,
                Hodder & Stoughton, London, 1972
Michael Harper, *A New Way of Living*,
                Hodder & Stoughton, London, 1972
W Graham Pulkingham, *They Left their Nets*,
                Hodder & Stoughton, London, 1973
Betty Pulkingham, *Mustard Seeds*,
                Hodder & Stoughton, London, 1977
Maggie Durran, *The Wind at the Door*,
                Kingsway Publications/Celebration, 1986
David Janzen, *Fire, Salt, and Peace*,
                Shalom Mission Communities, 1996

Community Wares
Music and worship resources, psalms, anthems, books
and recordings – see website store.

Guest Facilities
We offer a chapel, meeting and dining spaces, and
overnight accommodation for 13–17 people (one
guesthouse can be self-catering for 4–5 people). We
welcome individual retreatants and groups, men and
women. For further information contact Celebration's
hospitality director by mail, telephone or email.

Most convenient time to telephone:
        9.00 am – 5.00 pm Eastern Time (Mon-Fri)

Company of Mission Priests

CMP

Founded 1940

Website
www.
missionpriests.com

Warden's address:
99 Hilfield Avenue
Crouch End
London N8 7DG
Email: fathertimpike
@hotmail.com

Office Book
The Divine Office
(Vincentian
calendar)

**Community
Publication**
Occasional Newsletter

Associates
Laymen closely
associated with the
Company in life and
work may be admitted
as Associates of the
Company.

The Company of Mission Priests is a dispersed community of male priests of the Anglican Communion who, wishing to consecrate themselves wholly to the Church's mission, keep themselves free from the attachments of marriage and the family, and endeavour to strengthen and encourage each other by mutual prayer and fellowship, sharing the vision of Saint Vincent de Paul of a priesthood dedicated to service, and living in a manner prescribed by our Constitution, and with a Vincentian rule of life. For many years the company, although serving also in Guyana and Madagascar, was best known for its work in staffing 'needy' parishes in England with two, three, or more priests who lived together in a clergy house. Although this is rarely possible nowadays, because of the shortage of priests, we encourage our members who work in proximity to meet as often as practicable in order to maintain some elements of common life. The whole company meets in General Chapter once a year, and the Regional Chapters more frequently.

We were among the founding members, in the year 2000, of the Vincentians in Partnership, which works in accordance with the principles established by St Vincent de Paul, to support and empower those who are poor, oppressed, or excluded.

FATHER TIMOTHY PIKE CMP
(Warden, assumed office 2005)

Michael Whitehead	Mark McIntyre
Anthony Yates	Alan Watson
Allan Buik	Simon Atkinson
Brian Godsell	Peter Bostock
John Cuthbert	Kevin Northover
Peter Brown	Jonathan Kester
Beresford Skelton	Robert Martin
Michael Shields	Christopher Buckley
David Beater	Kevin Palmer
Michael Gobbett	Philip Meadows
John Vile	Andrew Welsby
Ian Rutherford	Derek Lloyd
Andrew Collins Jones	Alexander Lane
James Geen	
Colin Patterson	*Probationers:* 1
Philip North	*Aspirants:* 2

Bishop Visitor: Rt Revd Lindsay Urwin OGS,
Administrator at Walsingham

Little Sisters of Saint Clare

LSSC

Founded 2002

Mother Guardian
Dorothy-Anne
Kiest, LSSC
Franciscan House of
Prayer
20802 72nd Ave W
#303
Edmonds
WA 98026-9608
USA
Tel: 425 776 8182

Email:
motherguardian
@gmail.com

Website
www.
stclarelittlesisters.
org

Office Books
BCP, SSF Office for
Franciscan saints,
Holy Women, Holy
Men Celebrating the
Saints

Episcopal Visitor
Rt Revd Sanford
Z K Hampton, *retd*

The Little Sisters of St. Clare is a dispersed women's community founded on the Franciscan mission to make our Lord known and loved. Our desire is to bring the contemplative spirituality of St. Clare out of the cloister and into our churches.

We seek to live a contemporary expression of the rule of St. Clare in the world with solitude of heart and reverence. We desire to live a simple and consecrated life. For us this means a life of prayer and of inner stillness in which to listen to God. We honor St. Clare who found God in all creation. We accept the challenge of praying the daily office and we are strengthened by its offering to the world.

Our formation program is original and designed from our experience living the Gospel. It provides a supportive study program, time for reflection and conversation about Christian topics and spiritual practices. Professed Sisters participate and lead our formation curriculum that is offered at the Chapter level to all members.

We strive always to be mindful of our vocation to contemplative life and intercessory prayer, carefully maintaining the challenging balance between secular and religious life.

SISTER DOROTHY-ANNE KIEST, LSSC
(Mother Guardian, assumed office October 2006)

LSSC Sisters:

Abbess Gloria-Mary Goller	*Companion LSSC:*
Founder (retd), PCLS	Tovi Andrews
Mary-Agnes Staples	*Novices:* 2
Mary-Louise Sulonen	
Marie-Elise Trailov	Mary-Olivia Stalter
Jeanne-Marie Williamson	Mary-Clare Van Blair
Kathryn-Mary Little	
DedraAnn Bracher	*Associates LSSC:* 15

Obituaries
6 Sep 2009   Sister Mary-Frances Yanagihara
                              aged 59, professed 7 years

Associates
We have various categories of membership: profession for *Sisters* with a rule of life that includes at least one monastic vow; a simple rule for *Companions* and an ecumenical rule for *Associates*.

Companions are welcomed as they take a service role working closely with the Sisters. Associate membership is a way to stay connected with the community intercessory prayer requests. Associates support the Sisters through prayer and alms as they are able. Companions and Associates may elect to participate in our Chapter formation program. This is an opportunity to spend time in prayer and learn about spiritual practices that are central to the Franciscan ethos and contemplative living. Inquiries may be made to Sr. Kathryn-Mary Little at *kathrynlittle@wavecable.com*.

Other Addresses
Tovi Andrews, Comp/LSSC *(Secretary)*
25732 Pioneer Way NW, Poulsbo, WA 98370, USA   *Tel: 360 779 2610*

Sister Mary-Louise Sulonen, LSSC *(Formation Director)*
16300 State Hwy 305 #32, Poulsbo, WA 98370, USA   *Tel: 360 779 3662*

Guest and Retreat Facilities
Call Mother Guardian 425 776 8182, spiritual direction and personal retreat ministry.

Most convenient time to telephone:
Pacific Time, USA : 9.00 am – 11.30 am, 2.00 pm – 4.00 pm

Community Book
We have self published a little book called *Holy Weavings – A Tapestry of Reflections* by The Little Sisters of Saint Clare. We offer this to others for a donation of $15 to cover our costs and shipping. Write: Secretary LSSC, P.O. Box 364, Poulsbo, WA 98370.

Order of the Community of the Paraclete

OCP

Founded 1971

PO Box 61399
Seattle
WA 98141
USA

The Community of the Paraclete is an apostolic community offering an authentic Religious life of prayer and service. We were recognized by the Episcopal Church in 1992. The Paracletians are self-supporting women and men, lay and ordained, who have committed themselves to live under the Paracletian Rule and constitution. Our vision: we are a network of Paracletian communities learning how to grow spiritually and exercising our gifts in ministry. Members are in the states of Arizona, Florida and Washington, USA; and in Tokyo, Japan. 2011 saw the 40th anniversary of the founding of the original Paracletian Community in Philadelphia, Pennsylvania, USA in 1971.

Friends, Associates and Companions
FRIEND: any baptized Christian, with the approval of chapter.
ASSOCIATE: confirmed Episcopalian, active member of an Episcopal parish, or church in communion with the Episcopal Church or the Episcopal See of Canterbury; six months' attendance at local chapter, and the approval of chapter.
COMPANION: Any person who is a benefactor of the Order.

Website
www.
theparacletians.org

Monthly gathering at
St George's Episcopal
Church,
2212 NE 125th Street,
Seattle, WA

Monthly gathering at
St Michael's Episcopal
Church,
Yakima, WA

Eucharist, meal, study
and fellowship, every
third Saturday
5.30 pm – 9.00 pm

BROTHER JOHN RYAN OCP
(Minister, assumed office June 2009)
Tel: 206 363 6773   Email: rjhbro@mac.com

BROTHER MARVIN TAYLOR OCP *(Vice-Minister)*

Brother Douglas Campbell
Sister Ann Case
Sister Susanne Chambers
Sister Suzanne Elizabeth Forbes
Brother Carle Griffin
Sister Barrie Gyllenswan
Sister Patricia Ann Harrison
Brother Timothy Nelson
Sister Martha Simpson

Novices: 1   Postulants: 1

Community Publication
Paracletian Presence, distributed free

Office Book: Book of Common Prayer

Bishop Visitor
Rt Revd Nedi Rivera, Bishop of Eastern Oregon

Some members of OCP

The Third Order, Society of Saint Francis

TSSF

The Third Order of the Society of Saint Francis consists of men and women, ordained and lay, married or single, who believe that God is calling them to live out their Franciscan vocation in the world, living in their own homes and doing their own jobs. Living under a rule of life, with the help of a spiritual director, members (called Tertiaries) encourage one another in living and witnessing to Christ. The Third Order is worldwide, with a Minister General and five Ministers Provincial to cover the relevant Provinces.

THE REVEREND DOROTHY BROOKER TSSF
(Minister General, assumed office September 2005)
16 Downing Avenue, Pirimai, Napier,
AOTEOROA-NEW ZEALAND
Tel: 6 843 6779   Emails: dmbrook@clear.co.nz
or   *dorothy.brooker@gmail.com*

KEN NORIAN TSSF
(Assistant Minister General)
45 Malone Street, Hicksville, NY 11801, USA
Tel: +1 917 416 9579   Email: ken@tssf.org

Founded:

1920s
Americas

1930s
Europe

1975
Africa

1959
Australia with
East Asia & PNG

1962
Aoteoroa-New Zealand
with Melanesia

Statistics for the whole community

	Professed	*Novices*
Americas	439	46
Europe	1802	179
Australia & E Asia	238	36
PNG	58	30
Africa	94	23
NZ-Aoteoroa	94	9
Melanesia	78	46
Total	**2803**	**369**

Total Professed & Novices: 3172

Bishop Protector General
The Most Reverend Roger Herft, Archbishop of Perth, Western Australia

Office Book
Third Order Manual
The Manual includes a form of daily prayer called 'The Community Obedience'. Members are encouraged to use this in the context of Morning or Evening Prayer.

PROVINCE OF THE AMERICAS

KENNETH E NORIAN TSSF *(Minister Provincial)*
45 Malone Street, Hicksville, NY 11801, USA
Tel: +1 917 416 9579   Email: ken@tssf.org

Website of Province: www.tssf.org

Statistics of Province
Professed: 439; *Novices:* 46; *Postulants:* 46

Associates of the Society of Saint Francis
Welcomes men and women, lay or clergy, single or in committed relationships, young and old, to join us as Associates in our diverse Franciscan family.

Deaths since last Year Book
24 Aug 2009	Jaime Bedoya, professed 8 years
1 Oct 2009	Katherine Palmer, professed 26 years
3 Oct 2009	Elizabeth Greiner Luce, professed 19 years
4 Dec 2009	Harold Macdonald, professed 18 years
16 Jan 2010	Lindsay Warren, professed 20 years
9 Mar 2010	Heber Peacock, professed 23 years
28 May 2010	Kermit Bailey, professed 15 years
9 Oct 2010	Emmett Jarrett, professed 11 years

Provincial Publication
The Franciscan Times. Available online at www.tssf.org/archives.shtml

Bishop Protector: Rt Revd Gordon P Scruton, Bishop of Western Massachusetts

PROVINCE OF EUROPE

THE REVD JOANNA CONEY TSSF *(Minister Provincial)*
4 Rowland Close, Lower Wolvercote, Oxford OX2 8PW, UK
Tel: +44 1865 556456   Email: ministertssf@franciscans.org.uk

Administrator: HOWARD MCFADYEN, Les Standous, La Fontade 46300,
Gourdon, FRANCE   *Email: howard.mcfadyen934@orange.fr*

Website of Province: www.tssf.org.uk

Statistics of Province: Professed: 1802; *Novices:* 179

RIPs for In Memoriam at 2010 October Chapter
Joan Ashton *(Somerset)*; Nigel Barrett *(Guildford)*; Michael Foster *(Sussex)*; Howard Gribble *(Cornwall)*; Audrey Hall *(Essex)*; Kate Holford *(Kent W.)*; Sylvia James *(Mersey Valley)*; Douglas Mack *(Scotland)*; Michael Ward *(Wessex)*; Doris Wright *(Devon)*; Daphne Callender *(E. Anglia)*; Thelma Frost *(Cambridge)*; Jacqueline Line *(Wessex)*; Tom Strodder *(E. Anglia)*; David Datson *(Wyevern)*; Penelope Eckersley *(London W.)*; Hilda Hartshorn *(Northampton)*; Lorna Macpherson *(Cornwall)*; Vi Ruddick *(Guildford)*; Anne Thorpe *(E. Anglia)*; Hazel Wallis *(Sussex)*; Wendy Bromfield *(Beds & Herts)*; Peter Durnford *(Cornwall)*; Alice Favell *(Wyevern)*; Joyce Jagger *(Yorks W. & Skipton)*; John Joughin *(Newcastle)*; Richard Bird *(E. Anglia)*; Bett Cotterell *(London*

W.); Mary Johnson *(Oxford)*; Elizabeth Prior *(Cornwall)*; Joy Reed *(Sussex)*; Mary Woodward *(Northampton)*; Maureen Wookey *(Berkshire)*; John Hill *(Solent)*; Barbara Steiner *(Cambridge)*; Eileen Bird *(Yorks W. & Skipton)*; Diana Button *(Somerset)*; Michael Foster *(Somerset)*; Betty Latham *(London E. & Essex S.)*; Rita Martin *(London E. & Essex S.)*; Brenda McKenzie *(Solent)*; Jean Broome *(Midlands W.)*; Donald Penhaligon *(Cornwall)*; Joyce-Mary Sandles *(Canterbury)*

Provincial Publication
The Chronicle (twice yearly) & Third Order News (three times a year) – both available on our website. Contact: Communications Officer, Brian Berry, Birch Knoll, Mulberry Close, Crowthorne, Berkshire RG45 7 LG   *Email: brianberry43@aol.com*

Bishop Protector: Rt Revd Michael Perham, Bishop of Gloucester

PROVINCE OF AUSTRALIA, PAPUA NEW GUINEA AND EAST ASIA

REVD TED WITHAM TSSF *(Minister Provincial)*
139 / 502 Bussell Hwy, Broadwater, Western Australia 6280
Tel: +61 (0)8 9701 9430   Email: provincial.minister@tssf.org.au
Website of Province: www.tssf.org.au

Statistics of Province:

Australia & East Asia	*Professed:* 238	*Novices:* 36
Papua New Guinea	*Professed:* 58	*Novices:* 30

Deaths since last Year Book

18 Sep 2009	Janet Ferris	1 Dec 2009	Margaret Butterss
24 Jun 2010	Anne Robinson	23 Sep 2010	Jeanne Norris
1 Dec 2010	Noel Hanby		

Associates: From 2010, Regions in the Australian Province can invite people who wish to support the Third Order or who have an interest in Franciscan spirituality to be Associates of the Third Order. Details from the Regional Minister.

Provincial Publication: *Quarterly Newsletter* – available on request from the Provincial Secretary, David White TSSF, or from the website www.tssf.org.au/ Newsletter/   *Email: provincial.secretary@tssf.org.au*

Community History: Denis Woodbridge TSSF, *Franciscan Gold: A history of the Third Order of the Society of St Francis in the Province of Australia, Papua New Guinea and East Asia : Our first fifty years: 1959–2009.* Available from the Provincial Secretary.

Bishop Protector: The Most Reverend Roger Herft, Archbishop of Perth

PROVINCE OF AFRICA

REVD NOLAN TOBIAS TSSF *(Minister Provincial)*
PO Box 285, Simon's Town, SOUTH AFRICA
Tel: +2721 786 3564 & +82 749 6749 (mobile)   Fax: +2721 786 3564
Email: nolantobias@mweb.co.za
Website: www.tssf.org.za

Statistics of Province

	Professed	Novices
Central Region	14	0
Northern Region	24	18
Southern Region	49	1
Western Region	7	4
TOTAL	**94**	**23**

Bishop Protector: Rt Revd Merwyn Castle, Bishop of False Bay

Associates
The African Province includes a small number of Companions who are associated with, and pray for, the First Order, but are in the Third Order address list. The Secretary of the Companions is:
Mrs Joyce Gunston, Frail Care, Vonkehouse, Lourensford Road, Somerset West 7130, SOUTH AFRICA   *Tel: 021 21 852 1830*

Provincial Publication
Pax et Bonum (published three times a year). Available free of charge from the Provincial Publications Officer: Alan Rogers TSSF   *Email: AlanR@mcgind.co.za*
or the Newsletter Editor: Revd Canon Roy Snyman TSSF *Email: fr.roy@telskonsa.net*

PROVINCE OF AOTEAROA-NEW ZEALAND AND POLYNESIA WITH MELANESIA

REVD JOHN HEBENTON TSSF *(Minister Provincial)*
15 Farm Street, Mt. Maunganui, NEW ZEALAND
Tel: 07 575 9930 (home); 021 679202 (mobile)
Email: aynf.tp@clear.net.nz   or   jbheb@clear.net.nz

Website of Province: www.franciscanthirdorder.godzone.net.nz

Statistics of Province

	Professed	Novices
New Zealand	94	9
Melanesia	78	46
TOTAL	**172**	**55**

Provincial Publication: *TAU* Available from the Provincial Secretary: Terry Molloy
Email: tharmolloy@xtra.co.nz

Community History
Booklets by Chris Barfoot:
Beginnings of the Third Order in New Zealand 1956–74
Peace and Joy : Part 2 of the History of the Third Order, Society of St Francis in New Zealand

Bishops Protector
Rt Revd Philip Richardson, Bishop of Tarankai
Rt Revd Richard Naramana, Bishop of Ysabel *(for Melanesia)*

The Worker Sisters and Brothers of the Holy Spirit

WSHS & WBHS

Founded 1972 (Sisters)
& 1979 (Brothers)

Contact addressES:
Sr Deborah WSHS
(Canadian Director) 22
Elkorn Dr.
Suite 352
North York, ON
CANADA
M2K 1J4
Tel: 647 965 3196
Email: strdeborah
@hotmail.com

Sr Christine WSHS,
(American Director)
528 First St
Windsor
CO 80550
USA
Tel: 970 686 7135
Email: casturges
@msm.com

Website: www.
workersisters.org
& www.
workerbrothers.org

The Worker Sisters and Brothers of the Holy Spirit is a Covenant Community which seeks to respond to God's call through the power of the Holy Spirit, participate in Jesus Christ's vision of unity, become his holy people, show forth Fruit, and in obedience to his command, go forth into the world. It offers women and men, regardless of marital status, a path for individual spiritual growth through a life commitment to a Rule which provides an opportunity to experience prayer, worship, becoming, discovery, belonging, relating, commitment and mission. Membership is made up of:

First Order: Sisters – Lay Workers and Lay Sisters;
Second Order: Brothers – Lay Workers and Lay Brothers;
Third Order: Clergy Sisters and Clergy Brothers;
Companions: Lay and Clergy Persons;
Friends: Lay and Clergy Persons

The first three Orders are bound together under a Life Commitment to a common Rule which is Benedictine in orientation. Members do not live together, yet are not separated by geographical boundaries.

SISTER DEBORAH WSHS *(Canadian Director)*
SISTER CHRISTINE WSHS *(American Director)*
(Co-Directors, assumed office April 2010)

Members: 140
Novices: 3 *Postulants:* 3

Obituaries
1 Mar 2010   Sister Barbara Joan WSHS, professed 21 years
9 Mar 2010   Brother Robert Alban WBHS,
                         professed 24 years
18 Mar 2010   Sister Virgie Ruth WSHS, professed 34 years

Companions and Friends
COMPANIONS make a Life commitment to a Rule of Life. FRIENDS share in the prayer and spiritual journey of the community.

Other Address
Sister Kathleen Rachel WSHS, Director of Admissions, 2601 Sungold Dr, Las Vegas, NV 891134, USA

Office Book: Book of Common Prayer

Community Ecclesiastical Visitors
CANADA: Rt Revd Philip Poole, Friend WSHS/ WBHS,
                   Diocese of Toronto
USA: Rt Revd Barry Howe, Friend WSHS/ WBHS,
                   Diocese of West Missouri, *(retired)*

St Joseph's Retreat House and the Monos Centre

We provide Workshops, Retreats and Study Breaks in Christian Spirituality and New / Lay Monasticism

St Joseph's is the home of the 'Little Community of John & Mary' and Monos, 'A Centre for the Study of Monastic Spirituality and Culture'; set in the beautiful surroundings of the ancient Charnwood Forest and situated just a short walk from Mount St. Bernard's Abbey, Leicestershire. We offer opportunities for retreat or time out, home cooked food and the chance to join in with the life of the community; follow a simple office which is said 3 times a day, morning prayer 9.30am midday prayer around 12.15pm and evening prayer 7.30pm, or you have the opportunity to attend the monastic office at the monastery.

Our set workshops are run both at St Joseph's and the Abbey and include:

- The Spirituality of Work
- Monastic Tools for Everyday Christian Living
- Pilgrimage as Life, Including Making Your Own Coracle
- Franciscan Spirituality
- Desert Spirituality, Including Making Your Own Basket

For further details please contact us below:

**St Joseph's, Abbey Road, Oaks in Charnwood, Coalville, Leicestershire, LE67 4UA
Tel: 01509 506656
email: ant@monos.org.uk
web: www.monos.org.uk**

Some other communities

This section includes communities, either monastic or acknowledged, that whilst not Anglican in ecclesiastical allegiance are in communion with Anglicans.

There is also a community in the USA, inter-denominational in its origins, which includes Lutherans as well as Anglicans, as the ELCA is now in full communion with the Episcopal Church.

172

Mar Thoma Syrian Church

Mar Thoma Dayaraya

Founded 1996

Plachery PO
(Kalayanad)
Punalur 691 331
Kerala, INDIA
Tel: 04742222282
Email: rev.alexa@
gmail.com

**Night Prayer
& Morning Prayer**
5.00 am
3rd Hour 9.00 am
6th Hour 12 noon
9th Hour 3.00 pm
Evening Prayer
6.00 pm
Night Prayer 9.00 pm

This is one of four monastic communities of the Mar Thoma Syrian Church (a Church in Full Communion). It is a part of a monastic movement that goes alongside the better-known Ashram movement. There are six brothers and their monastery is in the hill ranges of Kerala. They live on a rubber plantation donated to the church by Captain Thomas Alexander in 1929 to run an orphanage of 30 boys now managed by the brothers.Their life is one of contemplative prayer and witness to those around by service in the orphanage and outreach in mission parishes in the local villages. They also take in ordinands and aspirants for ordination for experience of the life of prayer.

FATHER ALEXANDER ABRAHAM
Acharya (Abbot)

Brother Isaac Matthew   Brother Reji Kuriakose
Father P Philip   Brother Anish Thomas
Brother Sanil Alexander

Office Book
The Community uses a reformed version of the Shimtho in Malayalam.

Guest facilities: There is a guesthouse with five rooms as well as facilities for larger groups for a day.

MAR THOMA SANYASINI SAMAOHAM
Elanthor P.O., Pathanamthitta District, INDIA   *Tel: 0468 2361972*
Sister P.T. Mariamma *(Superior)*

CHRISTA PANTHI ASHRAM
Darsani P.O., Sihora – 483 225, INDIA   *Tel: 07624 260260*
Christa Panthi Ashram, Sihora, was established in 1942 under the leadership of Revd K T Thomas, Mr John Varghese and Mr M P Mathew, who both later became ordained. Today there are more than forty members, including permanent workers and volunteers. In addition to Gospel work, the activities of the Ashram include hospital work, village schools, a home for the destitute, agricultural work and a rural development programme.
Revd James Idiculla *(Acharya)*

CHRISTA MITRA ASHRAM
P.B. No. 3, Ankola P.O., North Kanara, Karnataka – 531 314, INDIA
Tel: 08388 230392, 230287 (0)
Started in 1940, this is one of the Ashrams of the Mar Thoma Evangelistic Association.

CHRISTU DASA ASHRAM
Olive Mount P.O., Palakkad – 678 702, INDIA   *Tel: 0492 272974*
Started in 1928 as an Ashram with celibate members, it is located in the north-eastern part of Kerala near the Tamil Nadu border.

Miss Mariyamma Thomas *(Superior)*

SANTHIGIRI ASHRAM
11/488, Edathala North, Aluva, Kerala – 683 564, INDIA   *Tel: 0484 2639014, 2839240*
Email: santhigiriasram@yahoo.co.uk   Website: www.santhigiri.in/index.html
This is a holistic healing and meditation centre.

SUVARTHA PREMI SAMITHI
Munsiari, Ranthi P.O., Pithorragarh, Uttar Pradesh, INDIA
Revd A K George and two lady workers went to Tejam and Munsiari on the border of Tibet and started work among the Bothi community. The Bhotias used to trade with Tibet until the 1949 invasion by China. The missionaries hoped to reach Tibet with the help of the Bhotias. Some from the Bhotia community accepted the Gospel and congregations have been founded at Munsiari and Tejam. At present, two groups are working here.

ECLA Lutherans in the USA

CONGREGATION OF THE SERVANTS OF CHRIST   Founded 1958
St Augustine's House, 3316 Drahner Road, Oxford, Missouri 48371, USA
PO Box 125, Oxford, Missouri 48371, USA   *Tel: 248 628 5155*
Website: www.staugustineshouse.org

Communities in Churches who have signed the Porvoo agreement

Porvoo created a community of Churches, the members of which have signed an agreement to "share a common life in mission and service". Anglicans in the British Isles and Iberia are currently members, with Lutherans from Denmark, Estonia, Finland, Iceland, Lithuania, Norway and Sweden.

ÖSTANBÄCK MONASTERY   Founded 1970, Benedictine monks
733 96 Sala, SWEDEN   *Tel: 0224 25088*   *Email: caesarius@swipnet.se*

HELGEANDSSYSTRARNA   Founded 1954, Benedictine sisters
Alsike Monastery, 741 92 Knivsta, SWEDEN   *Tel: 018 383002*
Email: alsikkloster@tele2.se

HELIGE FRANCISKUS SYSTRASKAP   Franciscan sisters
Clara Valley Monastery, Lindvägen 22, 443 45 Sjövik, SWEDEN   *Tel: 0302 43260*

Brothers of Saint John the Evangelist (OSB)

EFSJ

Founded 1972

1787 Scenic Avenue
Freeland
WA 98249
USA
Tel: 360 320 1186
Email:
efsj@whidbey.com

Website
www.
brothersofsaintjohn
.org

Morning Prayer
8.45 am

Noonday Prayer
12 noon

Vespers   5.30 pm

Office book
Book of Common
Prayer

Bishop Visitor
Rt Revd
Sanford Z K Hampton,
Diocese of Olympia

The community strives to promote interest, study and understanding of the vocation to the Religious life, and to sustain a Religious community on South Whidbey Island, WA. This monastic community is guided by the venerable *Rule of St Benedict*.

The Ecumenical Fellowship of Saint John was founded in Los Angeles in the spring of 1972 by five men – clergy and lay – from the Episcopal, Lutheran and Roman Catholic Communions of the Church. On Saint John's Day 1973, four of the founding group (two Lutherans and two Roman Catholics) made Promises of Commitment at Saint John's Episcopal Church in Los Angeles. After some years in Fallbrook, San Diego County, the Community moved to Whidbey Island in 1990. In 2000, we were blessed with the gift of ten acres of secluded and wooded acres, donated by Judith P Yeakel of Langley. Here the monastic house was built, and blessed on Holy Cross Day 2003. The 'Called to Common Mission' declaration of ELCA and TEC made it easy for Lutherans and Episcopalians to become one.

We were officially recognised as a canonical Religious community at the Diocesan Convention 2010.

BROTHER RICHARD TUSSEY EFSJ
(Superior, assumed office December 1973)
BROTHER DAVID MCCLELLAN EFSJ *(Prior)*

Sister Julian of Norwich DiBase
Brother Aidan Shirbroun
Brother Thomas Langler
Sister Frideswide Dorman

Novices: 3

Associates: We currently have three Associates.

Community Publication
BENEDICITE. Contact us via email or post; no charge other than freewill offering. It will also be available via email and as part of our website.

Community Wares: "Tanglewood Treats": jam, pecan pie, etc. (Tanglewood is the name of our monastery.)

Guest and Retreat Facilities: No overnight guests at present. We do have a building fund.

Most convenient time to telephone
10 am – 12 noon, 2 pm – 3 pm

Obituaries

Archbishop Rowan of Canterbury preaching in the new chapel at Mucknell Abbey during his visit on 25 March 2011, when he blessed the new Benedictine monastery.

Sister Clare CCK
(1911–2009)

Many people found Sister Clare a very special person. Brother Andrew, co-founder of the MBC with Mother Teresa, thought Sister Clare the epitome of holiness. When she was told this, she said she did not know what he meant. The most holy always see themselves as the greatest sinners.

Sister Clare was born Agnes Constance (Connie) Eime on 7 April 1911, the third of seven children, in a devout family, who were also generous in their hospitality to others in their home at Lameroo. Apart from her family, she was encouraged by Deaconess Mabel Walker, who helped her reach an early goal of being a Sunday School teacher. She later trained as a nurse and offered herself for missionary service. She was sent to Forrest River in NW Australia, where she shared her nursing skills and her faith with aboriginal girls there. After two years, she went to test her vocation with the Community of the Holy Name in Melbourne.

Agnes Constance was professed on 21 April 1949, taking the name Clare. In 1951, she was one of the first three Sisters sent to Dogura to work among Papua girls.

In 1975, she joined a group of CHN sisters who became enclosed so as to lead a life of prayer, and later answered a call to the solitary life. The Enclosed Sisters of CHN eventually evolved in the 1990s into the independent Community of Christ the King.

One of the secrets of Sister Clare's serenity – so attractive to others – was her use of the Jesus Prayer. It helped her to reflect from within the life of Christ, so it shone for others clearly, and therefore in her presence others found themselves drawn into that life.

Sister Clare died on 13 March 2009, a few weeks short of both her 98th birthday and her Diamond Jubilee of Profession.

Sister Mary-Frances LSSC
(1939–2009)

Sister Mary-Frances was born Frances Jo Masaki in Honolulu on October 21, 1939. Jo taught school in Hawaii, was married to Galen Yanagihara and had three children. In 1995, she and her husband moved to their retirement home on the Olympic Peninsula, in Washington State. She called their home in the woods, "a little piece of heaven".

She was a member of St. Luke's Episcopal Church in Sequim, serving on the altar guild and on the intercessory prayer team. God had more plans for Jo, leading her in 2001 to join The Little Sisters of St. Clare, a new Franciscan community, as a founding member. She took the name of Mary-Frances. She had great joy in her quiet life of simplicity and solitude.

She was strengthened by the rich gift of the community prayers and shared in the contemplative prayer work for the church and the world, as she fought cancer courageously. She said, "I try to keep my life simple. The Lord helps me in this regard. He is my guide through all my difficulties. He makes my burdens light. He slows my pace and brings peace to my days, by simply following his lead; he shows me the joy of living for him". She said she trusted "(Jesus) with every cell and fiber in my body, I trust him with my very soul ... He has always led me to the highest mountain and to joy".

She died on September 6, 2009. Her disciplined life of prayer and study resulted in encouragement and hope for the community. Memorial gifts helped the community to publish a book of reflections, poems and prayers called *Holy Weavings*. We treasure her words and pray to trust Jesus as she did.

Sister Winifred Mary CAH (1919–2009)

Sister Winifred Mary was born in 1919 into a devout Anglo-Catholic family. She became a teacher of children with special needs, first with the blind and then in a hospital in Birmingham. Trying her vocation in the Religious life was a thought for many years, but she felt a responsibility for her widowed mother. In the end, she put on a kind of celestial bet: "Lord, if I reach 50 before my mother dies, it won't be the right thing to do." Her mother died when she was 49. As she put it herself, it felt that "... God was calling me into the Religious life and that nothing else would satisfy me. That was what I was called to do and I never doubted it once."

She tried her vocation at Tymawr and then Edgware, but finally came to the Community of All Hallows, where her older sister Florence was already a professed member. After a few years in the school, Mother Mary asked her to begin work at Blundeston prison. It was the beginning of a remarkable ministry of twenty-six years, and then beyond through her continued correspondence with ex-prisoners and their families, sustained until very near the end of her life. This ministry is movingly recounted in her memoir: *The Men in my Life: a nun's story*.

Sister Winifred Mary did not feel that Jesus sent her to work at the prison, more that Jesus was present among the prisoners, a belief she held without sentimentality or illusion. It wasn't easy for her. There was a hidden cost. She said, "I found it very difficult at first, very difficult indeed. You see I was listening to things I never knew about, some terrible things, but somehow I got used to it because it was all normal to the men." She felt sustained by her Sisters' prayers, which she recalled helped her to go on. She would receive two awards for her prison work: the Butler award and an MBE. But her own reward was the lives she helped transform and the gratitude of the many who were moved by her acceptance without judgement and wisdom without condemnation. As she put it herself, "I loved my prisoners."

One characteristic of her presence was her humour, a childlike sense of fun. She loved telling jokes, and many will remember the twinkle in her eyes and the little chuckle as she reached the punch line. Her humour was undergirded by a deep contentment and thanksgiving. She had a profound trust in the Lord's providence, a deep knowledge of being held in love. It coloured everything she did: her work, her poetry, her household jobs, her skilled gardening.

She died on 11 November 2009 aged 90. The inscription on her Butler award could well sum up her life: "For ordinary work, extraordinarily well done."

Brother Edward SSF (1921–2010)

Brother Edward SSF, who died on the 25th February 2010 at the age of 88, was the second son of the Rt Hon Hastings and Mrs Eleanor Lees-Smith. His father represented Keighley in Parliament as a member of the Independent Labour Party, but despite the leftward leaning politics of the family, Christopher (Edward) grew up within a definitely upper-class milieu. He always claimed that he had been sent to an inner-city school – it just happened to be Westminster public school! While whole-heartedly committed to a life of poverty as a friar and to social justice in his work with and for others, he never lost touch with his roots and took delight in dropping the occasional name of a peer or politician with whom his family was connected.

Leaving the army at the end of the war with the rank of colonel, he graduated in history at Corpus Christi College, Oxford in 1949, was ordained deacon in 1950 and served in the great northern training parish of St Luke's, Pallion in Sunderland under Canon Gordon Hopkins. Like a number of other young priests who were committed to an incarnational pattern of ministry central to the Prayer Book Catholic tradition of the Church of England at the time, he went on to give his life to God not in parish ministry but within the Society of St Francis, which he joined in 1954 at Hilfield Friary in Dorset. He moved north in 1961 to help found Alnmouth Friary, becoming its Guardian in 1965. There he welcomed guests, led missions, organised camps, commandeered whoever was available to gather coal from the beach, and urged a Franciscan vocation on every young man who crossed the threshold: life in a parish on one's own outside SSF would most likely lead to 'drink, drugs, women or worse' as one young curate coming for retreat was warned.

The same energy served well when he left Alnmouth in 1974 to become Chaplain to the SSF Third Order. Edward interpreted the role as one of 'travelling salesman' for the Tertiaries as he zig-zagged across the UK in his blue Volkswagen Beetle, visiting parishes, encouraging local groups and recruiting new members. The poet Dante, Thomas More, the Cure d'Ars, Lech Walensa and Pope John Paul II were all roped in as famous members of the Third Order. 'Whenever there's been renewal in the Church or in Society Franciscan tertiaries have been at the heart of it'. SSF Third Order membership soared! His church history lectures

to First Order novices were no less enthusiastic, employing vivid colours and broad brush strokes rather than a fine pen. Edward's history may not have been entirely accurate, but it was memorable and fun. In recognition of his work for the Third Order and in nurturing vocations in the Church he was awarded the Cross of St Augustine in 1999 by Archbishop George Carey.

'Retirement' back to Alnmouth involved a gradual slowing down but the essentials remained: no more coaling expeditions, but guests to be encouraged, the village to be visited and the Friary and SSF to be campaigned for. He thoroughly enjoyed someone's 60th birthday party the evening before he died. Edward was a much loved brother, a humble friar and a true fool for Christ in the tradition of St Francis himself.

Father Gregory CSWG (1930–2009)

Father Colin CSWG writes:

I'd just like to thank you,' said Father Gregory, 'because in coming here I have been able to continue with my monastic life, which I came from New Zealand to do.' In its context, this was an astonishing remark. The ward sister, the physiotherapist, the occupational therapist, the palliative care registrar and I were sat around his bed in the orthopaedic ward of the hospital, having just had a conference to decide on his future care. It was May 2008. The cancer from his prostate had got into his bones and though some treatment had delayed its development, there was now no stopping it. He had fallen and broken his hip but the bones were beyond the usual method of repair. Six weeks in a busy orthopaedic ward would be a culture shock for anyone, especially a monk from an enclosed community, but he used it as an opportunity. 'I've got my Bible and my prayer rope, I don't need anything else,' he said. So he continued that steady offering of his life, praying for all around him,

being peaceful, patient and thankful. 'It's been wonderful to have him here,' the
ward sister said to me.

Born on 28 November 1930, Father Gregory was brought up on a farm in New
Zealand, had a scientific education and was ordained in Auckland in 1957. He came
to Crawley Down in 1960 to pursue the call to monastic life. On making his Life
Vows in 1973 he became the Superior and remained so until 2008. The inner work
of conversion of life and growth in dependence on the Holy Spirit went on all his
life and bore fruit in the loving, patient and joyful person that he was. He read
widely, especially patristic and Orthodox theology and the writings of St John of the
Cross and St Teresa of Avila. Father Gilbert Shaw, then Warden of the Sisters of the
Love of God, became his spiritual father and Father Gregory subsequently became
an exponent of the teaching of Father Gilbert. He wrote homilies, conferences and
booklets, produced the Community's Rule and developed its liturgy. He was the
spiritual father to the Community, providing guidance and direction and acting as
confessor to many who came to him, as well as to Religious and those living the
solitary life.

During his time as Superior, much work
was done on the property, especially
clearing back trees from the buildings and
developing the small farm with cows, hens,
vegetables and fruit. After a fire destroyed
the Community House in 1980, a new one
was built, as well as guest accommodation.
Since then three hermitages have been built
and a convent for the Sisters. In the midst of
all this he happily took his turn in brushing
floors or washing dishes.

He began to be ill in the middle of 2006 and
though there were periods of improvement,
he declined slowly until he died on 12
August 2009. Sometimes he struggled to
accept what was happening but overall
his faith and trust in the providence of
God shone through. After he was finally
anointed, a remarkable peace and gratitude
enfolded him and ten days later he gently stopped breathing.

We have a sentence in our Rule: *The enclosure should become a still centre in the heart
of the world, where the Community is always waiting on God, and invoking his Holy Spirit,
so as to embrace the whole world in its life of prayer and obedience to his will.* It occurred
to me after Father Gregory's death that his life's work had been to co-operate with
God in becoming a still centre himself – waiting on God, invoking the Holy Spirit,
embracing the world in his prayer and obedience.

Another sentence from the Rule sums him up: *If you want peace with God, be content
with what you have, and cease from wanting circumstances to be different.*

Organizations

The new home in the cathedral close at Salisbury of the Benedictines monks formerly at Elmore Abbey.

AUSTRALIA

Advisory Council for Anglican Religious Life in Australia
The Council consists of:

Rt Revd Godfrey Fryar, Bishop of North Queensland *(chair)*
Ms Ann Skamp, Diocese of Grafton, *(Secretary)* Email: *annskamp@aapt.net.au*
Rt Revd Keith Slater, Bishop of Grafton
Revd Michael Jobling, Diocese of Melbourne

Brother Robin BSB	Sr Carol Francis CHN	Sister Patricia SI
Mother Rita Mary CCK	Brother Wayne LBF	Sister Eunice SSA
Sister Sandra CSBC	Father Robert OGS	Br Alfred Boonkong SSF
Sister Linda Mary CSC	Abbot Michael King OSB	Father Christopher SSM

Members from New Zealand:
Mother Keleni CSN   Sister Anne SLG
Most Revd David Moxon, Bishop of Waikato *(liaison bishop)*
Observers:
Sister Jill Harding fcs *(for Catholic Religious Australia)*
Brother Graeme Littleton CT *(Community of the Transfiguration [Baptist])*
Revd Dr Helen Granowski TSSF *(Third Order Society of St Francis)*

EUROPE

Advisory Council on the Relations of Bishops & Religious Communities (commonly called 'The Advisory Council')

Rt Revd David Walker, Bishop of Dudley *(Acting Chair)*
Rt Revd John Pritchard, Bishop of Oxford
Rt Revd Humphrey Southern, Bishop of Repton
Rt Revd Anthony Robinson, Bishop of Pontefract
Rt Revd Dominic Walker OGS, Bishop of Monmouth *(co-opted)*

Communities' elected representatives (elected December 2010 for five-year term):

Sister Anita Cook CSC	Sister Mary Julian CHC
Father Colin Griffiths CSWG	Sister Mary Stephen Packwood OSB
Brother Damian SSF	Sister Rosemary Howarth CHN
Sister Elizabeth Pio SSB	Abbot Stuart Burns OSB
Sister Joyce Yarrow CSF	Mother Winsome CSMV

Co-opted: Father Peter Allan CR
Revd Canon Chris Neal *(Director of Mission & Community CMS)*
Revd Ian Mobsby *(Moot Community and representing new and emerging communities)*

ARC representative: Dom Simon Jarrett OSB
Conference of Religious Observer: Sister Kate McGovern OSF
Hon. Secretary: Father Colin Griffiths CSWG   Email: *father.colin@cswg.org.uk*

Conference of the Leaders of Anglican Religious Communities (CLARC)

The Conference meets in full once a year.

Steering Committee 2011

Father Colin CSWG
Sister Cynthia Clare SSM
Sister Dorothy Stella OHP

Sister Elizabeth CAH
Sister Monica CHN
Brother Stuart OSB

General Synod of the Church of England

Representatives of Lay Religious

Sister Anita OHP — (Elected 2006, re-elected 2010)
Brother Thomas Quin OSB — (Elected 2010)

Representatives of Ordained Religious

Revd Sister Rosemary CHN — (Elected 2002, re-elected 2005 & 2010)
Revd Thomas Seville CR — (Elected 2005, re-elected 2010)

Anglican Religious Communities in England (ARC)

ARC supports members of Religious communities of the Church of England. Its membership is the entire body of professed members of communities recognised by the Advisory Council *(see above)*. ARC holds an Annual Conference when members can come together both to hear speakers on topics relevant to their way of life and to meet and share experiences together. A news sheet is regularly circulated to all houses and ARC represents Anglican Religious life on various bodies, including the Vocations Forum of the Ministry Division of the C of E, The Advisory Council and the *Year Book* editorial committee. Some limited support is also given to groups of common interest within ARC who may wish to meet. Its activities are co-ordinated by a committee with members elected from Leaders, Novice Guardians, General Synod representatives and the professed membership. The committee normally meets three times a year.

Prior Simon OSB & Sister Susan Hird CSC
(representing Leaders)
Father Thomas Seville CR *(representing General Synod Representatives)*
vacancy (representing Novice Guardians)
Sister Anne CSJB, Sister Hilda Mary CSC, Sister Jean Margaret ASSP
& Sister Mary John OSB *(representing professed members)*
Sister Christine James CSF *(Administrative Secretary)*

More information about Anglican Religious Life (in England) or about ARC itself, may be obtained from: The Anglican Religious Communities Secretary, c/o Mr Jonathan Neil-Smith, Church House, Great Smith Street, London SW1P 3AZ
Email: info@arcie.org.uk   Website: www.thekingdomisyours.org.uk

NORTH AMERICA

Conference of Anglican Religious Orders in the Americas (CAROA)

The purpose of CAROA is to provide opportunities for mutual support and sharing among its member communities and co-ordinate their common interests and activities, to engage in dialogue with other groups, to present a coherent understanding of the Religious Life to the Church and to speak as an advocate for the Religious Orders to the Church. CAROA is incorporated as a non-profit organization in both Canada and the USA.

Brother Jude Hill SSF (*President*)
Father David Bryan Hoopes OHC (*Vice-President*)
Sister Elizabeth Ann Eckert SSJD (*Secretary-Treasurer*)

The Revd Dr Donald Anderson (*General Secretary*)
PO Box 99, Little Britain, Ontario K0M 2C0, CANADA
Tel: 705 786 3330   Email: dwa@nexicom.net

House of Bishops Standing Committee on Religious Orders in the Anglican Church of Canada

The Committee usually meets twice a year, during the House of Bishops' meeting. Its rôle is consultative and supportive.

Rt Revd James A J Cowan, Bishop of British Columbia *(chair)*
Most Revd Fred J Hiltz, Archbishop & Primate of Canada
Rt Revd George Elliot, Suffragan Bishop of York-Simcoe, Diocese of Toronto
Rt Revd Linda Nicholls, Suffragan Bishop of Trent-Durham, Diocese of Toronto
The Superiors of CSC, OHC, SSJD & SSJE
Revd Dr Donald W Anderson, General Secretary of CAROA
The Ven Paul Feheley, Principal Secretary to the Primate *(Secretary)*

General Synod of the Anglican Church of Canada

Religious Synod members:
Sister Elizabeth Ann Eckert SSJD
A second member to be appointed

National Association for Episcopal Christian Communities (NAECC)

The NAECC is an inclusive association that shares and communicates the fruits of the Gospel, realized in community, with the church and the world. It is primarily a forum for those who are living or exploring new or continuing models of religious commitment within the context of community.

Brother Bill Farra SCC *(Convenor)*
Brother Ken Murphy OP *(Recorder)*
Brother James Mahoney BSG *(Treasurer)*

Website: home.earthlink.net/~naecc/index.htm

Ecumenical & Inter-denominational

Conference of Religious (CoR)

The Conference of Religious is open to all Roman Catholic Provincial leaders of Religious Congregations in England and Wales. The leaders of Anglican communities may be Associate members, which, apart from voting rights, means they receive all the same benefits and information as the Roman Catholic leaders. CoR is run by an executive committee, elected from its members, which meets every two months. It deals with matters affecting men and women Religious, and various matters of interest to them. There is particular emphasis on peace and justice issues.

CoR Secretariat, P.O. Box 37602, The Ridgeway, London NW7 4XG
Tel: 020 8201 1861   Fax: 020 8201 1988   Email: confrelig@aol.com

Glossary
and
Indices

The chapel at the new CSF house in Metheringham, Lincolnshire, UK

Glossary

Aspirant
A person who hopes to become a Religious and has been in touch with a particular community, but has not yet begun to live with them.

Celibacy
The commitment to remain unmarried and to refrain from sexual relationships. It is part of the vow of chastity traditionally taken by Religious. Chastity is a commitment to sexual integrity, a term applicable to fidelity in marriage as well as to celibacy in Religious Life.

Chapter
The council or meeting of Religious to deliberate and make decisions about the community. In some orders, this may consist of all the professed members of the community; in others, the Chapter is a group of members elected by the community as a whole to be their representatives.

Clothing
The ceremony in which a postulant of a community formally becomes a novice, and begins the period of formation in the mind, work and spirit of the community. It follows the initial stage of being a postulant when the prospective member first lives alongside the community. The clothing or novicing ceremony is characterised by the Religious 'receiving' the habit, or common attire, of the community.

Contemplative
A Religious whose life is concentrated on prayer inside the monastery or convent rather than on social work or ministry outside the house. Some communities were founded with the specific intention of leading a contemplative lifestyle together. Others may have a single member or small group living such a vocation within a larger community oriented to outside work.

Enclosed
This term is applied to Religious who stay within a particular convent or monastery – the 'enclosure' – to pursue more effectively a life of prayer. They would usually only leave the enclosure for medical treatment or other exceptional reasons. This rule is intended to help the enclosed Religious be more easily protected from the distractions and attentions of the outside world.

Eremitic
The eremitic Religious is one who lives the life of a hermit, that is, largely on his or her own. Hermits usually live singly, but may live in an eremitic community, where they meet together for prayer on some occasions during each day.

Evangelical Counsels
A collective name for the three vows of poverty, chastity and obedience.

Habit
The distinctive clothing of a community. In some communities, the habit is worn at all times, in others only at certain times or for certain activities. In some communities, the habit is rarely worn, except perhaps for formal occasions.

Novice
A member of a community who is in the formation stage of the Religious Life, when she or he learns the mind, work and spirit of the particular community whilst living among its members.

Oblate
Someone associated closely with a community, but who will be living a modified form of the Rule, which allows him or her to live outside the Religious house. Oblates are so-called because they make an oblation (or offering) of obedience to the community instead of taking the profession vows. In some communities, oblates remain celibate, in others they are allowed to be married. A few oblates live within a community house and then they are usually termed intern(al) oblates. The term oblate is more usually associated with Benedictine communities.

Office/Daily Office/Divine Office
The round of liturgical services of prayer and worship, which mark the rhythm of the daily routine in Religious Life. Religious communities may use the services laid down by the Church or may have their own particular Office book. The Offices may be called Morning, Midday, Evening and Night Prayer, or may be referred to by their more traditional names, such as Mattins, Lauds, Terce, Sext, None, Vespers and Compline.

Postulant
Someone who is in the first stage of living the Religious life. The postulancy usually begins when the aspirant begins to live in community and ends when he or she becomes a novice and 'receives the habit'. Postulants sometimes wear a distinctive dress or else may wear secular clothes.

Profession
The ceremony at which a Religious makes promises (or vows) to live the Religious Life with integrity and fidelity to the Rule. The profession of these vows may be for a limited period or for life. The usual pattern is to make a 'first' or simple profession in which the vows are made to the community. After three or more years a Life Profession may be made, which is to the Church and so the vows are usually received by a bishop. In the Anglican Communion, Life Professed Religious can usually be secularized only by the Archbishop or Presiding Bishop of a Province.

Religious
The general term for a person living the Religious life, whether monk, nun, friar, brother, sister etc.

Rule
The written text containing the principles and values by which the members of a community try to live. The Rule is not simply a set of regulations, although it may contain such, but is an attempt to capture the spirit and charism of a community in written form. Some communities follow traditional Rules, such as those of St Benedict or St Augustine, others have written their own.

Tertiary/Third Order
This term is usually associated with Franciscan communities, but is used by others too. A Third Order is made up of tertiaries, people who take vows, but modified so

that they are able to live in their own homes and have their own jobs. They may also marry and have children. They have a Rule of Life and are linked to other tertiaries through regular meetings. In the Franciscan family, the Third Order complements both the First Order of celibate friars and sisters and the Second Order of contemplative Religious.

Vows
The promises made by a Religious at profession. They may be poverty, chastity and obedience. In some communities, they are obedience, stability and conversion of life.

Index of Communities by Dedication or Patron Saint

Index by location

Index of Community Wares & Services for Sale

MUSIC & WORSHIP RESOURCES
Community of the Resurrection, UK   48
Community of St Mary the Virgin, UK   68
Society of the Community of Celebration, USA   160

PRINTING
Community of St Clare, UK   54
Community of St Mary the Virgin, UK   68
Order of St Benedict, Camperdown, Australia   102

WINE
Christa Sevika Sangha, Bangladesh   28
Society of the Holy Cross, Korea   119

Index of Communities by Initials

Notes and Amendments

Notes and Amendments

Notes and Amendments